## Praise for *Value-Based Healthcare ( Including Frontline Strategies for 20 Clinical Subspecialties*

"This is the book I wish I had written. The jewels inside this manual are the specific tactics—what specifically needs to change in delivering healthcare services in order to bend the cost curve and fulfill our patients needs and expectations. Every example illustrates the key challenge for managers; changing a process in one specialty often means that people in other specialties also need to change what they do. This is about tightening the connections between silos of care to provide more continuously coordinated care.

"The authors have done the valuable task of culling the key insights and tactics from large disorganized body of sources—all to answer the 'what will we do to succeed?' question."

**Timothy G. Ferris, MD, CEO, Massachusetts General Physician Organization, Professor of Medicine, Harvard Medical School**

*"Value-Based Healthcare and Payment Models* is a gem! In the complicated world of payment and delivery system reform, this manual deconstructs the most challenging concepts for the novice yet provides sophisticated insights for even the most seasoned healthcare executive. From leading change, to valuable recommendations for infrastructure, to practical recommendations for specialty-specific engagement Terrell and Bobbitt have created the go-to guide for creating a successful ACO."

**Jennifer Wiler, MD, MBA, FACEP, Executive Vice-Chair and Professor, Department of Emergency Medicine, University of Colorado School of Medicine; Executive Medical Director and Co-Founder, UCHealth CARE Innovation Center; and Professor, University of Colorado School of Business**

"As the parent of a soon-to-graduate medical student, I wonder how my son will navigate his professional career through residency and a medical practice that is likely to be very different from the status quo. Fortunately, help is on the way. In *Value-Based Healthcare and Payment Models*, Bobbitt and Terrell have provided a road atlas for my son and the thousands of other newly minted doctors who will bear the responsibility of completing the transition of healthcare in the U.S. to a value-based system. Not that existing physicians wouldn't benefit from this work, especially those in the 20 fields of practice where the authors lay out methods and strategies for participating in specific changes in the way that medicine is practiced and paid for.

"One appealing feature of this work, in addition to its comprehensive information on reform opportunities and pitfalls, is its positive tone. I would expect readers of this work to emerge both well-educated and enthusiastic about changing the culture of medicine for the betterment of themselves and the health of our nation."

**Alan Bruce Steinwald, Health Economist and Member, Physician-Focused Payment Model Technical Advisory Committee, Washington, DC**

"An expertly written manual that illuminates the path to overcoming the gravitational pull of fee-for-service medicine and transitioning to value-based care delivery. Drs. Terrell and Bobbitt systematically and comprehensively break down the elements of value-based care delivery by key specialties and outline the steps needed to successfully deliver the high-quality, affordable care that purchasers and taxpayers expect, and patients deserve. It's a tremendously valuable reference guide for every physician and clinician seeking to understand value-based healthcare and how to deliver it. It's also a must-read for physician and administrative leaders navigating medical groups and care delivery systems toward transformative outcomes and a future that is value-driven."

**Jeffrey Bailet, MD, CEO, Altais; Chairman, Physician-Focused Payment Model Technical Advisory Committee; Former Executive Vice President, Blue Shield of California**

"In *Value-Based Healthcare and Payment Models*, Dr. Grace Terrell gives deep and actionable advice for physicians and leaders of healthcare organizations making the transition from fee-for-service to value-based care. Based on her extensive personal experience at the forefront of this movement, Dr. Terrell shares a number of useful frameworks for understanding culture change, alignment, clinical redesign, appropriate use of data and technology, and patient engagement. Uniquely, she gives detailed advice for many specialties on how they might practice differently in a value-based world. Like the *Washington Manual* carried by generations of physicians in their lab coats, this is an essential reference for anyone moving into the brave new world of value-based care."

**Rushika Fernandopulle, MD, MPP, CEO, Iora Health**

"Physician practices and other providers that are considering creating an Accountable Care Organization (ACO) or Clinically Integrated Network (CIN) will better understand the challenges they face and the steps needed for success by reading *Value-Based Healthcare and Payment Models*. The book makes it clear that merely creating a new layer of care coordination services is not enough for success; far more fundamental changes in care delivery and organizational culture are needed, and that requires active engagement and leadership by the frontline providers of care.

"Most importantly, rather than merely exhorting frontline providers to 'deliver higher-value care,' the book gives detailed examples of how physicians in more than a dozen subspecialties as well as multiple types of primary care providers can deliver better care at lower cost. The information on these specialty-specific care models is relevant to all physicians in those specialties, not just those who participate in ACOs, since the care models could be implemented everywhere if appropriate payment supports are available, thereby enabling the largest possible number of patients to benefit from higher-value care."

**Harold D. Miller, President and CEO, Center for Healthcare Quality and Payment Reform**

"Dr. Terrell's deep experience and insight into both the clinical and systemic transformations urgently needed in U.S. healthcare enable a clear, accessible, and important book with guidance for those leading this work. Few others could connect and translate the policy, practice, and operational changes into a useful blueprint. Dr. Terrell makes the complex and ambitious seem achievable."

**Elizabeth Mitchell, President and CEO, Pacific Business Group on Health (PBGH)**

"Terrell and Bobbitt have taken 'value-based' healthcare from a faith-based, aspirational concept to practical, realistic implementation designed to effect change. The book is particularly strong on providing clinically relevant approaches to engaging frontline practitioners across many specialties to improve value for their patients. A prodigious effort."

**Robert Berenson, MD, FACP, Institute Fellow, Urban Institute; Former Vice-Chair, Medicare Payment Advisory Commission**

"This book serves as the roadmap to value-based care that physicians have been waiting for. It is well-written, organized, and describes in detail how all providers might participate in the healthcare value chain–including specialists who have struggled to identify their role. A must-read for any physician or leader looking to successfully move their ACO or IDN into the future."

**Angelo Sinopoli, MD, Chief Clinical Officer, Prisma Health**

"This book is essential reading for any policymaker, physician, or administrator who is really trying to consider broad-scale changes that can have a tangible effect on patients. The authors have deftly captured the real elements of value-based care; reading this book should be a requirement for any health care leader. This book is a comprehensive, thoughtful read that encompasses business, politics, science and most importantly, the needs of patients in the United States."

**Kavita K. Patel, MD, MSHS, Former Deputy Staff Director on Health for Late Senator Edward Kennedy; Former Director of Policy for the Office of Intergovernmental Affairs and Public Engagement in the Obama White House; Fellow, the Brookings Institute**

"Dr. Grace Terrell has been a visionary leader of value-based care for decades. This book is a practical, useful guide to implement value-based care and should be read by frontline clinicians, physician group and health system leaders, policymakers, payers, and others implementing value-based care models."

**Patrick Conway, MD, Former CMO and Director of CMS Innovation Center at CMS**

"Terrell and Bobbitt have written an indispensable guide to moving to value for anyone working in the healthcare industry. A must-read for those interested in the future of the healthcare system."

**Paul N. Casale, MD, MPH, Executive Director of New York Quality Care, the Accountable Care Organization of New York Presbyterian, Columbia, and Weill Cornell Medicine**

"In all other aspects of our economy and our lives, we take for granted that we pay only for the value we receive. Why is healthcare so different? In *Value-Based Healthcare and Payment Models*, Grace Terrell, MD, and Bo Bobbitt, two national pioneers in value-based care, share stories and offer pragmatic suggestions as to how clinicians can thrive, not just survive, in a data-driven system that rewards high-quality outcomes. A must-read for primary care and specialty physicians looking for practical guidance from well-respected colleagues who were walking the talk of value-based care long before it was a buzz phrase!"

**Maureen K. O'Connor, JD, President, Whiterabbit.ai, former Chief Strategy & Innovation Officer, Blue Cross Blue Shield of North Carolina**

"A valuable reference guide for physicians and clinicians seeking to understand value-based healthcare and how to deliver it. It's also a great resource for physician and administrative leaders navigating the shift toward value-based care delivery, with a focus on how to engage specialists in this journey."

**Jennifer Gasperini, Senior Policy Advisor, National Association of ACOs**

"The ambitious title isn't an overstatement. This truly serves as a manual, helping physicians and provider organizations navigate the complexities of executing a volume-to-value strategy. Simultaneously visionary and practical, Terrell and Bobbitt go well beyond the case for change and challenges to transformation that most focus on, providing tangible approaches for each dimension of the move to value along with a best-in-class guide for the roles that each specialty can play in the future of healthcare. A must-read for anyone who wants to be effective in a more value-oriented healthcare environment—from those leading change at the organizational level to those on the front lines of patient care."

**Niyum Gandhi, Executive Vice President and Chief Population Health Officer, the Mount Sinai Health System**

"Some healthcare books are about showing what the authors know, or how policies must change, or how normal people can re-create themselves into marathon-running vegans. This timely book is about what physician-led groups of virtually every specialty type should do to thrive in a value-based world, a world that is still birthing, messily, but is clearly here to stay. Written by thoughtful and practical physician leaders who have distilled the chemistry of practice transformation chaos into a manual even economists can understand, this volume makes clear that only physicians can take these lessons to heart and implement them successfully. They should. Soon."

**Len Nichols, PhD, Director, Center for Health Policy Research and Ethics; Professor of Health Policy, George Mason University; Former Senior Advisor for Health Policy at the Office of Management and Budget During the Clinton Administration**

"This is a must-read how-to manual for any health professional or administrator seeking to circumvent the deep flaws and perverse incentives (and hundreds of billions of dollars in attendant waste) created by America's third-party-financed fee-for-service healthcare system. This book codifies years of hard-won practical experience in putting together Accountable Care Organizations by clearly articulating the challenges in assembling such arrangements and providing specialty-specific nuts-and-bolts guidance to physicians on how to make value-based care a reality."

**Christopher J. Conover, retired Health Policy Professor, Duke University; author of *The American Health Economy Illustrated*.**

"Success in value-based healthcare requires an historic blend of tenacity, collaboration, and evidence-based decision making. No matter the size of the market or its dynamics, with this book, the authors have done their part in capturing the essence of what executives and organizations must consider and implement to transform healthcare delivery within their organization and bring value to their stakeholders. The tenacity and collaboration are up to you!"

**Todd Ricotta, MHSA, MBA, Executive Director, Arizona Care Network**

# Value-Based Healthcare

## AND

# Payment Models

## INCLUDING FRONTLINE STRATEGIES FOR 20 CLINICAL SUBSPECIALTIES

Grace E. Terrell, MD, MMM, CPE, FACP, FACPE
Julian D. "Bo" Bobbitt, Jr., JD

American Association for
**PHYSICIAN LEADERSHIP**®

13     8 7 6 5 4 3 2 1
Copyedited, typeset, indexed, and printed in the United States of America

**PUBLISHER**
Nancy Collins

**EDITORIAL ASSISTANT**
Jennifer Weiss

**DESIGN & LAYOUT**
Carter Publishing Studio

**COPYEDITOR**
Pat George

*Grace Terrell:*

*To Tim, Katy, Mike, Robyn, Sidney, Eldora, Eugene, Mom and Dad.*


*Bo Bobbitt:*

*To my family, for their patient support while I pursue my healthcare improvement passion, and for their inspiration as role models.*

# ACKNOWLEDGMENTS

I would like to thank all of my friends and colleagues who have been part of the Cornerstone, CHESS, and Envision management teams and boards; the NC Medical Society Towards Accountable Care Consortium; the Oliver Wyman Health Innovation Center; and the Physician-Focused Payment Model Technical Advisory Committee. This book is the result of your wisdom and the passion you have shown in working every day to improve the healthcare delivery system for everyone. All of you are patriots and I thank you for your service.

—GRACE TERRELL

I would like to acknowledge and thank my colleagues at the Smith Anderson law firm, who are both dear friends and examples of professional lives well led. It has been a pleasure and honor to work at Smith Anderson generally, and with the exceptional value-based health law team there specifically, led by Robert Shaw, Shawn Parker, and Claire Dodd. I am doubly fortunate to have a similarly ideal group of friends and preeminent professionals with whom to work at Value Health Partners, led there by Dr. Gordon Wilhoit and Alex Nunez. My contributions to this book would have never occurred without you.

—BO BOBBITT

# TABLE OF CONTENTS

# About the Authors

**Grace E. Terrell, MD, MMM,** is CEO of Eventus Whole Health, a company focused on integrated value-based behavioral medicine and primary care in the long-term care space. She is a national thought leader in healthcare innovation and delivery system reform, and a serial entrepreneur in population health outcomes driven through patient care model design, clinical and information integration, and value-based payment models. She is the former CEO of Cornerstone Health Care, one of the first medical groups to make the "move to value" by lowering the cost of care and improving its quality for the sickest, most vulnerable patients; the founding CEO of CHESS, a population health management company; and the former CEO of Envision Genomics, a company focused on the integration of precision medicine technology into population health frameworks for patients with rare and undiagnosed diseases. Dr. Terrell currently serves on the U.S. DHHS' Physician-Focused Payment Model Technical Advisory Committee and on the board of the AMGA, and is a founding member of the Oliver Wyman Health Innovation Center. gterrell@eventuswh.com

**Julian "Bo" Bobbitt, JD,** is head of the value-based health law practice group at the Smith Anderson law firm in Raleigh, NC, where he serves as Of Counsel. He is also founder and president of Value Health Partners, LLC, a value-based care and payment strategic consulting firm. In these capacities he provides experienced strategic and legal counsel to healthcare stakeholders across the country who are making the transition to integrated population health with performance payment. Bobbitt speaks nationally to both legal and medical audiences and is regularly published on emerging policy and health law issues in value-based delivery and regulation. He has formed and/or provided strategic and business direction to dozens of integrated entities, whether ACOs, CINs, IPAs or merged entities. bbobbitt@smithlaw.com

# FOREWORD

In 2015, I had the honor of presenting the AMGA Acclaim Award to Cornerstone Health President Dr. Grace Terrell, one of the authors of this book, and her team. The Acclaim Award recognizes the nation's premier healthcare delivery organizations that are high-performing and that are measurably improving the quality and value of care. Cornerstone was recognized for their remarkable achievements in moving their system to value-based care by improving the patient experience and outcomes, continuously learning and innovating, and improving population health. With this publication, Grace and Julian "Bo" Bobbitt bring together their vast and varied experience and lessons learned to help your organization transform into an agile, value-based one that delivers superior quality care while lowering costs.

I have been privileged to work with Grace for many years as her relationship with AMGA (American Medical Group Association) has deepened. She has been a galvanizing force among our members' physicians and administrators, who lead over 440 prominent medical groups and health systems that together provide care for 120 million patients, or one in three Americans. Through workshops, lectures, and leadership in both private industry and government, Grace has dedicated her career to helping other organizations learn the lessons from Cornerstone Health and apply her years of experience in delivering high performance healthcare. This publication is yet another example of her sharing this knowledge and experience and will provide a vital resource for those who wish to transform their systems.

As president and CEO of AMGA and throughout my career, I have worked with hundreds of medical groups and thousands of healthcare leaders who want to enable meaningful change at their healthcare organizations. They want to deliver care that is high quality, safe, patient-centered, and affordable. They want to transform into a value-based organization that manages the per-capita cost of healthcare and improves the overall patient care experience while improving the health of their respective populations. Many of these leaders struggle, but their efforts often fall short of their lofty aspirations. Why? In some instances, they don't know exactly where to begin. Other leaders know what they want to do, but do not know the pathway to build the necessary infrastructure and implement new processes. Sometimes they lack the leadership knowhow to fully engage their physicians and workforce in the hard work required to change. These leaders get stuck, each in a different way, and need specific, practical solutions to help them move their organizations forward. This book provides that roadmap to value-base care.

Changing our healthcare delivery system is hard, and shifting from the transactional, fee-for-service, fragmented system to high-value, coordinated, patient-centered, and compassionate care requires a plan. This book provides a wealth of solutions that will help you navigate the journey to value, no matter where you are on that path. Grace and Bo are your transformation coaches, providing starting points for those early in this transformation, detailed workflow processes and infrastructure advice for those already on the journey, and sage leadership insights for those who need to motivate and inspire their physicians and care teams.

The authors draw upon their years of practical experience and the insights from hundreds of physicians who understand what it takes to make the move to value. The challenges they tackle include:

**Creating coordination:** What does coordinated care really mean, and how do you create effective teams of caregivers who provide the right care at the right time with the right people at the right cost?

**Promoting leadership:** How do leaders effectively communicate an inspiring vision that reaches the hearts and minds of the entire organization?

**Engaging specialists:** What are the roles specialists can play in a value-based system, and how do you measure their successful involvement?

**Prioritizing specific health conditions:** Which health conditions are most important for care redesign and have the best return on investment?

**Developing work plans:** What steps do you need to take, in what order, and which steps must you make sure not to skip?

**Enhancing culture:** How do you build a culture that fosters learning and promotes the behaviors and changes necessary to move the organization in the new direction?

**Understanding the financing:** What are the best health plan contract options that will support the required "upfront" investments and sustain the new practice model?

**Building the infrastructure:** What resources are required to support a value-based system, and how do you stage these investments?

**Information technology:** What capabilities does my organization need to manage clinical and claims data, create effective reports, and track performance?

**Finding early wins:** What are some of simple and quick interventions that will generate initial momentum and ensure subsequent progress?

I agree with the authors that value-based healthcare is inevitable. AMGA members, policymakers, regulators, employers, and health plans all concur that we must now change both how health care is financed and how care is provided. With this manual, leaders of health systems and medical groups can achieve these goals and align their physicians, management, care teams, payers, and patients to deliver exceptional care that will improve quality while lowering costs, resulting in better care, better patient experience, and more affordable health care.

**Jerry Penso, MD, MBA**
President and Chief Executive Officer, AMGA

# CHAPTER ONE

# Introduction

As value-based integrated population health, headlined by Accountable Care Organizations (ACOs), approaches a decade of evolution, value-based payment will become the dominant form of healthcare payment. Although the move to value will take many forms, ACOs are considered one of the prime vehicles to accomplish this change. With more than 1,000 ACOs in existence today and, at last count, 32.7 million patients enrolled in ACOs, several documented successful strategies have emerged.[1] Up to half of the U.S. population may be served by ACOs within the next five years.[2]

This manual shares many of these successful strategies to help pave the way for your journey to value-based care. It provides a framework for delivery system transformation that will be necessary to make good on the promise of higher-quality, lower-cost care for all Americans.

Before the Internet provided instantaneous information to help physicians practice more safely and effectively, most internists in training did not go anywhere without the *Washington Manual*, a spiralbound book that fit perfectly in the pocket of their white lab coat. The detailed information in that little gray book helped newly minted physicians take care of complex patients in a quaternary care center and manage conditions as complicated as diabetic ketoacidosis and acute myocardial infarctions.

The manual did not replace the mentorships of upper-level residents and attending physicians nor the wise questions of experienced nurses, but it did provide a framework from which novice physicians could function competently while they gained the necessary experience to practice effective internal medicine on their own. From that context, this manual is intended to provide a framework for primary care physicians, specialists, and health system leaders beginning their own journey in delivery system transformation, based on our experience with successful early movers to a value-based payment system.

The transition that healthcare systems face in the move to value is not unlike the transition that occurs when a medical student becomes an intern. If this manual is half as effective a tool as the *Washington Manual* was for interns, then we will be satisfied that our efforts to be helpful will have been worthwhile.

## HOW DID WE GET HERE?

If we stay on the current spending glide path, by 2035, healthcare costs in this country will be more than the total of all tax and other revenues collected, and by 2080, taxpayer-funded healthcare will equal all of our governmental revenues, meaning that everything else—defense, roads, education—must be funded by borrowing. In a 2014 report by the Commonwealth Fund, the United States "ranked last overall among 11 industrialized countries on measures of health system quality, efficiency, access to care, equity, and health lives." Significantly, the United States was noted to have the highest costs while also displaying the lowest performance.[3]

The Congressional Budget Office laid the groundwork for accountable care's "pay-for-value" underpinning when it reported that much of the blame for our runaway healthcare costs should be placed on our fee-for-service payment system where "providers have a financial incentive to provide higher-intensity care in greater volume, which contributes to the fragmented delivery of care that currently exists."[4]

The U.S. healthcare delivery system is undergoing a paradigm shift based on payment reform intended to drive value and improve the quality of care. This "volume-to-value revolution" is designed to reward those best able to provide efficient, high-quality services. Value-based business models require providers to undergo transformative organizational change to every facet of their operations. Reimbursement based on outcomes and taking on financial risk necessitates investment in clinical integration, redesign of traditional patient care models, and integrated information technology. Provider organizations that adequately invest in population health management capabilities and successfully shift to value-based contracts and capitated payments will have the greatest likelihood of success in the transformed healthcare market.

Payers, including Medicare, are pushing providers for increased accountability for the quality and cost of care delivered. Ongoing governmental policy changes since 2015 have greatly accelerated the healthcare market's move from pure fee-for-service to value-based reimbursement. In 2015, Department of Health and Human Services Secretary Burwell announced the department's goal was to move 50% of Medicare payments to value-based payment models by 2018; this goal was accomplished prior to the transition from the Obama to the Trump administration.

The Medicare Access and CHIP Reauthorization Act (MACRA) legislation further accelerated the broad move of the U.S. healthcare industry toward paying for medical services based on value rather that volume. The sustainable growth rate formula for physician payments was replaced with a fundamental shift to performance-based payments, with fee-for-service payments adjusted based on quality and cost through the Merit-based Incentive Payment System (MIPS) and the Advanced Alternative Payment Models (APMs) focused on population-level quality and outcomes performance that involve significant financial risk, but provide substantial bonus payments for those physicians who are in APMs rather than the modified MIPS fee-for-service based payment system.

Providers participating in qualified APMs will have a 5% basic bonus in Medicare fee rates from 2019 to 2024 and will not be subject to the penalties for poor performance in MIPS, which will increase over a five-year period to 9% reduction in fees.

Furthermore, organizations can qualify under MACRA for APM bonus payments by moving their non-Medicare patients to APMs, not just by changing how they receive payment for Medicare patients.

Over the next few years, these policy changes will greatly accelerate the transition of the healthcare delivery system to one differentiated by performance at the global system level. The ACO-covered lives are projected to increase from the current 37 million lives to 177 million lives by 2020—a more than 600% increase.[5]

The 21ˢᵗ Century Cures Act enacted by Congress in December 2016 further accelerated federal healthcare payment reform via its emphasis on reducing administrative burden for providers addressing health information technology barriers, such as information blocking, interoperability, and the expansion of telehealth services. Current CMS Administrator Seema Verma continues to emphasize the reduction in regulatory burden and flexibility while also focusing policy on increasing incentives for providers to assume more risk in value-based payment models. In January 2019, she announced CMS is exploring ways to apply value-based payment models beyond Medicare and encourage more providers to buy into the programs and work with additional payers.

The Trump administration, like the Obama administration before it, is committed to the transition to value-based care. The administration is pushing the envelope to accelerate the progression of contracts from shared savings to full capitation with market-based reforms emphasizing individual choice, decreased regulatory burden, and increased competition.[6]

Healthcare providers need a new set of skills and tools to successfully navigate this accelerating transition. As reimbursement moves from volume-based to value-based, the department-centered organizational model of most legacy healthcare providers must be re-organized around specific populations, conditions, and focused asset capabilities. Efficiency on a population level rather than volume-based unit level will become increasingly important for financial viability, with chronic condition management, "focused-factory" capabilities for bundled payments, and service offerings organized around specific patient populations driving profitability more significantly than investment solely in capacity. Strategic alliances across the continuum of care and investment in clinical and information integration will become increasingly important drivers of profitability.

The resources and capabilities necessary in the reforming healthcare delivery system are inadequate for the demand as the fee-for-service system shifts to value-based payment models. Proven models for success and adequate infrastructure are in short supply because the capabilities involving strategy, people, process, and technology required for the new delivery system paradigm are not intrinsic in current healthcare organizations' structural framework, which has been built to maximize success in the fee-for-service payment system.

Given that governmental and commercial payers are moving to a value-based model of reimbursement over the next two to five years, it is remarkable that 95% of health provider organizations in the United States have no specific strategy for moving to that model. Even though physician reimbursement will increasingly be based on quality outcomes and patient satisfaction, there are few holistic, physician-inspired solutions that will support the people, process, and technology transitions required to lower operating costs and increase the quality of care.

The solution is to change the culture of the care team through innovative and proven care model redesign, reduce healthcare operating costs by providing process and technology tools to dramatically increase productivity and efficiency, and increase healthcare operating margins by providing process and technology tools to manage contracts and risk.

Because most patient populations require a full suite of healthcare services, providers must be able to enter into strategic partnerships with internal and external stakeholders across the entire spectrum of the healthcare delivery system network. Future integrated delivery networks will be focused around care models that operate at the intersection of the population segments and health conditions. New structures, such as internal care coordination and condition management hubs, Clinically Integrated Networks (CINs), and high-performance networks (HPNs) will be required to provide the quality, breadth, and efficiency of healthcare services being demanded by the new paradigm.

## THE NEW HEALTHCARE IS A TEAM GAME

Building on the momentum of other growing trends toward changing payments to incentivize better population health and lower costs such as the Medicare Shared Savings Program (MSSP) and MACRA will radically change America's healthcare delivery landscape. The transformation of the delivery model has been progressing in recent years from fee-for-service (which has had the unfortunate unintended consequence of paying more money for more, not better care) to pay-for-value (which rewards better outcomes at lower cost). However, to a large degree, the transformation has been implemented slowly. MACRA has fixed deadlines and significant financial bonuses and penalties and should not only significantly impact provider Medicare fee reimbursement but motivate other payers to shift as well.

A fundamental premise of value-based care is to achieve better health status and reduce avoidable *overall* costs for patient populations. This is almost impossible to achieve if providers continue practicing in silos, within a fragmented and uncoordinated "non-system." Put another way, practicing in integrated care teams is the proverbial low-hanging fruit in the new healthcare to drive "value," defined for purposes of this manual as achieving the highest quality at the lowest costs.

Surveys show that the majority of affected providers with substantial Medicare Beneficiary populations are totally or mostly unfamiliar with MACRA.[7] Anecdotally, it is clear that even fewer comprehend that the now-delayed "cost" measurement on which they will be graded within its MIPS and Advanced APM components of

MACRA will generally judge them on the *overall* costs for the patients they encounter, not just their own costs.

This is as radical as it is poorly understood. For example, as Mark McClellan, MD, PhD, wrote recently, though a primary care physician receives 6%–8% of this sum, the patients of a typical primary care physician in this country consume roughly $10 million annually in healthcare costs.[8] The MSSP, MACRA MIPS, and Advanced APMs models clearly require and incentivize coordinated care across the care continuum. The impact of MACRA virtually guarantees that value-based payment will be a dominant payment model.

Other private and public payment initiatives like Accountable Care Organizations continue to grow as well. For example, the "accountable" part of Accountable Care Organization denotes that all providers now depend on each other, across specialties, to manage the health status and total overall costs of their patient populations. No longer is doing well as an individual enough.

The bottom line is that the influence of MACRA removes all doubt that value care is inevitable and that thriving in such an environment, where providers are compensated based on the *overall* costs of their patients, requires interaction across specialties. The new healthcare is a team game.

## THE MOVE TO VALUE IS NOT GOING AWAY

MACRA was passed by both chambers of Congress with strong bipartisan support.[9] Implementing regulations have now been promulgated by both the Obama and Trump administrations.[10] HHS Secretary Alex Azar's announcement of five new value-based primary care payment models on April 22, 2019 integrates direct input from primary care clinician stakeholders and is based on underlying principles designed to reward value and quality:

- Prioritizing the doctor-patient relationship;
- Enhancing care for patients with complex chronic needs and high need, seriously ill patients;
- Reducing administrative burden; and
- Focusing financial rewards on improved health outcomes.[11]

Importantly, the five primary care models introduced are designed for primary care physicians in practice types across the organizational spectrum, from small, independent practices to integrated delivery networks. Primary Care First is designed for physicians in small, independent practices, whereas the Direct Contracting models are designed for ACOs, IDNs, and Medicare Advantage plans. These ambitious programs are designed to move 25% of Medicare patients out of the fee-for-service arrangement with primary care physicians and into value-based payment models.

Similarly, on July 10, 2019, HHS Secretary Azar and CMS Administrator Verma announced five new payment models focused on nephrologists and designed to transform kidney care: the End-Stage Renal Disease Treatment Choices Model, the Kidney Care First Model, and variations of the Comprehensive Kidney Care Contracting Models (Graduated, Professional, and Global). They also announced a proposed Radiation Oncology Model targeted to radiation therapy providers. These models are a harbinger of value-based care focused on specialists.

# CHANGE IS HARD

Without question, we are moving to a team-oriented value-based payment model for integrated population health. This will require a disruptive transformation of healthcare delivery. Such a fundamental change is difficult for people and organizations, and there is a natural tendency to resort back to fee-for-service business practices even once in an integrated or alternative arrangement. Additionally, change is difficult even when there is universal support, which this movement has never purported to have.

**The move to value is an opportunity for physicians and other health system leaders to drive positive change and create a sustainable, affordable healthcare delivery system.** The so-called healthcare Triple Aim is based on the idea of delivering the right care at the right time at the right price. We should all embrace with enthusiasm the unprecedented opportunity to redesign the healthcare system to achieve these aims. These new payment models are the opening for physicians and other healthcare leaders to think about new and better ways of providing healthcare services and participate in the redesign opportunity of a lifetime.

**A new set of skills is required for physician and other healthcare leaders to accomplish this goal.** These skills include a working knowledge of design thinking and change management and an understanding of the new payment models and contracting parameters. Those who will be most successful in the move to value will be those who bring these new skills to the table in a way that integrates the vast expertise in patient care delivery already part of our skill set.

As discussed in more detail later, there is no way to thrive under the new model without collaborating and "integrating," as it were, with other providers; moving to value care is no longer optional. This manual moves in a prioritized fashion to help overcome the obstacles that have befallen unsuccessful ACOs and to unlock the approaches and strategies found in the most successful ones.

Value-based care done right is truly disruptive. It requires a major culture shift by stakeholders and a major reengineering of care delivery. It is no surprise that the most successful ACOs are the ones that have been at it the longest. Richard Zane, MD, while serving on the NEJM Catalyst Insights Council, stated, "I feel our current system of healthcare is so flawed and rife with anchoritic processes and perverse disincentives that the only likely way we'll achieve the transformation is through disruption. . . . [O]ut-of-the-box thinking is difficult for entrenched health systems because many are totally hooked on fee-for-service medicine."[12]

# CHAPTER TWO

# Elements of Value-Based Healthcare

Value-based care is built on designing new models of care with new payment models and building teams and finding strategic partners to design effective care across the spectrum of the healthcare delivery system.

The concept of "value" is often misunderstood. Value does not imply lowest price, nor does it indicate, in economic terms, a single choice of price. Rather, value is a fair return on goods or services, based on relative worth or utility for a given price. Within the context of the healthcare delivery system, value-based care indicates a care delivery system in which high-quality healthcare is delivered at an efficient price, in contrast to the fee-for-service system where there is a standard fee based on providing an individual service not tied to quality.

In a fee-for-service system, the service provider is incentivized to provide the highest volume of the service they have at the highest price possible to negotiate at the minimal level of quality necessary. Although most physicians endeavor to provide the best possible care for their patients, fee-for-service only rewards volume at the minimal quality necessary to provide the service. This increases cost and waste and does not encourage quality or innovation.

Value-based healthcare is built on the assumptions that high-quality, efficient, and effective healthcare ought to be provided and can be provided if physicians and health systems are paid differently. But it is more than just a payment system.

## COMPONENTS OF DELIVERY SYSTEMS

Often productive discussions about health system improvement are dampened by the failure to properly categorize the various components of the delivery system in ways that clarify how they fit together as a whole. Like the parable of six blind men touching an elephant and describing only a component of the elephant from their limited perspective, limited knowledge often leads to the mistaken belief that one has the whole truth. This can skew healthy debate and eliminate creative solutions to complex problems.

These components of the delivery system can be integrated more effectively once their unique elements are better understood:

1. **Medical Conditions.** Clinicians have been trained to think about their work from the perspective of pathological processes to be prevented or diagnosed and treated. The disease model of human health can be divided into various patterns of medical conditions.
   - **Prevention and well care:**
     – Screening
     – Immunizations
     – Lifestyle counseling
     – Wellness programs
   - **Evidence-based medicine guideline adherence:**
     – Antibiotic use in upper respiratory tract infections
     – Chronic diabetes management
   - **Preference-sensitive shared decision making:**
     – Early-stage prostate cancer management
   - **Early identification and exacerbation control:**
     – Chronic obstructive pulmonary disease
     – Irritable bowel syndrome
   - **Integrated progressive condition management:**

- – Congestive heart failure
- – Coronary artery disease
- **Integrated complex condition management:**
  - – End-stage kidney disease
  - – Multiple sclerosis
  - – Lung cancer

2. **Population Health.** Those trained in public health tend to think about the entire population of a community and divide the population into groups of individuals with various states of health in order to organize health resources. Groups include:
   - Healthy and independent
   - Health risk factors
   - Early-stage chronic disease
   - Complex conditions
   - Late-stage or polychronic conditions
   - End of life

3. **Episodes of Care.** Much of the healthcare system is designed around the episodes in which healthcare services are delivered with the technologies, facilities, and resources needed organized around providing care in specific episodes. Types of episodes and examples of services include:
   - **Well Care**
     - – Pharmacy
     - – Primary care office
     - – Employer-based clinics
     - – Health department
     - – *Services:* immunizations, lipid screening, mammography
   - **Minor Episodes**
     - – Employer-based clinic
     - – Minute Clinic®
     - – Primary care office
     - – Urgent care
     - – *Services:* evidence-based diagnosis/treatment, health education
   - **Major Episodes**
     - – Ambulatory surgery center
     - – Community hospitals
     - – Infusion center
     - – Medical clinic
     - – *Services:* acute care, chronic complex care management, procedures and surgeries
   - **Catastrophic Care**
     - – Academic medical centers
     - – ICUs

> – Trauma centers
> – *Services:* burn units, Level 3 neonatal intensive care units

- **Long-term Care**
  - Long-term care hospitals
  - Rehabilitation centers
  - *Services:* PT/OT, ventilator management
- **Skilled Nursing Care**
  - Skilled nursing facilities
  - *Services:* physical therapy
- **Home Care**
  - Home health services
  - Home dialysis
  - Hospital-at-home
  - *Services:* infusions, PT/OT, speech therapy, behavioral medicine, medication management
- **Palliative Care**
  - Hospice
  - *Services:* pain management
- **Telecare**
  - Behavioral medicine
  - Primary care
  - Rural health
  - Teledermatology
  - Teleradiology
  - *Services:* employer benefits, enhanced access, expertise access

4. **Managed Care.** Managed care is focused around benefits design and financial incentives designed to improve the use of limited resources. Ideally, benefits are designed to incent neither over- nor underutilization. Managed care includes:
   - Benefits design
   - Co-insurance
   - Deductibles
   - HMOs
   - Narrow networks
   - PPOs
   - Preauthorization
   - Tiered formularies
   - Wellness programs

5. **Payment Models.** How providers of healthcare services are paid for their work makes up the bulk of where most healthcare reform efforts are currently focused because of the belief that fee-for-service payments improperly promote overutilization and do not incentivize high-quality care. But fee-for-service will

continue to have a place within the healthcare payment system, particularly for straightforward service transactions as might be provided in an urgent care or through primary care telemedicine services.

- **Fee-for-service:** Despite the widespread criticism of this payment model due to its implicit incentivization of overutilization and inadequate controls of quality, this payment methodology may still be ideal for high-volume, efficient services transactions (such as urgent care visits) provided evidence-based medicine is required for payment.
- **Pay-for-performance**: Pay-for-performance permits variance in payment based on quality, patient safety, patient satisfaction, and other performance outcomes, but requires new information systems to access and measure performance.
- **Care-coordination payments:** Coordination of care engenders innovation in the provision of non-facility-based services to improve patient management.
- **Bundled payments:** The bundling of payments for major episodes of care where coordination of diverse services is required encourages quality and efficiency. Although most effective bundled payments involve discrete ser-vices—total knee replacement, for example—there is a growing interest in bundling services for chronic disease processes.
- **Risk-adjusted payments:** Appropriate risk adjustment permits payment variance depending on the complexity of the patients being provided services.
- **Population-based payments:** Organizations taking on risk for the total cost of care of a population may benefit from risk-adjusted capitated payments that encourage innovations in service delivery.

6. **Delivery System Models:** How the healthcare delivery system organizes itself to provide services takes on many different forms throughout the world, with particular complexity within the United States:
   - Accountable Care Organizations (ACOs)
   - Clinically Integrated Networks (CINs)
   - Independent medical groups, hospitals, nursing facilities, and other healthcare providers
   - Nationalized universal healthcare: National Health Service of the United Kingdom
   - Patient-centered medical homes
   - Patient-centered specialty homes
   - Public health services; state and local health departments
   - Universal insurance with private providers of services
   - Veteran's Administration hospitals and clinics

To move to value successfully, healthcare providers should understand the elements of all six of these components independently and as an integrated whole. It is particularly important to understand how care models and payment models integrate.

Successful value-based care depends on designing models of care that improve the quality and lower the cost of care for which appropriate payment models are designed to permit successful, sustainable business models.

Not all care delivery innovations require a new payment model. Often, other tools are more suitable for achieving desired changes in care delivery. An important distinction between care delivery innovations requiring a new payment model and those requiring other changes is whether the innovations could be accommodated within existing payment mechanisms. Care delivery innovations that do not require a new payment model may fall into three big buckets:

1. Development of new codes for payment
2. Payment for new or different services
3. Quality improvement strategies

Consider the following value-based options:

- Uncomplicated urinary tract infections in otherwise healthy women can be addressed by evidence-based protocol via telemedicine, decreasing the expense and inconvenience of traditional office-based care. This service could be paid for via traditional fee-for-service but at reduced cost.
- Condition-based management fees can be provided to specialty medical homes providing whole-person care models to patients with complex chronic conditions such as multiple sclerosis or cancer.
- Bundled payments could be provided to a "focused-factory" that provides comprehensive services for hip replacement including surgery, anesthesia, hospital services, post-operative rehabilitation. Shared decision making, evidence-based protocols, and measurements of outcomes would be crucial elements in establishing performance criteria upon which to base payment.
- Perhaps a population-based global payment would engender a focus on the frail elderly, who often have high costs with poor outcomes. To reduce the total cost of care and improve quality, a team-based care approach across settings (home, hospital, SNF, hospice, outpatient rehab) may be undertaken by ACOs, HMOs, and MA plans receiving global payments for a population.

From this perspective, the components of value-based care are part of a continuum of payments models coupled with appropriate services and models of care for various types of health conditions, as illustrated in Table 2-1.

TABLE 2-1. The Components of Value-Based Care

| PAYMENT MODEL | CONDITION | SITE OF SERVICE | CARE MODEL |
|---|---|---|---|
| Fee-for-service | Urinary tract infection | Telemedicine, urgent care, primary care office | Evidence-based medicine protocols |
| Condition-based management fees | Multiple sclerosis | Specialty clinic | Whole-person care model |
| Bundled Payments | Total knee replacement | Focused-factory | Outcomes measures, shared decision making, EBM protocols |
| Population-based global payments | Frail elderly services | Team-based care across settings | ACOs, HMOs, CINs, other risk-bearing entities |

# CHAPTER THREE

# The Thorniest Problems Facing ACOs, and Solutions to These Challenges

*"The most significant challenge of becoming accountable is not forming an organization, it is forging one."* [13]

The three biggest challenges to value care success are: (1) changing the culture, (2) getting the necessary actionable data, and (3) integrating care models and business models.

## CHALLENGE 1: CHANGING THE CULTURE

By "changing the culture" we are focusing on physicians who have both the ability and desire to work together in multispecialty teams to promote population health. This is a transformative change that is far out of typical physicians' comfort zone because they are being pulled from a fragmented system and a culture that rewards independent decision making. The legacy fee-for-service compensation model actually created a sense of competition of fighting over the shrinking healthcare dollar. All the analytics tools in the world will be useless if no one wants or knows how to use them.

Yes, culture change is huge. Yes, it is hard. But when done right, physicians will see the professional and economic opportunities for practicing a better way and getting paid to do it. They will then embrace the move to integrated population health. Table 3-1 compares the traditional and the new health system cultures.

**TABLE 3-1.** Traditional vs. New Physician and Health System Culture

| TRADITIONAL | NEW |
|---|---|
| 1. Top-down command-and-control hierarchy | 1. Engage and empower through horizontal, shared decision making |
| 2. Turf protection | 2. Build collaboration and teamwork through shared commitment and shared ideas |

*Continued on next page*

**TABLE 3-1.** Traditional vs. New Physician and Health System Culture (continued)

| TRADITIONAL | NEW |
|---|---|
| 3.  Them vs. Us | 3.  Develop strong relationships; all for one, one for all, and everyone for the patient |
| 4.  Guarded motives and agendas with low transparency | 4.  Focus on total transparency and open communication |
| 5.  Over-emphasis on professional autonomy and individualism | 5.  Balance autonomy and accountability |
| 6.  Distant, disparate motives | 6.  Develop trust and mutual respect by looking through another's eyes |
| 7.  Siloed, misaligned visions | 7.  Build clinical integration through cultural integration |
| 8.  Too much focus on individual success, reputation, and benefit | 8.  Achieve collective success and shared purpose by asking, "How will this benefit the patient?" |
| 9.  Fee-for-service, volume-centric focus | 9.  Transition to fee-for-value to improve overall quality of care |
| 10.  Over-emphasis on beating the competitor and winning at any cost | 10.  Create a brand recognized for the delivery of high-value, data-driven, evidenced-based, patient-centered, collaborative care |
|  | 11.  Promote physician leadership and inclusivity by distributing organizational control among constituents; produce physician leadership not physician followership |

It's all well and good to critique the current physician/health system culture and describe an ideal state, but how on earth do we get from our current state to this new, presumably better one? It may be easier than you think.

Physician burnout is at an all-time high. The dysfunctions of the current fee-for-service delivery system, including the regulatory burden, ham-handed payer-driven managed care intended to be blunt instruments to decrease overutilization, and short, ineffective office-based transactions with patients, have most physicians looking for a better way. Fostering vigorous engagement of motivated and knowledgeable physicians is perhaps value-based payment's greatest strength.

In summary, one cannot neglect efforts to help justifiably skeptical physicians better understand that the major shift to integrated value-based care is a better and more rewarding way to practice. America is asking physicians to redesign the country's healthcare system the right way and is paying them to do it. By driving best practices for a CIN's or ACO's entire patient population, they can improve care for thousands of patients, not just one at a time. Once this culture shift is made, it truly can be the Golden Age of medical practice.

The most important element, yet the one most difficult to attain, is a team-oriented culture with a deeply shared commitment to reorganize care to achieve higher quality at lower cost. A fully functional ACO will catalyze the transformation of health delivery. According to the Advisory Board Company, "While strong hospital-physician alignment has always been a cornerstone of success, the necessary degree of future collaboration, partnership, and risk-sharing will dwarf what has come before it. Hospitals and physicians will have to recognize, embrace, and leverage their growing interdependence to create organizational structures and incentive models that are strategically aligned and mutually rewarding."[14]

### Challenges for Physicians

Physicians favor autonomy and individualism over collaboration. This mindset is inculcated in clinical training and reinforced daily in care delivery. Reimbursement rewards an individualistic "eat what you kill" mentality. The level of involvement needed to effect changes in quality and cost, however, is more than just banding together for contracting purposes. Physicians must be willing to change utilization, referral, and care-management patterns. In many settings, specialists will need to release primary control of patient care decision making to the medical home primary care physician.

Physicians are justifiably cynical about "next best things," such as HMOs, gatekeeping, and capitation, and have little experience with or time for organization-level strategic planning. But, "[I]f providers do not change their decision-making and behavior, ACOs will go the way of most PHOs and IPAs . . . to the boneyard. More importantly, the healthcare crisis will persist, and more drastic solutions will be mandated."[15]

### Challenges for Hospitals

Will hospitals be willing to embrace a true ACO structure, which will likely drive down hospitalizations and readmissions? Will they be willing to distribute shared savings as intended, to incentivize and reward those who attained the savings through high-performance care delivery and improved coordination? Or will they try to take any savings dollars "off the top" to make up for the lost revenue from the reduction in avoidable hospitalizations and readmissions? Will the increased market share from joining an ACO make up for the lost revenue?

Exacerbating these business risks for sharing governance with physicians and committing without reservation to an orientation of higher quality and lower costs is a deeper cultural barrier: control. Hospitals are complex organizations, and a degree of control over operations and direction has been historically important for their viability.

## The Solution

In chapter four we take a deeper dive into the necessary components of organizational readiness needed for successful change, including the characteristics of a higher-performing health system, culture and systems thinking, leadership, professionalism, strategy, innovation and design thinking, change management, and execution. We draw on the work of some of the expert thinkers in these areas and apply their insights to healthcare and our move to value.

But there is no need to delay the implementation of effective strategies while you are learning more. Table 3-2 presents a summary of the most effective strategies employed by successful ACOs that you can begin to implement now.

**TABLE 3-2.** Seven Proven Strategies for Physicians
to Embrace and Lead Value-Based Care

| |
|---|
| 1. **Establish an initial education and awareness program.** Feature live presentations supplemented with written materials, blog postings, and access through each physician's secure portal, which provide the initial offerings of a self-guided learning library. |
| 2. **Identify respected physician champions** who, with the ACO/CIN leadership, receive more concentrated briefings. Teach the future teachers, as it were. |
| 3. **Be led by physician champions.** Physicians have strong representation across governance but are led by clinical committees and disease-state specific subcommittees. Physicians *must* determine what they deem best practices. This peer-reviewed list must equate with excellent medical care. |
| 4. **Select clinically valid metrics** to track compliance yardsticks with the best practice behavior desired. |
| 5. **Collect accurate data on performance.** Share results transparently. Distribute shared savings and other incentive payments on a merit basis relative to performance. However, payment amounts need not be substantial to engage physicians in active change *if* the results shared with respected peers are associated with excellence in care and team play. |
| 6. **Educate chronically poor performers,** then provide a period of probation. If necessary, they must be dropped from the ACO. This reinforces engagement, as high performers are recognized. |
| 7. **Share short but frequent value-care tips** to keep the drumbeat of awareness going. |

# CHALLENGE 2: OBTAINING ACTIONABLE DATA THROUGH TECHNOLOGY

A common complaint of ACOs and other entities engaged in integrated population health delivery with performance-based compensation is the inadequacy of analytical support. Integrating disparate providers across the continuum of care engaged in not only reacting in a coordinated way to illnesses presented, but also proactively raising the health status of the entire patient population requires a robust technology chassis. Sometimes that analytics platform is elusive if not impossible to find.

This dilemma is exacerbated by lack of user understanding of the new purposes of value-based care technology. In other words, if the provider does not understand the value of accessing and sorting information, even the perfect analytics toolkit will be useless.

Successful implementation of new technology often requires major redesign of traditional workflows. The instinct to simply bolt new technology on top of traditional processes leads to inefficacy and contributes to physician burnout. Further, much as Amazon has upended the traditional retail model of physical shopping centers, disruptive technology will be capable of replacing much of the traditional office-visit model of healthcare.

It is predicted that patients will physically engage with hospitals and physicians less and less and instead seek care through virtual delivery systems. "A lot of these parts of care can be done without human interaction," says Joanne Roberts, SVP and chief value officer at Providence St. Joseph Health, Kenton, Washington.[16] Health systems and clinicians who continue to work through the lens of transactional medicine, focused on technology based on facilities, procedures, office visits, and revenue cycle management, will fail to take advantage of the potentially greatly improved healthcare delivery system that becomes possible as a result of new technology platforms.

## The Solution

For years, healthcare technology focused on two things: (1) capturing the patient's medical record digitally and (2) facilitating billing. The technology functionalities for value-based care are quite different. Financial and network management must be integrated with clinical data and equipped to handle sophisticated reimbursements. Sophisticated analytical tools for patient stratification, clinical risk quantification, and predictive modeling are a crucial part of population and clinic risk management. Integrated evidence-based medicine, clinical pathways, and protocols must be designed into the clinical care models across sites and into the clinical systems at the point of care.

Evidence-based platforms and rules engines with standard bundles and episode definitions can be used to define clinical delivery and performance. An automated point-of-care decision support system with automated patient registry with active monitoring and clinical resource management including referral tracking and intelligent schedule can be built as part of core clinical technology infrastructure. Patient engagement through patient portals and online tools for shared decision making also requires integration into a technology platform. Performance management, comparative effectiveness tracking, and tracking of quality and performance improvement is crucial, as is the ability to safely and efficiently exchange clinical and administrative data with third parties.

Ideally, the technology "chassis" for the ACO will have the robust functionalities described below, but also will be capable of supporting the other value-based payments currently provided by Medicare and others: (1) the value-based care codes and (2) MACRA MIPS reporting and score optimization.

Technology provides essential data collection, reporting, and decision support, but is often the largest expense of an ACO. These tensions need to be reconciled as the technology investment decisions of an ACO are made. It is crucial to "meet them where they are" and utilize all useful existing technology, based on the feasibility analysis. The required capabilities can be prioritized by first building on and leveraging the existing legacy technologies and then extending that foundation with targeted enhancements based on proper IT governance and management principles.

There is no ideal technology solution, but population health technology leaders are continuing to improve the solutions available on the market. For clinicians and managers used to traditional healthcare fee-for-service and first generation EMR technology, a new mindset needs to emerge: *design thinking* needs to be applied by frontline leaders partnering with technology vendors to build out effective technology platforms serving the needs of provider organizations with varying degrees of technological capabilities. The NEJM catalyst project surveyed healthcare leaders and found that the top three barriers to applying design thinking to healthcare were limited buy-in from decision makers, limited understanding of design, and insufficient training in design.[17]

Many organizations fail to execute on the analytics investments they have made. In the move to value-based payment models, failure to embed analytics into business processes throughout the enterprise may lead to an organization's extinction. Value-based contracts are based on the ability to identify opportunities and mitigate risks that impact clinical and financial performance. Failure to develop an analytical culture at both the clinical and enterprise level greatly jeopardizes successful delivery system transformation.

Competitive analytics capabilities require integrated predictive analytics rather than simply relying on laggard reporting capabilities upon which much of the fee-for-service payment system is built. With adequate investment in predictive analytics and its application to clinical and business processes throughout the organization global payment contracts can be de-risked substantial, and performance improvement progress along an accelerated path.

The application of design thinking to the "wicked problems" of health information technology can be facilitated by elevating the appreciation of the need for, and understanding of the tenets of, new healthcare technology. Chapter four takes a deeper dive into information integration as part of implementing models of care. In the meantime, Table 3-3 and Table 3-4 provide summaries of the data collection goals for ACOs and technology capabilities to get you started.

**TABLE 3-3.** Data Collection Goals for ACOs

| |
|---|
| 1. Collect near real-time data from disparate sources into a single longitudinal health record integrated with the EMR for each patient, enabling every provider who has contact with the patient to have complete access at the point of care, accompanied by decision supports reflecting the ACO's agreed-upon best practices. |
| 2. Provide a patient population health status gap analysis, tailored performance measurement reports, reporting, and shared savings distribution analysis down to the individual physician level. |
| 3. Provide patient and caregiver engagement functionalities and appropriate telehealth and telemedicine functionalities. |

**TABLE 3-4.** Ideal Technology Capabilities for ACOs

| | |
|---|---|
| 1. | Extraction of actionable data at the point of care, including having a longitudinal health record and decision support derived from the initiatives and best practices selected by the ACO. |
| 2. | Standardized data entry for interoperable EHRs. |
| 3. | Aggregated reporting (*i.e.*, quality measures, admissions, ER utilization, and readmissions), GPRO compliant, tailorable to user preferences, drill down capabilities, embedded in EMRs. |
| 4. | Financial calculations and distributions. |
| 5. | Gap analysis capability; starting with claims data, have capacity to identify the impactable population. |
| 6. | Health information exchange—Collect data from disparate sources in near-real time; integrate actionable data into the EHRs. |
| 7. | HIPAA privacy and security safeguards. |
| 8. | Leakage/referral compliance tracking. |
| 9. | Linkage to value-based care coding and MACRA. |
| 10. | Medication reconciliation and compliance. |
| 11. | Patient engagement tools: My Care Pad, Care Circles, targeted education reminders and alerts, appointments, mobile devices. |
| 12. | Predictive analytics. |
| 13. | Profiles of hospitals and post-acute care facilities. |
| 14. | Reality check—Square costs with needs once "wish list" created. |
| 15. | Referral management tools. |
| 16. | Reports, including care-management and care-coordination reports, care plan creation, dashboards, alerts, transition of care workflow. |
| 17. | Risk stratification rules engines; query-ability. |
| 18. | Staffing needs in-house and contracted, from data entry to mentoring. |
| 19. | Tailored reports measuring matters deemed important by the ACO to meet payor reporting requirements and ACO benchmarks tied to meeting selected care goals. |
| 20. | Vendor profiles and costs. |

# CHALLENGE 3: INTEGRATING CARE MODELS AND BUSINESS MODELS

Frontline healthcare providers who become enthusiastic about value-based healthcare usually become so because they believe it will provide them opportunities to improve the care they deliver to their patients. The hope is that being paid in a new way will allow them opportunities to provide care in ways that are limited in a fee-for-service payment system. However, care delivery innovations and payment innovations are two entirely separate domains and failure to integrate innovation in both will lead to failure in both.

Clinical leaders often focus more on care model redesign than on payment model redesign because they experience the impact of the care model first-hand in their day-to-day practice of medicine, but often do not have the technical expertise in payment policy needed to fully integrate care model innovation into comprehensive payment model innovation, nor do they have the technical assistance to do so.

Likewise, payers, administrative leaders, and policy experts whose focus is mainly in the arena of healthcare business models and payment policy are frequently mystified by the passionate objections from frontline clinicians with reforms intended to improve the payment system. They often start from a position that changes in payment methodology will naturally lead to changes in patterns of patient care that can improve quality and lower costs.

Clinicians, on the other hand, know that payment policy reform often has unintended consequences that may directly and adversely impact their ability to provide good care to their patients. However, they have difficulty foreseeing the strengths and weaknesses of proposed payment policy reforms from the overall cost and quality of care at the macroeconomic level because they are trained to provide healthcare services in a one-on-one relationship with individual patients, not populations of patients.

## The Solution

For those frontline providers who have a great idea for improving patient care, the care delivery model must be integrated into a defined, sustainable payment model. Not all care delivery innovation requires a new payment model. An important distinction between care delivery innovations requiring a new payment model and those requiring other changes is whether the innovations could be accommodated within existing payment mechanisms. Often, other tools are more suitable for achieving the desired changes in care delivery.

Care delivery innovations that do not require a new payment model may fall into three categories. First, quality and efficiency improvement strategies may improve the delivery of care within a traditional fee-for-service payment structure. Following evidence-based guidelines in care delivery such as those espoused in the Choosing Wisely® campaign is one example.

Second, a new code within the traditional Medicare or commercial fee schedule may need to be developed or a currently available code may need to be used in a new care model. The chronic care and transitions of care codes are examples of codes that may provide reimbursement for redesigned processes or may need to be broadened in scope by policymakers through traditional fee schedule processes.

Third, payers may need to provide coverage for a new medical device or service and pay for it in a traditional fee-for-service mechanism. For example, the provision of telehealth services has recently been increased by new, distinct fees in the Medicare fee schedule which will have broad applications that could lead to innovation in care delivery.

Understanding how care delivery model innovation fits within the current established traditional fee-for-service or alternative payment models is crucial to financially successful business models. *CMS' Innovator's Guide to Navigating Medicare* is a useful reference in determining whether a new code for payment or new device coverage is the appropriate strategy for a care model innovation versus participation in an alternative payment model such as an ACO or bundled payment model. The CMS Innovation Center website (https://innovations.cms.gov) provides information about participation in existing alternative payment models and about upcoming models they are introducing such as the new primary care initiatives.

Frontline providers who are used to approaching healthcare by delivering innovation first through the lens of care model design and subsequently through the lens of payment redesign could take a stepped approach by first defining the care delivery model, then determining if an alternative payment model is required, and defining that payment model, including directly addressing cost, quality, and infrastructure requirements.

The real solution to improving cost and quality in the healthcare delivery system lies in designing care models that improve outcomes for patients. Although well-designed payment reform will incentivize improved care, the core transformation must occur at the clinical level, not merely at the reimbursement level.

The process for developing new models of care includes defining the clinical specialties and interventions designed to drive cost and quality improvements and defining which patients would be served. Defining any new technology and operational requirements needed to enable the care delivery models can help structure the payment model through its assessment of reporting staff, reimbursement platforms, and compensation models.

If an alternative payment model is necessary to achieve the care delivery innovation, defining the payment model should include how this model differs from existing payments, defining the type of payment, and tying how quality is tied to payment. Chapter four provides a deep dive into care model redesign methodology and chapter five provides a detailed look at value-based payment. Table 3-5 and Table 3-6 offer some basic categories to help you begin thinking about how to integrate care model redesign with sustainable business models.

**TABLE 3-5.** Types of Payment Models

| BASIC PAYMENT MODEL TYPES | EXAMPLES |
|---|---|
| Fee-for-service | Traditional Medicare |
| Fee-for-service linked to quality and value | PQRS, MIPS |
| Alternative payment models built on FFS | CPC, BPCI, MSSP |
| Population-based payments | Some next-gen ACOs |

**TABLE 3-6.** How to Build Integrated Care and Business Models

| | |
|---|---|
| Determine what patient populations are to be included in the care model | • Healthy and independent people<br>• People with health risk factors<br>• People with early-stage chronic disease<br>• People with acute illnesses<br>• People with complex chronic illnesses<br>• People with late-stage complex conditions<br>• People at the end of life |
| Determine what components of care are to be included | • Total cost of care<br>• Professional services<br>• Facility services<br>• Pharmacy services<br>• Laboratory services |
| Determine segment health conditions | • Episodes of care<br>• Types of care |
| Determine episodes of care | • Preventive care (AWV/immunization)<br>• Minor episodes of care (urgent care)<br>• Major episodes of care (joint replacement)<br>• Catastrophic care (sepsis/trauma)<br>• Chronic care (diabetes, epilepsy)<br>• End-of-life care (hospice) |
| Categorize medical conditions | • Independent conditions (hypothyroidism)<br>• Preference-sensitive conditions (low back pain)<br>• Progressive, degenerative conditions (CHF)<br>• Conditions with episodic manifestations (gout, MS)<br>• Complex episodic conditions (COPD)<br>• Systemic conditions (metastatic lung cancer) |
| Match payment methodology to episodes and conditions | • PCMH for prevention/chronic conditions<br>• Bundled payments for acute episodic care<br>• Bundled payments/care coordination for chronic complex conditions<br>• FFS with P4P for simple transactional care (urgent care/telemedicine primary care) |
| Determine which providers and services should be involved in the care | • Primary care<br>• Specialty care<br>• Facilities<br>• Home care<br>• Telemedicine<br>• SNFs |
| Evaluate what information needs to be integrated | • Care coordination<br>• Cohort management<br>• Clinical, financial data<br>• Clinician engagement |

# CHAPTER FOUR

# A Deeper Dive into Building Sustainable Value-Based Care

## ASSESSING ORGANIZATIONAL READINESS

### Characteristics of a High-Performing Health System

As health systems built to be successful in the current fee-for-service health system prepare for healthcare payment reform, they should assess organizational readiness for this change as a crucial first component of a capabilities evaluation. High-performing healthcare systems in the current ecosystem may not have the assets and culture necessary for continued success in the transforming market. It is thus essential to understand the inherent characteristics in organized systems of care with exceptional performance from a current market point of view and from the perspective of the impeding market changes.

Many researchers have attempted to qualify the characteristics of a high-performing healthcare system, with most focusing on cultural characteristics rather than organizational capabilities. For example, in a study of 693 medical groups in 2005, Stephen Shortell and colleagues developed a framework in which clinical quality of care, financial performance, and organizational learning capability of medical groups were assessed in relation to environment forces, resource acquisition and resource deployment factors, and *a quality-centered culture*.[18]

Quint Studer likewise emphasizes cultural factors in performance: no tolerance for low performers; alignment among senior leaders; effective leadership training; effective leadership evaluation systems; consistent leadership; and standardization of best practices.[19] The perennially re-published *The Well-Managed Healthcare Organization* articulates four critical issues in developing excellence in the foundations of high-performing healthcare organizations:

1. Emphasizing mission, vision, and values.
2. Building a culture that listens, empowers, trains, and rewards.
3. Measuring performance, seeking benchmarks, and negotiating realistic goals.

4. Maintaining close relation with all stakeholders.[20]

In a similar perspective, the Camden group's depiction of hospital high performance focused on several cultural competencies:

- Defined strategic vision.
- Consistent leadership.
- Talent management (don't tolerate the lower performers).
- Culture of accountability.
- Change management and adaptability.
- Transparency.
- Outcomes.
- Alignment with physicians through clinical integration.
- Patient engagement.
- Innovation and care redesign.[21]

The Commonwealth Fund tackles the issue of high performance from the macroeconomic level of the entire health delivery system for the United States, citing an overarching mission "to help everyone, to the extent possible, lead long, healthy, and productive lives." The Commonwealth Fund's approach emphasizes that critical characteristics of such a system include "commitment to a clear national strategy for achieving the mission and establish a process to implement and refine that strategy; delivering care through models that emphasize coordination and integration; and establish and tracking metrics for health outcomes, quality of care, access to care, population-based disparities, and efficiency."[22] The commission identifies the most critical sources of system failures and offers a framework for addressing them that emphasizes core goals and performance improvement priorities for high-quality care, efficient care, access and equity, and system and workforce innovation and improvement.

In contrast to these approaches that focus on cultural or system change characteristics, the American Medical Group Association has developed a highly specific seven-domain framework for characterizing a high-performing health system. This framework is sufficiently granular to permit capabilities assessment at the individual health system level in order to develop a strategy for significant transformation.[23]

Rather than focusing on the loftier qualities of "leadership excellence" or "culture of quality" as seen in the other approaches, the American Medical Group Association's High-Performing Health System™ defines specific criteria necessary for achieving high performance from an operational framework. The seven domains do not presume a particular form of health system structure is superior to another, so long as the requisites of the seven domains are fulfilled. Thus, the framework can be used by any number of healthcare delivery systems, including independent multispecialty medical groups, integrated healthcare delivery systems, Clinically Integrated Networks (CINs), Accountable Care Organizations (ACOs), and Independent Provider Associations (IPAs).

The seven domains of the AMGA's framework are:

1. **Accountability**. The provider entity assumes shared financial and regulatory responsibility and accountability for successfully managing the per-capita cost of healthcare, improving the overall patient experience, and improving the health of their respective populations.

2. **Care Coordination**. The provider entity uses a team-based approach that supports collaboration and communication among the patient, physician, and licensed or certified medical professionals who are working at the top of their field across medical specialties and healthcare settings to improve the patient's wellbeing. This activity includes:
   - A *single plan of care* across healthcare settings and across healthcare providers who furnish care to the patient; and
   - *Shared decision making*, which is a collaboration between the patient and healthcare provider that empowers the patient in the decision-making process and provides the patient with objective information concerning:
     – The risk of seriousness of the disease or condition to be prevented or treated;
     – Available treatment alternatives; and
     – The costs and benefits of available treatment alternatives.

3. **Compensation Practices That Promote the Other Domain's Objectives**. The provider entity uses compensation structures that provide incentives to physicians and licensed and certified medical professionals to improve the health and outcomes of populations. These compensation practices may include, but not be limited to, incentives that are affiliated with:
   - Patient experience; or
   - Quality metrics, such as chronic disease measures and prevention compliance within a physician's managed population.

4. **Efficient Provision of Services**. The provider entity successfully manages the per-capita cost of healthcare and improves the overall patient care experience and the health of their respective populations.

5. **Organized System of Care**. The provider entity includes a multispecialty medical group or other organized system of care and:
   - Provides a continuum of care, including prevention and ambulatory care, for a population of patients; and
   - Is integrated or has partnerships with other care sites, which may include, but not be limited to, acute care hospitals, long-term acute care hospitals, inpatient rehabilitation facilities, skilled nursing facilities, home health agencies, ambulatory surgery centers, and hospices to provide the appropriate care setting for each patient's needs.

6. **Quality Measurement and Improvement Activities**. The provider entity conducts quality measurement and improvement activities across sites of care and between patient visits to improve the health and outcomes of populations, including:

- Preventive care and chronic disease management for targeted groups of patients;
- Ongoing patient outreach programs, such as patient registries, to improve the health of those populations;
- Participation in continuous learning, such as collaboratives, and the conduct of benchmarking on utilization rates and patient outcomes with other peer groups;
- Use of research and/or other mechanisms, such as applied data analytics, to validate clinical process and outcomes data to determine effectiveness;
- External reporting and transparent internal reporting on clinical outcomes, variability, and timely performance improvements; and
- The conduct of patient experience surveys, which would be made publicly available.

7. **Use of IT and Evidence-based Medicine**. The provider entity meaningfully uses interoperable information technology, scientific evidence, and comparative analytics to:
   - Aid in clinical decision making and improve patient safety;
   - Help monitor patients and track preventive services; and
   - Aid in the prescribing of prescription drugs.

Based on this framework, AMGA and the Dartmouth Institute developed an assessment program for high-performing health systems that provides a detailed analysis at multiple levels of an organization's actionable information. The purpose is to provide guidance on prioritization and resource alignment, employee transformation engagement, identification of what is working and what is not, identification of gaps and blind spots in organizational flow, and determination of where actions align with vision.

The assessment is designed to help leaders determine if the organization can confidently and repeatedly execute capabilities to meet the new challenges in payment reform and find organizational gaps that can restrict the harmonization needed to fully address the changing healthcare landscape. Designed for use by all levels of the organization, it identifies which resources are aligned with organizational strategy and which are not in order to align personal with strategic vision across the organization.

The assessment provides a method for prioritizing capabilities that require improvement and educational materials to help leaders educate personnel on key value-based care concepts. The assessment tool is benchmarked across a large spectrum of healthcare organizations but is customized for the organization being assessed.[24]

## Culture and Systems Thinking

*"Thus, American medicine, which has increasingly relied on the culture's male values of heroism and efficacy to legitimate its interventionist healthcare, has faced serious*

*challenges from competitors justifying their own presence in the healthcare field with the female values of nurturance and forethought."*[25]

*"Managers are not confronted with problems that are independent of each other, but with dynamic situations that consist of complex systems of changing problems that interact with each other. I call such situations messes. . . . Managers do not solve problems, they manage messes."*[26]

Organizational culture is often used to explain the success or failure of change efforts. But what does that mean? If culture is defined as "a social domain that emphasizes the practices, discourses, and material expressions, which, over time, express the continuities and discontinuities of social meaning of a life held in common," then understanding what organizational practices inform the social domain of the life held in common will be crucial to changes an organization moving to value will need to adapt.[27]

The process of sense-making required for widespread organizational change should include an early focus on known organizational work processes, accountability processes, governance processes, and inculcation of formal mission, vision, and values (including informal values) manifest in permitted patterns of behavior and interaction. Whether an organization's workforce "walks the talk" with respect to its mission, vision, and values or behaves in ways incongruent with the lofty messages hung on walls and marketed externally is a crucial distinction that must be evaluated early in a change process.

The study of change in organizations typically is undertaken using one of two basic models: the *rational choice model* and the *population ecology model*. The rational choice model presumes that change is pursued as the outcome of a rational, strategic process of decision making in which the organization actively chooses one course of action over another (usually in response to environmental threat). The population ecology model presumes that change is the outcome of environmental selection processes that are outside of the control of any individual organization.[28]

Conceptualizing the culture of an organization as the elaborate rules and requirements to which the organization must conform in order to receive the social and political support and legitimation necessary to survive, and the behaviors undertaken to conform to these rules, is a way of melding these two models into a coherent framework. From that framework, a systems-thinking approach can be applied to organizational culture as it impacts capacity for effective change.

An integrated healthcare delivery system is the quintessential *complex adaptive system*. A complex system is defined as "a system in which large networks of components with no central control and simple rules of operation give rise to complex collective behavior, sophisticated information processing, and adaptation via leaning or evolution."[29] In contrast, a complex *adaptive* system is a "complex macroscopic collection" of relatively "similar and partially connected micro-structures" formed in order to adapt to the changing environment and increase its survivability as a macrostructure.[30] It is distinguished from a complex non-adaptive system in which learning and adapting do not occur.

Anatol Rapoport characterized the main themes of general system theory as *preservation of identity* amid *changes, organized complexity*, and *goal-directedness*.[31] Complex adaptive systems, including integrated healthcare delivery systems, can preserve their identity amid changes and complexity by directing leadership and governance to specific strategic goals.

Systems are more than the sum of their parts. They exhibit adaptive, dynamic, goal-seeking, self-preserving, and sometimes evolutionary behavior. Information holds systems together and determines how they operate. Human systems operate around a common purpose and use information feedback about system constraints to manage and adapt behavior.

Systems must be managed for resilience, even within the context of their self-organization. Healthcare organizations are non-linear systems that operate on a continuum. Deciding where to draw a boundary around a system for purposes of management is a crucial task for leadership and should be focused on the input that is the most important to the system. The multiple inputs and outputs that act on a system comprise its limits and determine its growth. There are always limits to growth of any system. If they are not self-imposed, they will be system-imposed based on the greatest constraints.[32]

Complex adaptive systems have multiple places in which to intervene in order to improve system output. Management has several options, including balancing and reinforcing feedback loops; managing the flow of information; developing rules around behavior, including incentives and penalties that define the scope and boundaries of behavior and freedom; honing the purpose, function, or goal of the system; and changing the mindset or paradigms of the system. For a healthcare delivery system, a paradigm change may be shifting from a focus on delivering inpatient care to managing a population. Emergence of self-organizing behaviors throughout the organization to adapt to this paradigm shift is the crucial system characteristic healthcare leaders must recognize and manage in order to be successful.

The critical element of collaboration necessary in a successful culture in complex adaptive systems is based on the understanding that collaborative environments impact behavior in positive ways that can mitigate system failure. Common attributes of collaborative cultures include:

1. Frequent, cross-functional interaction.
2. Leadership and power spread around the organization.
3. People are accessible regardless of their level in the organizations.
4. Reduce fear of failure.
5. Broad input into decisions.
6. Cross-pollination of people.
7. Spontaneous or unscheduled interaction.
8. Less structured interaction.
9. Formal or informal interaction.
10. Tools fit work styles.[33]

For large complex healthcare organizations, fostering such attributes can be challenging and may require a mindful leadership focus to prevent stagnation due to hierarchical infrastructures and a tendency to self-organize into silos and fiefdoms. Although most of us would find it difficult to deny any negative connotations to collaboration conceptually, the truth is that collaboration must be disciplined and managed like any other process. Collaborating in unreceptive environments can have a toxic effect on organizational culture and the ability to accomplish strategic objectives. Over-collaborating when it is unnecessary is inefficient, as it is implementing the wrong solution due to a groupthink mentality born out of poor collaboration efforts.

The resolution to poor collaboration efforts is to develop leadership practices around disciplined collaboration. This requires properly assessing when to collaborate (and when not to) and instilling in people both the willingness and the ability to collaborate when required. Morten Hansen's disciplined collaborative framework is a three-step process of evaluating opportunities for collaboration, spotting barriers to collaboration, and tailoring collaboration solutions.[34]

## Leadership

The crucial role of effective leadership in the successful transformation to a value-based healthcare delivery system cannot be overstated, yet the process of guiding people, teams, and organizations through change is sometimes poorly understood. Position power, inherent in a particular organizational role, is not adequate in and of itself. Nor are a particular set of traits, such as charisma, extroversion, intelligence, or conscientiousness, adequate to develop effective leaders.

The healthcare delivery system fits easily into the VUCA world, as it is fraught with **v**olatility, **u**ncertainty, **c**omplexity, and **a**mbiguity. Bob Johansen asserts that managing the VUCA world requires a new set of skills that differ from the traditional approaches to leadership development and executive training. It is the essential role of leaders to make a better future, not passively accept whatever is coming one's way. The requisite 10 new skills Johansen describes are relevant to healthcare[35]:

1. **Maker Instinct**: *The ability to exploit your inner drive to build and grow things, as well as connect with others in the making.* In order to transform healthcare, creative capacity is essential, as is connecting with others in new networks.

2. **Clarity**: *The ability to see through messes and contradictions to a future that others cannot yet see. Leaders must be clear about what they are making but flexible about how it gets made.* In healthcare, the chaos of the present often clouds the vision of the future state. Leaders must navigate with clarity and flexibility in order to successful drive change.

3. **Dilemma Flipping**: *The ability to turn dilemmas into advantages and opportunities.* Problems are solvable, but dilemmas are not. Healthcare leaders in the VUCA world mainly deal with dilemmas. Dilemma flipping is a skill in which one can hold "two opposing ideas" in the mind simultaneously—that an unsolvable

challenge is both a treat and an opportunity—and identify hidden opportunities rather than hopelessness in the situation. Dilemmas of the future will be unsolvable, recurrent, complex, messy, threatening, confusing, puzzling, and potentially positive.

4. **Immersive Learning Ability**: *The ability to immerse yourself in unfamiliar environments, to learn from them in a first-person way.* In many respects, the case study approach to medical education and simulation labs to build technical skills is already imbedded in medical culture. However, leading healthcare transformation at the system level will require this skill set at a much more systemic level, as development of new care models and payment models up-end the traditional healthcare infrastructure.

5. **Bio-empathy**: *The ability to see things from nature's point of view; to understand, respect, and learn from its patterns. Bio-empathy is simply the attempt by leaders to stay in touch with and learn from natural cycles.* A conscious awareness that healthcare functions as an ecosystem is how this skill is translatable in the delivery system. By beginning from the perspective that human beings are part of nature and our health is determined by our place in nature, including our food, housing, and social world, healthcare leaders can broaden their understanding of the functions of healthcare delivery from a more "whole-person" point of view.

6. **Constructive Depolarizing**: *The ability to calm tense situations where differences dominate and communication has broken down and bring people from divergent cultures toward positive engagement.* The healthcare delivery system as it is currently constructed is divided into individual tribes (doctors, nurses, administrators, social workers) and silos (hospitals, pharma, payers). Successful healthcare leaders must decelerate the tensions arising from competing interests in order to promote real system change.

7. **Quiet Transparency**: *The ability to be open and authentic about what matters without being overly self-promoting.* Humility as a leadership skill is difficult in healthcare, which tends to promote personality cults. Transparency and self-effacement at the organizational level will become increasingly inculcated into healthcare due to the regulatory measures to increase transparency in quality, cost, and patient satisfaction.

8. **Rapid Prototyping**: *The ability to create quick early versions of innovations, with the expectation that later success will require early failures.* The pace of change in healthcare right now is such that leaders must use innovative techniques to learn from people's pains.

9. **Smart-Mob Organizing**: *The ability to create, engage with, and nurture purposeful business or social change networks through intelligent use of electronic and other media.* Population health management must organize around a transformed health system built upon disease-specific "smart mob" self-organizing patient groups. This

is an upside-down, inside-out approach compared to the traditional healthcare facility-based hierarchically designed delivery system.

10. **Commons Creating**: *The ability to seed, nurture, and grow shared assets that can benefit all players and allow competition at a higher level.* For healthcare leaders, this requires the insight to break away from traditional perspectives on healthcare competition and market-share approaches. Value-based care will realign industry dynamics. Payers and providers may develop strategic partnerships rather than seeing each other as rivals in a perpetual zero-sum game negotiation over fees. The churches, community services, and safety-net organizations will consciously become part of the healthcare delivery ecosystem.

The Center for Creative Leadership developed the DAC model for nurturing individual leaders. The model provides experience at direction setting, alignment nurturing, and commitment building[36] (see Figure 4-1). A desired outcome requires effective leaders to integrate these three functions into a working whole. Experience, technical skills, and high intelligence take a back seat to the emotional intelligence traits of self-awareness, self-regulation, motivation, empathy, and social skills in order to meet the needs of highly complex leadership environments.

During rapid change in an organization, people's emotions can prohibit effective action. It is the leader's responsibility not only to manage the organization's actions, but also to be attuned to the emotional challenges of organizational change. The leader must "prepare an organization for change and help people cope as they struggle through it." The leader's focus is people alignment, motivation, and inspiration.[37]

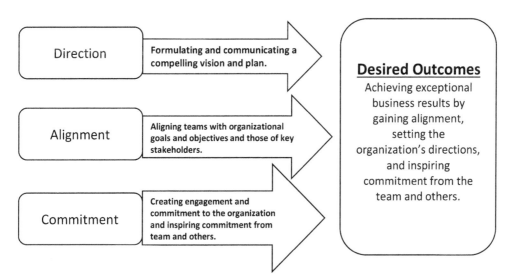

**FIGURE 4-1.** Center for Creative Leadership's Leadership Development Framework

Leadership effectiveness is enhanced by seeking understanding, establishing priorities, and then planning actions. It also ultimately depends on excellent communication skills. Telling stories is one of the most effective ways that leaders can communicate. Deeply embedded in pre-literate tribal culture, storytelling remains a basic human social function and is one of the greatest tools for change and providing cultural meaning. As author Barry Lopez writes in *Crow and Weasel*:

> *"Remember only one thing. The stories people tell have a way of taking care of them. If stories come to you, care for them. And learn to give them away where they are needed. Sometimes a person needs a story more than food to stay alive. That is why we put these stories in each other's memories. This is how people care for themselves."*[38]

We are fortunate in healthcare to be blessed with myriad stories about how our actions affect the patients we serve. Listening for stories that are linked to our mission helps leaders inspire a vision.

## Professionalism

Much of the work around the study of professionalism is focused on understanding it as "how society structures expertise with respect to power, privilege, and organizational structures."[39] However, the foundations of professionalism are built on not just a claim of expertise, but also an ideology of a higher goal of service that transcends its specialized knowledge.[40]

*Webster's Third International Dictionary* defines a profession as "a calling, requiring specialized knowledge and often long and intensive preparation including instruction in skills and methods as well as in the scientific, historical, or scholarly principles underlying such skills and methods, maintaining by force of organization or concerted opinion high standards of achievement and conduct, and committing its members to continued study and to a kind of work which as for its prime purpose the rendering of a public service."[41]

Commitment to a higher public service and possession of a specialized body of formal knowledge are characteristics that some use to distinguish professionals from managers.[42] In complex healthcare organizations, the need to bridge the cultural divide between healthcare clinical professionals and administrative managers and to develop and integrate effective leadership across the organization depends on integrating commitment to a higher public service into the understanding of the nature of professional work. The leadership necessary for successful change is more likely to be found as physicians, nurses, and senior management rally around the higher goals inherent in improving patient care.

The four basic activities of leadership are (1) setting direction, (2) gaining commitment to the direction, (3) executing, and (4) setting a personal example.[43] Securing commitment for widespread organizational change can be more successful by incorporating the goals and duties inherent in professionalism as part of the messaging surrounding organizational change.

Medical workers often hear rhetoric around organizational commitment to the Institute for Healthcare Improvement's Triple Aim of improving the patient experience of care, improving the health of populations, and reducing the per-capita cost of healthcare, but do not tie it back to professional responsibility at the individual level. Professionalism binds one to a code of values; to holding each other accountable to maintaining one's skills and competence; and to having integrity to the social covenant to those one has been entrusted to serve. By incorporating the concepts that the social covenant is based on the Triple Aim, not just the individual relationship with an individual patient, professionalism can be incorporated into the leadership imperative for organizational change.[44]

One powerful way to tie professionalism back to organization goals and commitment to the Triple Aim is to tell powerful patient stories that illustrate conflicts between higher professional obligations and individual behavior that did not live up to those obligations. Most healthcare professionals aspire to provide care that is excellent and will react strongly to stories indicating institutional or professional behavior that does not fulfill that aspiration.

## Strategy

All businesses have the same strategic choices: They can continue with the status quo; they can sell their assets to another organization that may be able to use them more effectively; they can collaborate with other organizations in strategic partnerships that create multiplicative value from the combined assets; they can innovate; or they can transform.

Every organization has a "default future," the future that will occur if no action is taken to alter it. The default future consists of expectations, fears, hopes, and predictions, all based on past experiences.[45] Because healthcare organizations are participating in the most rapid transformation of any industry in U.S. history, there is insufficient certainty in the future direction of healthcare to bank on such a passive approach.

The process of transformation involves more than operational excellence married to change management. Rather, leadership must eliminate the default future by choosing to re-write it, putting language to an alternative future that is superior; creating a tangible, clear vision of that future; and creating a good strategy to get there. A vision without a good strategy is a hallucination. The process of developing a good strategy is crucial to successfully mitigating a default future to one that drives the organizational mission forward.

Eliminating the default future by articulating a vision and creating good strategy to reach it is the quintessential task for leadership. A leader's most important responsibility is to identify challenges in the current environment that are impeding progress and determine a coherent strategy for overcoming them. What is a strategy? It is not a goal, hope, or aspiration. It is not performance improvement. From a business point of view, it is "the intelligent allocation of limited resources through a unique system of activities to outperform the competition in serving customers."[46]

Strategies solve real problems. A good strategy makes an accurate diagnosis of the problem, creates a guiding policy for problem solving, implements a coherent administration of tactics, focuses on risks and how to mitigate them, and understands the competitive advantage of the approach being taken.

For physicians, these strategic steps should sound familiar: accurate diagnosis, guiding principles for problem solving, coherent administration of tactics, risk mitigation, and understanding advantages of one approach over another. They are the heart of the diagnostics and treatment process that is the core of clinical medicine. From that context, the process of making the right choices as essential to good strategy should be a comfortable skill set for physicians to develop outside of the clinical setting.

Both clinical choices and strategic choices are best approached from an assessment of strengths and capabilities. The essence of strategy is to identify the assets and capabilities of an organization and then effectively execute actions that will use them to create value. A methodology known as "capabilities-driven strategy" organizes this approach into a series of steps that permit the design of coherent structures that create competitive advantage.[47]

For healthcare organizations developing a successful progression to value-based payment models, this capabilities-driven strategic plan provides a coherent methodology around which to organize successful change efforts. Figure 4-2 illustrates Leinwand and Mainardi's framework—a model from which to build a capabilities-driven strategic roadmap.

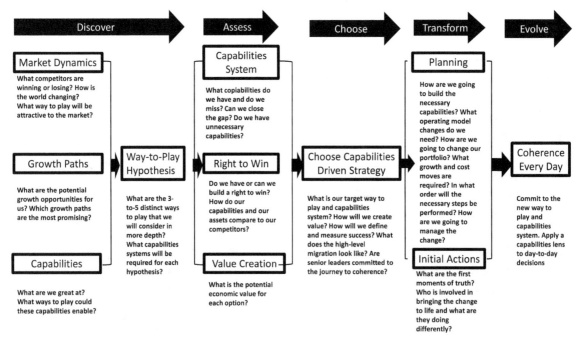

FIGURE 4-2. Leinwand and Mainardi's Capabilities-Driven Roadmap

Strategy essentially is a fitting process that marries the constraints of the external environment with the capabilities of the internal environment and the values and culture of the organization. The external environment determines what an organization *should do*. The culture and values of the organization determine what it *wants to do*. The internal environment determines what it *can do*. The discovery, assessment, selection, transformation, and evolution process of a capabilities-driven strategy can organize these environmental and cultural organizational factors into a coherent design.

Significant research indicates that strategic thinking has a substantial positive impact on the bottom line of business; the primary cause for revenue loss is poor decisions about strategy.[48] Yet, organizations rarely cultivate true strategic thinking adequately. Strategic thinking is about the ability to generate new ideas that lead to competitive advantage.[49] Effective strategy is difficult to craft, risky to accept, and challenging to implement. A disciplined approach to strategy begins with a focus on strategic intent, which should be directed toward the goals and objectives of an organization.

Goals and objectives are the "what" of organizational intention, while strategy and tactics are the "how." Rich Horwath's GOST framework[50], illustrated in Figure 4-3, outlines the relationship between these interrelated concepts in a form that can clarify the process of developing strategy.

**FIGURE 4-3.** Horwath's GOST Framework

Strategic intent is directed at identifying the gaps between organizational aspirations and resources and developing the strategy to fulfill those ambitions. The strategic planning process typically is conducted in a six-step process:

1. Define the mission.
2. Establish objectives to fulfill the mission.
3. Perform an external and internal environmental scan.
4. Form a strategy.
5. Implement the strategy.
6. Evaluate and evolve the strategy.

Michael Porter's work on business strategy articulates the need to establish competitive advantage by delivering superior value through what one uniquely delivers to the market. This is consistent with the capabilities-driven strategic approach because it identified the resources and activities that are competitively relevant. Strategic competition means choosing a path different from others. Porter's framework is outlined in Table 4-1.[51]

**TABLE 4-1.** Porter's Competitive Advantage Framework

| BE THE BEST | BE UNIQUE |
|---|---|
| Be number one | Earn higher returns |
| Focus on market share | Focus on profits |
| Serve "best" customer with "best" product | Meet diverse needs of target customers |
| Compete by imitation | Compete by innovations |
| ZERO SUM: A race that no one can win | POSITIVE SUM: Multiple winners, many events |

A "strategic inflection point" is a dramatic change in the environment that makes an organization alter the way it does things or risk extinction. The current healthcare delivery system environment is at such a point. Often competitive advantage is conferred on those companies that can be the first to recognize and respond to a major change in the environment that affects their activities.

## Innovation and Design Thinking

To survive during environmental change, organizations and systems must learn to adapt at a pace that keeps up with the change. To thrive, the systems must have the capability to innovate and to execute the innovations effectively. However, the paradox is that ongoing operations in systems are set up to be performance engines in which repeatability and predictability are inherent standards. Therefore, the process of innovation is always and inevitably in conflict with ongoing operations.[52]

An innovation is any project that is new to the organization and uncertain in outcome. The difficulty in successfully executing innovations is part of the conflict between ongoing operations and new ideas, which are disruptive to reliability and predictability at the operational level. Therefore, using an organization's typical business processes to drive and execute innovation is fraught with risk.

Innovation is about generating new ideas and successfully executing them within a system. Urging individuals to "be creative" or "think outside the box" is not an effective process for stimulating innovation. Rather, there are specific tools and techniques that an organization can use to drive innovation. Having a dedicated team focused on innovation or setting aside dedicated time for those otherwise working in ongoing operations is essential to the innovation process, followed by a focused approach to identify a problem to be addressed.

Having a time set aside to "innovate a new care model" for care of end-stage kidney disease patients is not useful. Setting aside time for content experts to work together to identify problems current ESKD patients have in receiving the best care *is* useful. Having a team with content experts who bring different perspectives to the problem *is* useful.

The first part of the innovation process is the discovery process of drawing on the experiences of those with content knowledge or varying perspectives to identify problems in the current model and therefore question the assumptions of the status quo. These opportunities for improvement can then be outlined in a schematic of what the idea will look like when it is built. Effective innovators draw heavily from analogy, identifying others who have already solved the problem or similar problems and subsequently building a business model around it.

The innovation process involves assessing and testing the idea prior to widespread implementation in order to learn and adapt in real time, as the inevitable design flaws become more apparent. Finally, the innovation must be adapted into the ongoing operations and become part of the performance engine itself. At that point, reliability and predictability must inherently be part of ongoing management and operations so formalized new processes are implemented.[54,55]

Rethinking the entire business enterprise design needs to be part of the process of innovation for today's healthcare organizations. This involves identifying the core elements of the enterprise that are truly valuable rather than assuming this is inherent in ongoing operational processes and current assets. For all aspects of the business, the correlation with the system key business goals must be evaluated, in addition to the operational connection to the company's core identity. Additionally, the ongoing performance level of all crucial core aspects of the business must be quantified in order to achieve higher value.

From this perspective, understanding the organization's core competencies—what it truly is good at—should be part of the innovation process because the core competencies and highest performing assets have the highest likelihood of significantly improving value by developing a culture of innovation within the context of managing ongoing operational performance.

At its core, innovation is unpredictable. Therefore, developing ongoing processes for measuring outcomes and formulating spaces for ongoing learning must be built into the culture. Innovation is more than an optimization and improvement process for ongoing operations. It is a fundamental process of rethinking the entire operating model in the business ecosystem.[56] For healthcare delivery systems, this requires questioning all aspects of the delivery of healthcare, from facility-focused processes of care delivery to the assumptions about the role of professionals in the delivery process. This is a form of design thinking that traditionally has not been a strong part of healthcare service delivery.

Design thinking refers to a process of integrating innovation, customer experience, and brand value. The good ideas that come out of the innovation process must lead to business transformation that drives value. In healthcare, some of the innovation remains in the ongoing work in core healthcare technologies. But the far greater task for the healthcare industry right now involves design thinking for service that is patient-centric and focused completely on the patient experience.

Thomas Lockwood asserts that becoming a design-minded organization involves 10 steps to integrate design thinking into the organization. These steps can be incorporated into the healthcare delivery system in order to adequately drive the pace of change necessary to survive:[57]

1. **Develop empathy for the customer**. In healthcare, our patients are our customers. Taking a patient-centric perspective on care delivery will accelerate service innovation.

2. **Engage unique design processes**. This means integrating design management processes into core business functions. In healthcare, development of cross-functional teams with the focus on defining the problem, discovering opportunities, looking for patterns and connections, and prototyping, measuring, and then ultimately incorporating the innovation into ongoing processes should be an iterative process built around a patient experience-focused culture.

3. **Connect with corporate culture**. The integration of design into corporate culture involves determining cultural norms and drivers, determining how design can support the norms, building awareness around the value of design, setting appropriate design partners, integrating design processes into corporate business policy and practice, measuring the value gained by design, and training and empowering others in design-thinking methods. Because design thinking is a relatively unfamiliar concept in most healthcare organizations, a significant amount of work may be required to educate the workforce about its powerful, uplifting concepts.

4. **Set design strategy and policy.** Design is what makes strategy a reality. Its output is the process that brings innovation to the market. Healthcare organizations must align their strategy with ongoing design work that embeds in teams, structures, and resource investments.

5. **Align business strategy and design strategy**. Traditional business processes discuss strategy as the way to accomplish organizational goals and objectives, and tactics as the specific techniques used to implement the strategy. Embedding design thinking into this traditional approach means understanding tactics through a design mindset. Design thinking in healthcare can create patient-centric approaches to tactics that will accelerate successful innovation.

6. **Design for innovation and transformation**. Much of healthcare improvement in traditional healthcare organizations in the past 15 years has been focused on incremental process improvement, such as techniques found in lean and six sigma

methodologies. These techniques tend to be focused on ongoing operational functions rather than the transformational changes needed for the healthcare delivery system at the macro level. At this juncture in our industry, design must be focused on system improvement that is transformative rather than incremental.

7. **Design for relevancy at each touchpoint**. Design must be not only at the product level, but also at the level of communication, information, environment, and service. For a complex adaptive healthcare system, this means all aspects of the ongoing operation must be impacted by design thinking.

8. **Focus on the customer experience**. The patient experience is more important in healthcare at a basic ethical level than it would be in many other industries. It involves patient safety, evidence-based medicine, service delivery, facility design, and, professional obligations and commitment to patient wellbeing. For most healthcare professionals, the joy of work is at least partially fulfilled in recognizing the ongoing importance of our work in the lives of those we serve.

9. **Empower creativity**. Design is a discipline that engages human creativity in workable, functional ways. For the complex environment of the healthcare delivery ecosystem, design thinking provides structure to creative work, which is necessary in an environment where so much is at stake, as it is for our patients.

10. **Be a design leader**. Many of the most successful businesses in the world have succeeded because design thinking was embedded in the culture. Apple, Dyson, and Target are three companies known for design thinking. But where are the healthcare companies known for design thinking? In the future, healthcare organizations that develop this skill will drive the industry forward and develop an ongoing competitive advantage.

## Change Management

*"The trouble with the future is that is usually arrives before we are ready for it."* — *Arnold Glasnow*

*"If you don't know where you are going, any road will take you there."* —*The Cheshire Cat, Alice's Adventures in Wonderland, by Lewis Carroll.*

During periods of rapid change, people must operate with one foot in the past and the other in the future. Living in both worlds simultaneously is difficult and exhausting. However, as Michael Porter's work has demonstrated, an organization's long-term competitiveness is not tied to short-term operational effectiveness, but to the ability to outperform its rivals with an established difference it can preserve.[58]

Sustainable competitive advantage for legacy healthcare systems requires exceptional change management processes due to the increasing pressure to do more with less as the healthcare industry undergoes historic transformation. We know from experience that periods of rapid industry transformation are accompanied by disorientation and confusion. The organizational work of reengineering and restructuring during industry transition will more likely succeed with effective change management. Moreover, successful innovation is an economic advantage for companies across industries, with greater than 60% of profits deriving from innovation across industries.

### The Change Management Process

The overarching purpose of change management is to accelerate the speed with which people move successfully through the change process so that anticipated benefits are achieved more quickly.[59] Change and innovation can be more effectively managed by understanding the processes that lead to successful organizational change. John Kotter's work in this area delineates an eight-stage change process:[60]

1. Establish a sense of urgency.
2. Create a guiding coalition.
3. Develop a vision and a strategy.
4. Communicate the change vision.
5. Empower broad-based action.
6. Generate short-term wins.
7. Consolidate gains and produce more change.
8. Anchor new approaches in the culture.

*Establishing a sense of urgency* is a crucial first step for organizations to change successfully. Examining the markets and competitive realities is essential, including identifying and discussing crises, potential crises, and major opportunities. Allowing too much complacency can be a critical error in change management.

Winners in transitioning industries adapt to change at the beginning, recognizing the need to rethink strategy early in the cycle. They begin to rationalize change early, begin reengineering early, and focus on adding merit, including integration strategies across industry-wide value chains. Effective change managers focus on quality, investments in information technology, and strategic partnerships. In contrast, late adaptors who focus on preserving the status quo and on keeping their institution safe rather than reengineering or at least tinkering are unlikely to be successful.

The window to the future closes early in the change cycle. Therefore, sources of organizational complacency must be identified and addressed. Kotter describes nine sources of organizational complacency, outlined in Table 4-2.[61]

A dysfunctional culture is one whose shared values and behavior are at odds with its long-term health. During periods of transition, it is the responsibility of senior leadership to identify the sources of complacency that threat the organization's continuing health and establish a sense of urgency. Using information about the organization's competitive situation to facilitate a general discussion is an important component in establishing urgency, but in and of itself it is insufficient. Data provide information, but analysis alone does not lead to change. The core patterns associated with successful change always affect the emotions as well as the rational, thinking brain.

TABLE 4-2. Kotter's Nine Sources of Organizational Complacency

1. An absence of a major or visible crisis.
2. Too many visible resources.
3. Lower overall performance standards.
4. Organizational structure that focuses employees on narrow functional goals rather than overall strategic objectives.
5. Internal measurement systems that focus on the wrong performance index.
6. A lack of sufficient performance feedback from external sources.
7. A "kill-the-messenger-of-bad-news'" low candor, low confrontational culture.
8. Human nature, with its capacity for denial, especially if people are already busy and stressed.
9. Too much "happy talk" from senior management.

Kotter describes the core pattern associated with successful change as one in which individuals are helped to see the need to change through compelling visualization that affects their emotions. The individuals are then open to behavior change. Kotter contrasts this successful "see, feel, and change" process with the typical and ineffective "give analysis, think, and have new thought" process used in many organizations.[62] His cross-industry research on effective change leads him to conclude: "Our main finding, put simply, is that the central issue is never strategy, structure, culture, or systems. All those elements and others are important. But the core of the matter is always about changing the behavior of people, and behavior change happens in highly successful situations mostly by speaking to people's feelings."[63]

Establishing a sense of urgency through storytelling can be effective. Effective leaders tell a compelling story that wins hearts, not just minds. Managing the sense of urgency to transform ultimately must take into account whether the individual believes the benefit of the change outweighs the cost, whether it outweighs the risk involved, and whether the expected outcome of the change outweighs any difficulty in implementing the change.[64] But these factors will come into play only when the individual has experienced an emotional response to a story at a deeply personal level.

The "burning platform" can establish the sense of urgency in a story by describing the psychological pain that lack of change may lead to. However, great transformational efforts will not be sustained by fear alone. The story must include a compelling picture of a possible, more desirable future. People must begin to tell each other, "We need to change things. Here's a better future. Let's go!"

Successful change management requires *building an effective guiding team* to lead the transformation. This group must have adequate organizational power to lead the change and the ability to work well as a team. Failing to create a sufficiently powerful guiding team will likely halt effective change, especially in large, complex organizations. Improvement methods in these systems are challenged by the need for integration, coordination, and synchronization of effort among many people and systems; unanticipated disruptions from system change; delayed responses due to multiple layers of organizational bureaucracy; and the need for behavioral change on a mass scale.[65] The guiding team must therefore have adequate positional power, credibility, expertise, and leadership skills.

The stakeholders in a change management process have three sources of their "stake": power, agency, and constituency. Power is held by those who control resources and/ or have vetoes. Agency is facilitated by those with relevant expertise. Constituencies can be direct, such as employees and patients, or indirect, such as community leaders or policymakers. Without an adequately powerful guiding team, power, agency, and constituency forces will be ineffectively addressed to permit sustainable change.

It is the guiding team's responsibility to *develop a vision and strategy* to help direct and achieve the change effort. Underestimating the power of an effective vision—one that is manageable, desirable, feasible, focused, flexible, and communicable—can be a crucial error.[66] The strategy is the logic of how the vision can be achieved. Common mistakes in developing an effective vision include not creating an ideal future state that can be "seen" in the storytelling; developing a vision as a small-group exercise for senior executives; crafting the vision but never cascading the message to the front lines; and developing a vision but allowing some of the organization's leadership to be uncommitted to and unaligned with the end state envisioned.

The vision is a picture of the future for people to step into. A clear vision defines the change being embarked upon and details the reasons the change is necessary. A compelling vision defines the end state with specific measures of success and answers the question, "How will we know when we get there?"[67]

*Effectively communicating the change vision* is a critical part of successful change management; under-communicating will undermine the best-laid change plans. The guiding team's role is crucial in this endeavor, not only with effective verbal messaging, but with role-modeling the behavior change expected of frontline employees. Leadership by example is a crucial part of the communication strategy.

Other key elements of effective communication of the change vision include simplicity, repetition, and use of multiple forms of communication. The vision of the future state should be easily describable to family and friends. Leaders should seek and model opportunities to use metaphor, analogy, examples, and storytelling. They also should be able to acknowledge pain points and challenges while reinforcing opportunities and the vision of the future state.

The five types of reaction to change are resistance, apathy, compliance, conformance, and commitment.[68] Effective change must *empower broad-based actions* throughout the organization. The more people feel that are able to act—and do act—on the vision and the more they feel supported by leadership in their efforts to do so, the faster sustainable change will occur. Understanding the cultural and structural barriers to change in the system and eliminating those obstacles will empower employees to identify and change obstacles that undermine the vision and change efforts.

Stakeholders' perceptions about the integrity of the organization's leadership depends on how much the leaders empower them to contribute to the success of the change. Leaders should encourage stakeholders to take risks that can actively advance the vision; they should not punish them if their efforts are not successful. To achieve widespread commitment, leadership must listen to the concerns, acknowledge the anxieties, and remove the obstacles that limit employee empowerment. By understanding where and how change will create pain or loss in the organization, people can more quickly move from resistance to engagement in improving the change process.

Incorporating flexibility into the way the vision is achieved will provide more freedom for the broader talent of the organization to participate in implementation. Sustaining passion during short-term setbacks and pressures and supporting personnel who experience these setbacks will empower staff and enhance the transition to full commitment to the change.

During the chaotic transition, *creating short-term wins* is crucial to building momentum as people try to fulfill the vision. Designing for, publicizing, and celebrating short-term successes is an effective tool for overcoming resistance. Short-term wins provide evidence that the sacrifices are worth the effort and rewards change agents for their commitment. Designing the change process into small, frequent, incremental steps rather than large, discontinuous efforts results in a continuous change culture that allows a more effective competitive advantage strategy, as the organization is capable of accepting and adapting to change at a pace that allows it to maintain relevance with industry change.[69] Figure 4-4 illustrates the differences between continuous and discontinuous change.

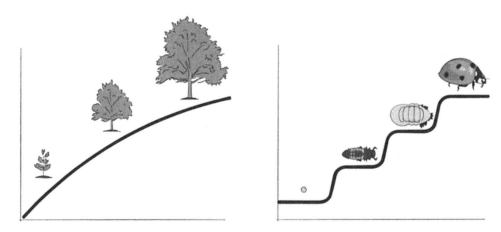

**FIGURE 4-4.** Continuous vs. Discontinuous Change

In the process of developing a culture of continuous change based on small, incremental wins, it is important to ensure that people *don't let up* after some of the early change efforts are implemented. Declaring victory too soon will lead to inadequate improvement that will not sustain the change over time. Wave after wave of changes should be a planned part of the process until the vision is fulfilled. Consolidating gains and producing more change leverages the incremental outcomes to further extend the system change.

Policies and structures that are not compatible with the vision should be altered over time in an integrated strategic fashion. Hiring, promoting, and developing the human capital most aligned with the vision will accelerate commitment at the institutional cultural level over time. Reinvigorating the change process with new projects and change agents is a desirable outcome of long-term change management.[70]

Sustainable change requires that the new approaches *be anchored in the culture of the organization.* Creating better performance through customer (patient)-centric behavior requires articulating the connection between individual behavior and organizational success and developing means to ensure leadership development and succession planning compatible with the organizational mission outlive transitions in leadership.

Readiness for change requires removing obstacles and reorganizing to reduce friction points; sustaining change requires ongoing cultural support. Cultures that support innovation develop stories, rituals, and symbols around the future vision—stories of transformation journeys with illustrations from many areas and levels of the organization. Rituals are those key organizational moments of pause when one can build community and cultural consensus, such as beginnings, endings, benchmarks, and recruitment. Redundancy of these crucial components throughout the organization reinforces change and innovation as a cultural value at the system level.

Organizational culture is a control system that is the normative order around which work is done. Symbolic evidence, such as the language in written materials, human resource practices, reward structure, mentoring, physical design, and artwork, can be embedded in the work of the organization to sustain a culture of innovation. Its role in promoting and sustaining innovation should be a thoughtful part of the work of leaders in the organization.

At both the individual and organizational level, change is a process by which there is a transition from the present state to a future state. Characteristics of the transition include low stability, high stress, undirected energy, and conflict. Past patterns of behavior may become overly valued due to the pain of the transition state, and issues of control become more important due to the stress of change.

## *Maintaining People Through Change*

William Bridges emphasizes that change is situational, whereas transition is psychological and must be managed from that point of view. His three phases of transition are: letting go of the old ways, going through the in-between time, and coming out of transition into the future state.[71] Regardless of the potential positivity of the future state, transitions involve loss, which must be acknowledged in order to overcome resistance to change. Much of the change management work on transitions has drawn from Elisabeth Kübler-Ross's work, in which she identified the stages of grief as progressing from denial, to anger, bargaining, depression, and acceptance.[72]

As Machiavelli stated, " . . . the reformer has enemies in all those who profit by the old order."[73] The ultimate price of resistance may be organizational failure if not managed proactively. The price of prevention is paid up front, involves high initial investment, and targets the bodies and souls of people whose project motivation is mission and success driven. A healing price, on the other hand, is paid late, targets compliance, and has high and ongoing maintenance costs. Therefore, successfully implementing change requires extensive attention to the people and their psychological wellbeing.

Getting people to let go of the present state requires identifying who has lost what and accepting and acknowledging the reality and importance of subjective losses, including acknowledging losses openly and symbolically. Treating people with respect, expecting and accepting signs of grieving, and letting people take a piece of the old ways with them can accelerate acceptance of the new reality.

Organizations should not be surprised at overreaction and will need to give information repeatedly because of the difficulty of processing information when one is overly stressed. When appropriate, compensation for losses should be planned for. Marking endings with rituals can provide closure and clarity, while specifically defining what has ended and what has not can help individuals identify the continuity of what really matters.[74]

Transitions can be painful but potentially creative times as well. Creating temporary systems for cultivating this creative space can be effective in supporting individuals during times of extensive change. In complex organizations, developing communal social systems organized around creative processes can break through resistance. Authoritarian, micro-managed processes are not conducive to empowering people for effective change. Developing an organizational culture that supports learning and high performance during transitions is an antidote to complacency and resistance. Providing information about the purpose of the changes, showing how the organization is supporting individuals during the change, and reframing the change as an exciting opportunity are all important aspects of managing people through transitions.

Howard Gardner has done substantial research on how individuals change their mind about something. Table 4-3 outlines the findings of his research in this area.[75]

By focusing on these seven factors during the transitional creative period, leaders can reinforce the concepts undergirding the change plan, leading to more personal resilience in the face of change.

## Execution

The best strategy in the world will provide no value unless it is effectively executed. If strategy is a way of planning for the future to respond to the ever-changing environment and achieve our goals, tactics are the specific actions undertaken to execute strategy. Strategy is crafted to impose order on the chaos of reality. Successful execution of strategy requires specific sets of behaviors and techniques that must be operationalized. Good execution requires accountability; accurate measures of performance; clear, specific, actionable goals; and positive reward for achieving objectives. Execution is

TABLE 4-3. Gardner's Seven R's of How People Change Their Mind

| 1. **Reason** | The rational approach involves identifying relevant factors, weighing each in turn, and making an overall assessment. For large, complex health systems with a highly educated workforce, cogent, logical reasoning must underlie any and all change messages. |
|---|---|
| 2. **Research** | Relevant data complements the use of arguments. An academic medical center facility will more likely be convinced of a change message with adequate supporting data. |
| 3. **Resonance** | Whereas reason and research appeal to the cognitive aspects of the human mind, resonance denotes the affective component. This is Kotter's emotional component. In healthcare, most individuals will respond with substantial positive emotion to powerful stories about patient care. |
| 4. **Representational Re-descriptions** | A change of mind becomes convincing to the extent that it lends itself to representation in several different forms, which can reinforce one another. For example, the concepts of the Triple Aim, volume-to-value payment reform, and the Institute of Medicine's Six Aims for Crossing the Quality Chasm reinforce one another in healthcare transformation. |
| 5. **Resources and Rewards** | The provision of resources can be an instance of positive reinforcement for one course of behavior and thought rather than the other. There is now widespread consensus that the fee-for-service payment system leads to overutilization. Significant healthcare reform efforts are therefore focused on identifying alternative payment systems. |
| 6. **Real-World Events** | Sometimes an event occurs in the broader society that affects many individuals, not just those who are contemplating a change. Events such as the 2015 passage of MACRA is an external, real-world event that has physicians more focused on healthcare system change than previously. |
| 7. **Resistances** | The hassles of change are the counterpoising force to the six other factors. In the current healthcare delivery system, many are substantially rewarded financially. Understanding the losses such individuals and institutions face with delivery system reform is important in developing a point of view about healthcare's future. |

about focus and action and it depends on collaboration and teamwork among leadership, management, and frontline staff.[76]

Strategic failures may result from faulty strategy, but more frequently they come from failures in the *execution* of the strategy. Rich Horwath states that managers tend to make one of five common errors in strategy execution:[77]

1. Faulty strategy
2. Unclear resource requirements
3. Poor communication

4. Weak accountability

5. Lack of calibration

Other than "faulty strategy," these errors are in the realm of execution rather than analysis and planning. Stanley Ridgley's categories are labeled somewhat differently but address the same risks. He delineates five execution pathologies that can cause the best of strategic visions to go awry:[78]

1. Lack of responsibility

2. Overreach

3. Communication and coordination breakdown

4. Poor intelligence

5. Inertia

Leadership is critical for successful execution of change strategies; leaders must take responsibility for ensuring clarity around who is accountable for what. At the same time, they must be certain the organization and its personnel have adequate capabilities to carry out the plan's laudable goals and objectives. Deliberate and effective communications plans and coordinated efforts help deploy the strategy throughout the organization and weaken resistance to change.

Execution is the linking of strategy to people, and it involves many actions, including performing capabilities gap analysis, developing a communications plan, and building an operational plan. Action plans must be broken down into measurable processes that are tied back directly to individuals who are held accountable for their outcomes. Contingency plans should be a component of execution but must not enable inertia. Inertia has two characteristics: a body at rest tends to remain at rest and a body in motion tends to remain in motion. Organizational inertia includes the concepts not only of lack of action, but also tendencies to maintain a specific direction in a specific course of action.

Chaotic environments require flexibility and speed in changing courses when conditions change. Methodologies such as lean, six sigma, and Kaizen events can be incorporated into operations to defend against organizational inertia. Breaking down processes into their primary elements is an essential part of an action plan that can then tie back people and organizational structural resources to strategy. Prioritizing actions, including eliminating some choices and putting others on the back burner, then permits a more cogent management process.[79]

## IMPLEMENTING NEW MODELS OF CARE

Three components must be implemented in order to successfully transform a healthcare delivery system.

*First, an organization must change the way it provides care to its patients.* Providing a broad set of capabilities across the continuum of care that improves quality, lowers costs, and enhances patient safety, satisfaction, and access requires a complete realignment of current capabilities into integrated care models. Development of care models must address:

- Improved inpatient care efficiency.
- Use of evidence-based lower-cost treatments when appropriate.
- Reduction in adverse events.
- Reduction in preventable readmissions.
- Improved prevention and early diagnosis.
- Reduction in unnecessary testing and referrals.
- Reduction in preventable ER visits and admissions.
- Improved management of complex patients.
- Care planning integrated across providers and care settings.

Design thinking with proven techniques can be implemented as part of this change process.

*Second, an organization must invest in clinical and information integration.* Building team-based care models and properly aligning physician incentives are key drivers to success, but they are insufficient without integrating high-impact specialty care models with primary care medical homes. An integrated medical neighborhood across the continuum of care drives performance at the system level that cannot be achieved by a siloed approach of medical homes in primary care and acute care settings focused on bundled payments or episodic-based condition management.

The ability to integrate clinical and financial information across the continuum is also a crucial component of integration. Performance improvement requires integrated information at the system level in order to manage clinic performance and financial risk and have functional effective analysis of business and clinical processes.

*Third, an organization successfully transitioning from volume to value must change the way it is reimbursed.* The healthcare delivery system is moving from fee-for-service contracts across the continuum to pay-for-performance, gain-share, and global-capitation models; however, the current transition period, in which most payments are in volume-based models but investment must be made to prepare for capitation models, is messy and difficult and the financial planning and contract negotiation needed for success requires capabilities many health systems do not have. Institutions that adequately manage the transition to value-based contracts likely will be the survivors in the value-based payment world.

## Population Health

Population health is a *"cohesive, integrated, and comprehensive approach to health care that considers the distribution of health outcomes within a population, the health determinants that influence distribution of care, and the policies and interventions that impact and are impacted by the determinants."*[80]

The National Priorities Partnership convened by the National Quality Forum in 2008 set out to address four major healthcare challenges that affect all Americans: eliminating harm, eradicating disparities, reducing disease burden, and removing waste. A population health framework for setting national health policy goals arising from this work was structured around five determinants of health integrated around specific policies and interventions. The determinants of health in the framework were medical care, individual behavior, social environment, physical environment, and genetics.

Specific policies and interventions focused on improving health outcomes and health-related quality of life at the population level and the disparities among the population as it pertains to mortality and quality of life led to policy prioritization in six key areas identified based on opportunities for the greatest impact: *patient and family engagement, population health, safety, care coordination, palliative and end-of-life care,* and *overutilization.*[81] From this framework and its subsequent impact on federal and state payment policy, including PPACA and MACRA, the so-called "silos" in the healthcare delivery system are being dismantled, with providers expected to cooperate to advance seamless, coordinated care that traverses settings, health conditions, and reimbursement mechanisms.[82]

The consequential reality for the traditional healthcare delivery system is that it needs to be redesigned around the tenants of population health in an economically sustainable fashion while the payment system and care delivery system continue to evolve. This requires traditional healthcare services be restructured with respect to delivery system design (how care is delivered), information integration, and payment system design.

The health systems of the future will be population health managers and will have invested in population health infrastructure required for coordinated delivery of services across the spectrum of care. The population health management infrastructure has five core management components that are built on a chasse of a core clinical technology infrastructure with integrated data exchange and aggregation. These seven components of population health management are:

1. Clinical model design and management.
2. Core clinical technology infrastructure.
3. Financial and network management.
4. Integrated data exchange and aggregation.
5. Performance management.
6. Patient engagement.
7. Population and clinical risk management.

The population health management capabilities required to enable these components include key elements that must be built or acquired. Wake Forest Health System's population health continuum (see Figure 4-5) was designed by population health specialists with clinician input at Wake Forest Health System to think comprehensively about the health system's resources to create an overarching infrastructure for meeting the needs of the entire population the system serves.

**Population Health Continuum**

IT Tools/Analytics/Patient Alerts/Patient Engagement/HCC Coding Support/Telehealth/Health Information Exchange

| | Primary Care | Specialty Care | Acute Care | | Transitional Supportive Care Services | Post-Acute Network Partners | Community Support Programs |
|---|---|---|---|---|---|---|---|
| **Tier 4:Highest Risk/End of Life** | Palliative Care | Hospice | SNF | | Home Health | Inpatient Rehab | • CenterPoint |
| | CARE PLUS EXTENSIVIST PROGRAM | DIALYSIS CENTERS | | | TRANSITIONS NP Home Visits in partnership with Paired Health/hand off to PCP clinic | | • Northwest Community Network |
| **Tier 3: Rising High Risk/Complex Social Needs/Complex Chronic Disease/Frequent ED and Inpatient Utilization** | Central health navigation NPs- backbone of case management structure to support primary care | Population Clinics/two tracks: a. Specialist-led with embedded PCP- neurology/oncology/behavioral health | EMERGENCY DEPARTMENT PROGRAMS / Supportive Care RNs | INPATIENT PROGRAMS: Care Management/Care Coordination Service/Disease Led -nephrology -CHF -stroke -COPD | Health on Call Discharge Follow-up ANCHOR Social Work program for patient discharged home Payer/Care Managers, Medicaid/Medcost/B CBS/primary home of hone follow up | Palliative Team Staffing / Partner Homes / Care@Home / WFBMC IP Rehab Unit | • Senior Services • Carenet |
| | **Patient-centered medical home** | b. B. PCP with specialist linkage and embedded RN/social work/behavioral medicine | | | | | |
| **Tier 2: Chronic Disease Diagnosis** | Patient Care Advocates (CMAs filling gaps in care | | | | | | |
| | | | | | | | • Winston Salem State • Community Advocates • Faith Congregations • Health Department • Community Care Center • Southside FQHC |
| **Tier 1: Low Medical Complexity/Social Needs** | Patient portal –drive low risk to MyWakeHealth | | | | | | |
| | Mobil app care gap reminders | | | | | | |
| | | | **Central Support** | | | | |
| PT/OT | Faith Health-inclusive of Advanced Care Planning | Pharmacy/ Carewell | Palliative | | Behavioral Health | Social Work | |

**FIGURE 4-5.** Wake Forest Health System's Population Health Continuum

Because the move from fee-for-service to population health management requires a fundamental shift in the way health systems do business, the ability to prioritize investment in population health enablement is crucial for ongoing financial stability and success. The development of new clinical care models, integrated information systems, and value-based contracts must be staged strategically around what services may provide the greatest and most immediate return on investment during the transition to value-based care.

Successful population health management requires segmentation of the population into smaller, more actionable groups around which care models can be developed. This risk- segmentation approach can be quantified financially by integrating both clinical and non-clinical data sources on the targeted population segments and modeling assumptions regarding cost reductions based on proven care model approaches, such as those developed by CHESS (see Figure 4-6).

This classic pyramid indicates that an initial focus on the highest-risk patients is most efficient. However, data indicate that a positive margin in capitated contracts requires management of both high-risk patients and moderate-risk patients.[83]

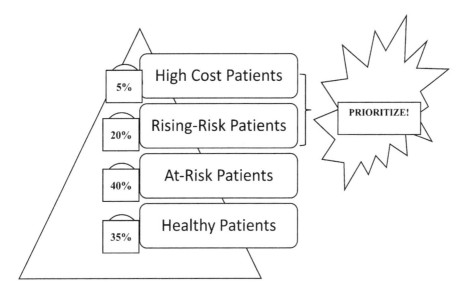

FIGURE 4-6. CHESS's Population Segmentation Framework

## Clinical Model Design and Management

Sometimes clinicians doing the complex day-to-day tasks that comprise their medical practice and healthcare managers focused on the smooth financial and clinical operations of their organizations do not step back from their work to consider all its core elements and how the elements fit together to provide good patient care. When they do so, they may be able to re-imagine how these healthcare services could be provided more effectively. Breaking down a clinical service model into its functional parts can enable the creative work necessary to design models of care that provide a better value to patients, as illustrated in Table 4-4.

## Core Clinical Technology Infrastructure

Although fee-for-service focused health systems tend to view their core clinical infrastructure from the perspective of facilities, equipment, and human resource management, the core clinical infrastructure needed for value-based care must be designed less around facilities and more around integrated information necessary to manage resources efficiently (see Table 4-5).

## Financial and Network Management

The essential business processes around which fee-for-service payment systems are designed are focused on maximizing revenue across service lines through growth and volume as well as expense control. Budget processes are focused on efficiency at the individual service unit level and revenue cycle management is focused on adequate payer contracting for fees and coding and collection processes with capital planning based on maximizing profitable service lines.

These factors also are important in value-based healthcare, which is often built on top of an underlying fee-for-service infrastructure still inherent in current payer relationships. However, new sources of revenue exist in value-based care, such as care-coordination fees, gain-share of savings, bundled payments, and payment differential based on quality performance. The ability to understand the costs of services provided, including the total cost of care, requires new sources of financial information, such as which service providers are more resource-efficient and what services, even if provided at a loss at the unit level, decrease the total cost of care and therefore contribute in risk-based and gain-share contracts to overall revenue.

Some value-based infrastructure must be invested in up front and reserves often are required to offset any potential losses. Financial management must be considered as a whole rather than simply looking at incremental revenue generation through increased volume-applied use of resources. Table 4-6 details the components of financial and network management.

**TABLE 4-4.** Framework for Clinical Model Design and Management

| CLINICAL MODEL DESIGN AND MANAGEMENT | | | |
|---|---|---|---|
| **ENABLEMENT CAPABILITY** | **DESCRIPTION** | **KEY COMPONENTS** | **FUNCTION** |
| **Care Coordination/ Transitions of Care** | System that enables clean handoffs between care settings | • Automated discharge planning and management, with visibility and communication to continuity of care<br>• Formal handoff processes, responsibility, and accountability across continuum of care<br>• Identification of care quarterback/lead for step-down, recovery/rehab, remote monitoring/home care/ ambulatory follow-up care coordination | • Minimizes redundancy, ensures continuity of care, keeps patient at center of care, reduces readmissions, and reduces complication and cost |
| **Clinical Process Development** | Demonstration and/ or development of clinical process models and key metric | • Clinical improvement programs<br>• Clinical outcomes, performance, process measurements<br>• Clinical workflow mapping and process | • Ability to demonstrate and manage clinical outcomes, delivery, and value proposition |

TABLE 4-4. Framework for Clinical Model Design and Management (continued)

| CLINICAL MODEL DESIGN AND MANAGEMENT | | | |
|---|---|---|---|
| **ENABLEMENT CAPABILITY** | **DESCRIPTION** | **KEY COMPONENTS** | **FUNCTION** |
| **Comparative Effectiveness/ Benchmarking** | Supports logical and national performance comparison and benchmarking | • Identification, collection, reporting, tracking of metrics<br>• Referral costs and performance reporting<br>• Transparency within delivery system network and reporting to patients/members and stakeholders | • Demonstrate quality and value proposition |
| **Credentialing/ Top of License Parameters** | System that creates and manages delivery-system-level credentialing and privileging for practitioners to provide highest-level care possible, support and flag identification and implementation of opportunities for all clinical to practice up to the top of their license | • Centralized credentialing (performance criteria) giving system-wide privileges<br>• Tied to resource management to flag opportunities for lower-cost personnel to provide care<br>• Top of license identification | • Consistent standards and hurdles for clinical practitioners to ensure quality delivery and adherence to EBM and quality standards |
| **Definition of Clinical Area** | Process to clearly define and delineate scope of services for different treatment areas | • Defined structure for reimbursement: quality and performance bonuses, bundled payments/case rates, risk-based payments, shared savings (e.g., clinical triggers for start of bundle)<br>• Definition of clinical activities for inclusion in perfor mance stricture of service bundle contracting (e.g., DRG, CPT codes) | • Critical to ensure plan and provider entity are fully aligned on what services are covered and how<br>• Demonstrates clear areas of structured clinical focus for the ACO—clinical integration, clinical quality, clinical differentiation |

**TABLE 4-4.** Framework for Clinical Model Design and Management (continued)

| CLINICAL MODEL DESIGN AND MANAGEMENT | | | |
|---|---|---|---|
| ENABLEMENT CAPABILITY | DESCRIPTION | KEY COMPONENTS | FUNCTION |
| Evidence-based Medicine Pathway Development and Protocol Management | Framework to define content and tools to build/infuse evidence-based medicine pathways into treatment plans and order sets | • Aligned with plan-approved EBM pathways<br>• Clinical workflow platform<br>• Dynamically adaptable to changes in research/evidence base; automated flow through to protocols and workflow<br>• EBM rules engine laying out pathways<br>• Mapping of activities/events triggered by EBM pathways (e.g., visits specs, treatment checklist, dosing levels)<br>• Tied to reimbursement for performance process metrics (e.g., EBM) | • Formalization of practice standards to recue treatment variation/redundancy, improve outcomes, support clinical quality and compliance |

**TABLE 4-5.** Components of Core Clinical Infrastructure

| CORE CLINICAL INFRASTRUCTURE | | | |
|---|---|---|---|
| ENABLEMENT CAPABILITY | DESCRIPTION | KEY COMPONENTS | FUNCTION |
| Connected Clinical Information System | Interconnected clinical platforms to support management of care within and across settings<br>For the health system: inpatient/event care, activity/ambulatory care, chronic/ongoing care | • Clinical documentation/notes<br>• CPOE<br>• Embedded clinical decision support<br>• E-prescribing<br>• Interoperable EHR with clinical linkages between and across ambulatory and acute<br>• Real-time data access | • Improves quality, reduces cost, improves predictability of treatment and outcomes for system, plan, and patient<br>• Increases treatment compliance by simplifying array of touch points/requirements<br>• Supports management of continuity of care |
| Intelligent Scheduling | System that enables health system to align patient's care visit needs with delivery setting, location, practitioner, and visit type | • Determination of patient visit parameters<br>• Expanded hours for visits, support, and triaging<br>• Internet scheduling<br>• Priority appointments<br>• Schedule prioritization/triaging | • Ensures patients receive appropriate level of care for situation |

**TABLE 4-5.** Components of Core Clinical Infrastructure (continued)

| CORE CLINICAL INFRASTRUCTURE | | | |
|---|---|---|---|
| **ENABLEMENT CAPABILITY** | **DESCRIPTION** | **KEY COMPONENTS** | **FUNCTION** |
| **Point-of-Care Decision Support** | Tools that enable real-time patient care decisions based on dynamic clinical information | • Automated, real-time, inpatient monitoring and risk assessment to identify and support patient interventions for HAI, complications, negative events<br>• Comparisons with general and condition-specific clinical guidelines<br>• Gaps in care/alert generators<br>• Real-time, ongoing analytics to identify care intervention opportunities | • Helps providers make clinical decisions with best available information for specific patient situation<br>• Support patient safety, risk reduction, complication avoidance, cost reduction |
| **Referral and Network Management** | System that maps full array of organizations/practitioners that deliver care for attributed individuals | • Identification of providers out of network that serve as referrals<br>• Map of providers found in network<br>• Map of providers that serve in contracted service role | • Helps system best allocate resources to meet patient needs and effectively control costs |
| **Resource Management** | Platform that enables resource optimization of personnel, equipment, and other assets to target lowest-cost setting, top of license care, and tailored visit specifications | • Asset/resource profitability optimization<br>• Capacity planning<br>• Group purchasing<br>• Resource scheduling (personnel, capital, rooms) | • Helps system best allocate resources to meet patient needs and effectively control |
| **Shared Documentation** | Platform to share patient-level treatment plan and clinical information across full care continuum (both within system and across network/contracted entities) | • Ability for practitioners to collaborate on documentation and care planning<br>• Consolidation of care delivery documentation and reporting into single source of truth<br>• Linkage of care delivery documentation to health plan reporting (and subsequently to reimbursement)<br>• Synthesis of treatment plan data for presentation to a variety of stakeholders | • Improves efficiency and reduces both redundancy and fragmentation of care |

**TABLE 4-5.** Components of Core Clinical Infrastructure (continued)

| \multicolumn{4}{c}{**CORE CLINICAL INFRASTRUCTURE**} | | | |
|---|---|---|---|
| **ENABLEMENT CAPABILITY** | **DESCRIPTION** | **KEY COMPONENTS** | **FUNCTION** |
| **Tracking, Monitoring, Reminders** | Collection of dynamic patient health information to inform provider point-of-care decisions and enable patient self-management | • Monitoring of prescription compliance and compliance alerts<br>• Patient health status tracking and alerts<br>• Practice tracking and monitoring of patient compliance with treatment plans | • Enables faster intervention, helps avoid costlier treatment downstream, helps patients manage their condition/react to changes in health status |

**TABLE 4-6.** Components of Financial and Network Management

| \multicolumn{4}{c}{**FINANCIAL AND NETWORK MANAGEMENT**} | | | |
|---|---|---|---|
| **ENABLEMENT CAPABILITY** | **DESCRIPTION** | **KEY COMPONENTS** | **FUNCTION** |
| **Budget Determination** | Cost tracking and processing tools to support flow of FFV funds within and outside provider organization | • Enhanced cost accounting<br>• Patient-level costing<br>• Provider stakeholder-level costing | • Helps ACO make sound cost-based decisions and understand source of costs |
| **Compensation/ Incentives Alignment** | Development and implementation of compensation systems for clinical and non-clinical staff that align incentives to financial, clinical, and organizational objectives | • Exchange of performance and compensation information between plan and provider entity | • Aligns payment share with stakeholder role and value delivered |
| **Contract Management** | Strict oversight of new, dynamic payment methods and performance metrics | • FFV contract reconciliation<br>• Reimbursement adjustments | • Holds all parties accountable for value delivered based on established payment/ performance terms |
| **FFV Disbursement** | Capabilities to share/ manage payments within and across delivery system | • Transfer of payment to provider entity<br>• Sharing of payment within the delivery system and across contracted entities | • Aligns payment share with stakeholder role and value delivered<br>• Transparent management of disbursement (performance payments and gain-sharing) across ACO/CIN/JV/Alliance participants |

TABLE 4-6. Components of Financial and Network Management (continued)

| FINANCIAL AND NETWORK MANAGEMENT | | | |
|---|---|---|---|
| ENABLEMENT CAPABILITY | DESCRIPTION | KEY COMPONENTS | FUNCTION |
| **Network Assessment/ Formation** | Evaluation of potential provider delivery-side stakeholders to identify network boundaries | • Organization/practice/ provider selection<br>• Continual re-evaluation to tighten network<br>• Network adequacy must be assured across the continuum of care | • Ensures ACO is formed on strong delivery system foundation with proven track record |
| **Novel Reimbursement Model Facilitation** | Capability to process and pay diverse array of value-based reimbursement methods in addition to standard FFS | • Application of risk-adjustment methods to global payments<br>• Flexibility to support processing of traditional and enhanced FFS (covering new services)<br>• Processing new types of retrospective, performance-based payment (quality bones, shared savings, etc.)<br>• Processing of prospective payments (care coordination fee, capitation/global fee) | • Enables delegation of risk through value-based reimbursement arrangements and simultaneous FFS payments to contracted entities |
| **Patient Financial Management** | Ability to tie actual care delivered to value-based benefit construction and adjudicate claims accordingly | • Real-time patient liability estimation/collection<br>• Real time tracking of eligibility/financial status for patient | • Holds patients accountable for decisions and enables provider entity to more readily, rapidly collect patient portion of reimbursement |
| **Product Contract Development** | Establishment of value-based contracts in conjunction with select FFS contracts to cover in-network and out-of-network services | • Compliant with exchange-based actuarial requirements<br>• Incentive-based impact on price premium<br>• Shared price setting (payer and provider entity) | • Positions delivery system competitively from a pricing standpoint; helps attract/retain individuals and employers |

*Continued on next page*

**TABLE 4-6.** Components of Financial and Network Management (continued)

| FINANCIAL AND NETWORK MANAGEMENT | | | |
|---|---|---|---|
| **ENABLEMENT CAPABILITY** | **DESCRIPTION** | **KEY COMPONENTS** | **FUNCTION** |
| **Provider Contract Development** | Establishment of value-based contracts in conjunction with select FFS contracts to cover in-network and out-of-network services | • Network contracts between plan and provider entity<br>• Out-of-area/network contracts<br>• Intra-provider contracts between ACO and services to fill gaps in care continuum<br>• Inclusive of ancillary services, specialty care, acute, post-acute, and community resources | • Promotes competition in local market; enables appropriate disbursement inside and outside of delivery system network |

## Integrated Data and Secure Information Exchange

Value-based care is built upon the integration of clinical and financial information in new ways to improve both the quality and cost of healthcare. Unfortunately, healthcare information systems built for fee-for-service revenue cycle management and delivery of services in clinics and facilities are not designed for the free flow of information in formats that will be maximally useful in value-based care. The siloed information systems in fee-for-service healthcare need to be surveyed with respect to what they can deliver for value-based care and what they are missing. The organization must invest in the necessary capabilities that are missing.

Fortunately, the market for efficient population health management tools continues to develop increasingly sophisticated applications to manage costs, quality, and value-based financial performance. Often the necessary data sources are siloed. Payers may have claims data that they are unwilling to share. Electronic medical records from multiple sources may not be integrated across various sites of service or across delivery systems. Understanding what sources of information are needed and how to securely integrate the information is a first step in prioritizing information investments in value-based care. Table 4-7 details the components of data integration and secure information exchange.

TABLE 4-7. Components of Data Integration and Secure Information Exchange

| ENABLEMENT CAPABILITY/ FUNCTION | DESCRIPTION | KEY COMPONENTS |
|---|---|---|
| **Clinical Data Stores** | • Clinical data warehouse for comprehensive access to clinical data for near-real-time access for patient management and to support population management<br>• Clinical data warehouse optimized for clinical data analysis<br>• Operational data store (ODS) for access and service needs | • Supports continuity of care management, recognition of improvement opportunities, clinical performance analysis, improvement in care delivery and system performance |
| **Evidence-Based Medicine/ Computerized Order Entry** | • Access to EBM guidelines<br>• Actual care delivered vs. agreed-upon EBM pathways<br>• Documented management of exceptions | • Real-time management of the most complex, highest-cost patients |
| **Health Plan Data** | • Administrative data<br>• Claims data<br>• Enrollment data<br>• Financial data<br>• Pharmacy data | • Availability of activity and performance data to support delivery system efficiency, cost, and delivery planning |
| **Provider Data and Clinical Inputs** | • Automated quality and clinical compliance reporting<br>• Clinical diagnostics and standard reporting<br>• Lab, imaging, and diagnostic results | • Care coordination<br>• Clinical performance<br>• Supports clinical input to prospective risk management |
| **Provider Treatment Cost and Quality** | • Cost and efficacy comparisons of treatment alternatives<br>• Cost and quality tracking of system, practices, and providers for specific care delivery areas | • Enables provider and patient accountability |
| **Remote Monitoring** | • Patient biometric and other health data from remote devices | • Event avoidance, avoiding readmissions, improving patient management and outcomes, patient quality of life, and improved care transitions |
| **RHIO HIE Clinical Information Access** | • Access for import and export of patient clinical data and standardized reporting for care management<br>• Defined interfaces and links within the system, with the health plan, with external providers and stakeholders<br>• Visibility to patient status, activity, health management | • Integration of care, improved appropriateness of care, reduced redundancy of test and clinical activity, accuracy, reduced errors, improved quality and patient experience |

## Patient Engagement

Value-based healthcare is a team sport, and patients are the central members of the team. Understanding how to engage patients as part of the team is crucial and is best undertaken from the perspective of the patient. Engaging patients-as-consumers does not come naturally to most healthcare providers, nor does the idea of having patients serve on boards and quality committees. For many healthcare leaders, the experience of being a patient is eye opening. An emphasis on access, shared decision making, and openness to feedback is a good place to start in the crucial efforts to engage patients in their own healthcare. Table 4-8 details the components of patient engagement.

TABLE 4-8. Components of Patient Engagement

| PATIENT ENGAGEMENT | | | |
|---|---|---|---|
| ENABLEMENT CAPABILITY | DESCRIPTION | KEY COMPONENTS | FUNCTION |
| e/Telehealth | Expanded access and availability to care beyond the traditional visit setting | • Access to MDs and APPs for treatment and/or advice and clinical support on synchronous or asynchronous basis<br>• Facilitated specialists' access for appropriate or PCMH-based simultaneous consults<br>• Remote visits<br>• 24/7 counsel, automated or asynchronous check-ins, e-visits, status reporting via multiple contact options | • Member satisfaction and enablement of member-centric delivery system<br>• Provides multiple access points and convenient access to care to improve prevention, access, compliance, tracking management of chronic conditions, management of low-level acute events<br>• Reduce total costs to member, employer and system; reduce inappropriate utilization of ER and lower-level usage of urgent care |

TABLE 4-8. Components of Patient Engagement (continued)

| PATIENT ENGAGEMENT | | | |
|---|---|---|---|
| ENABLEMENT CAPABILITY | DESCRIPTION | KEY COMPONENTS | FUNCTION |
| **Information Portal** | System that houses holistic information and resources (clinical, support) tailored to patient preferences; can range from access to hospital and physician practice-specific diagnostic and clinical activity to full PHR that aggregates all patient information while also allowing patient-entered information and reporting, and providing self-management tools | • Diagnostics and lab results, as well as after-visit summaries and discharge planning<br>• Education specific to health status/condition<br>• Incentives VBB tracking tied to health goals<br>• Longitudinal summary of treatment plan<br>• Member self-management via care-focused PHRs and health content<br>• Patient financial planning<br>• Patient self-reporting of alternative treatment sought/received<br>• Tailored cost and quality tools tied to comparative effectiveness, provider profiles | • Increased patient engagement, accountability, satisfaction through greater access and control<br>• Patient-authorized access to non-ACO providers |
| **Integrated Customer Service** | Service center integrated with medical care management and coordination resources to support patient engagement, coordinated outreach coaching, visibility and tracking of activity and touchpoints, and to provide streamlines access to information | • Ability to manage patient hot handoffs between entities<br>• CRM platform supporting integrated clinical and administrative support<br>• Inbound/Outbound targeted contact management<br>• Seamless access and multichannel experience<br>• Track customer service activity, accountability, and closure across system<br>• Transparent access to performance reporting across identified service responsibilities and roles | • Leverage contact opportunities to drive intervention and increase efficiency and effectiveness of healthcare management programs<br>• Patient satisfaction through seamless experience, customized service models, reactive and proactive service problem resolution |

**TABLE 4-8.** Components of Patient Engagement (continued)

| PATIENT ENGAGEMENT | | | |
|---|---|---|---|
| **ENABLEMENT CAPABILITY** | **DESCRIPTION** | **KEY COMPONENTS** | **FUNCTION** |
| **Intelligent Scheduling** | Scheduling/triaging of patients to align needs with delivery setting, practitioner, and visit type | • Determination of patient visit parameters, complaints, and key issues prior to visit<br>• Flexibility, open access, expanded hours for visits, support<br>• Online scheduling<br>• Priority appointments, automated alerts on waiting time<br>• Schedule prioritization, triaging, and access to most appropriate clinical or resource | • Ensures efficiency of visits and utilization of clinical resources<br>• Ensures patient receives appropriate level of care for situation<br>• Patient satisfaction and ease of use |
| **Member Patient Navigation and Care Collaboration** | Designated resources, processes, tools, and platform to help patients (and families/care coordinators) navigate full spectrum of care | • Facilitation and empowerment of family members assisting with patient care<br>• Facilitation of referrals to specialists<br>• Monitoring and steerage of provider touchpoints<br>• Prospective calendar of scheduled, expected provider interface<br>• Streamlines interface with community resources, web support groups, other care providers | • Duplicative and unnecessary care can be minimized though coordination of care processes across the spectrum of provided services<br>• Ensures patients and their family members are able to receive necessary services efficiently in the complex, fragmented, health care delivery system |
| **Shared Decision Making** | Sharing and transparency of information to promote dialogue, understanding, and patient engagement in tradeoffs or informed choice between treatment options, ideally utilizing "comparative effectiveness" information in consumer-friendly form | • Comparative effectiveness tools for treatment options<br>• Cost and quality-driven practitioner information<br>• Enable simultaneous access, delivery to physicians and patients at point-of-need | • Heightens patient engagement and helps reinforce health system objectives, supports patient accountability, ensure informed consent |

TABLE 4-8. Components of Patient Engagement (continued)

| PATIENT ENGAGEMENT | | | |
|---|---|---|---|
| **ENABLEMENT CAPABILITY** | **DESCRIPTION** | **KEY COMPONENTS** | **FUNCTION** |
| **Tracking, Monitoring, Reminders, Alerts** | Collection of dynamic patient health information to inform provider point-of-care decisions and enable patient self-management | • Health status monitoring and alerts<br>• Patient satisfaction/stress surveys<br>• Self-assessment and triage tools for episodes of illness | • Compliance with preventive care<br>• Enables faster intervention, event avoidance, helps avoid costlier treatment downstream, helps patients manage their condition/react to changes in health status |

## Population and Clinical Risk Management

Value-based care requires an understanding of the population being care for, not just the individuals who present to the clinic or emergency room on any given day. Knowing who is healthy, who is at risk for getting sick, and who is getting adequate and necessary services is important. Risk assessment tools, appropriate condition-based risk clinical coding, and adequate access to demographical data are essential elements for value-based care. The Triple Aim of providing the right care at the right time at the right place begins with population and clinical risk management (see Table 4-9).

TABLE 4-9. Components of Population and Clinical Risk Management

| POPULATION AND CLINICAL RISK MANAGEMENT | | | |
|---|---|---|---|
| **ENABLEMENT CAPABILITY** | **DESCRIPTION** | **KEY COMPONENTS** | **FUNCTION** |
| **Clinical Risk Quantification** | Analysis of patient-specific and panel-level data to forecast future care needs and costs and identify potential patients or populations for intervention that have the greatest potential impact | • Prospective patient and panel-level risk scores based on enrollment management data (evaluated continuously in real time)<br>• Risk-adjusted bundling for episodes of care<br>• Patient stratification into clinical risk segments (for care models and programs) | • Enables plans, CINs, and ACOs to delegate appropriate risk, elect payment models, and negotiate benchmarks with transparent information |

*Continued on next page*

TABLE 4-9. Components of Population and Clinical Risk Management (continued)

| POPULATION AND CLINICAL RISK MANAGEMENT | | | |
|---|---|---|---|
| **ENABLEMENT CAPABILITY** | **DESCRIPTION** | **KEY COMPONENTS** | **FUNCTION** |
| **Enrollment Management** | Collection of key patient information at the time of intake | • Patient history/ demographics<br>• Family history<br>• Consent for data sharing<br>• Program preferences<br>• Benefit structure delineation<br>• Patient registry<br>• Clinical and certified health risk assessment<br>• Clinical data<br>• Patient eligibility | • Provides robust set of patient information to drive population health management analysis and activities<br>• Provides risk-based input to support risk-adjusted payment structures |
| **Patient Attribution** | Where missing member enrollment and active designation, provide transparent rules dictating assignment of patient to ACO and designated care coordinator and care team | • Access to historical utilization to drive assigned attribution<br>• Review and cross-check/ confirmation with ACO-aligned providers(s)<br>• Confirmation and alignment with patient<br>• Identification of gaps in care<br>• Use by providers, care coordinators, case managers, and other clinical staff to manage information flow, identification of accountability, performance tracking, and to report quality outcomes data to payers | • Ensures patient is at the center of care and that specific providers are responsible for outcomes |
| **Predictive Modeling and Patient Stratification** | Analysis of patient-specific and panel-level data to forecast future care needs and costs and identify potential patients or populations for intervention that have greatest potential impact | • Leverages full set of data captured in enrollment management<br>• Patient-level cost forecasting<br>• Identifications of at-risk individuals<br>• Prioritization and stratifications of segments and individual patients | • Informs quantification of clinical risk, helps steer patients into CM/ DM programs, and stratifies and prioritizes daily intervention and resource alignment |

## Components of Patient Care Redesign

Healthcare delivery transformation at the health system level requires a focus on the entire spectrum of the population and the various components of the healthcare delivery network in an integrated framework. In a fee-for-service payment system, an integrated framework is less feasible because volume-based reimbursement is organized around a departmental or facility approach to services directly tied to specific fees. However, as payment moves toward more value-based methodologies, the organizational model can be shifted from departments and facilities to populations, conditions, and episodes of care.

As payment reform drives a shift to value-based methodologies such as bundled payments, capitation, and chronic condition management, integrated delivery systems have the opportunity to redesign patient care more effectively and efficiently across the healthcare network. An organizational framework that focuses care models at the intersection of the population segments and health conditions can deliver care in a manner that will enhance provider accountability and integration.

Populations can be subdivided by health condition into broad categories of the healthy independent, those with health risk factors, those with early-stage chronic conditions, those with complex conditions, those with late-stage or polychronic conditions, and those at the end of life. Further demographic divisions focused on the social determinants of health such as race, gender, income level, vocation, insurance form, and educational level can be integrated into care model design to sharpen specific care models by refining basic population health approaches.

Superimposed on the population segmentation is a health delivery system organizational model focused on health condition segmentation by the degree of condition complexity and the need for care coordination. Care models can be organized into episodic care models, condition-based care models, and population-based care models, and each can be tied to specific value-based payment models that can be linked to one another in an integrated health delivery network.

Episodic condition care models are most effective for service models that are tied to a unique point in time. Routine and well care can be provided effectively in episodic condition models and may not necessarily need to be tied to traditional healthcare providers. For example, convenience care clinics and retail pharmacies can provide simple, episodic services in a cost-efficient manner. Examples of services include treatment of sore throat, upper respiratory tract infections and simple urinary tract infections, and administration of vaccines. In this care model, best designed for healthy, independent portions of the population, focus should be on evidence-based medicine, decrease in variation, and access and convenience.

Major and minor episodes of care, such as joint replacement surgery, cholecystectomy, or appendectomy, likewise should be based on evidence-based protocols, reduction in variation, and convenience, but will require a higher degree of complexity with respect to services rendered. Bundled payments are well-suited for minor and major surgical procedure service management. The "focused-factory" approach will be the development of high-volume, high-quality, and low-variation centers of excellence that will improve care relative to lower-volume facilities.

The third type of episodic care model is organized to provide efficient care for catastrophic episodes. For example, major motor vehicle-associated trauma may impact any portion of the population at any time. The requirements to efficiently and effectively provide such services may differ by co-morbidities of an individual patient, but protocoled trauma center services have shown to have superior outcomes and can be designed around comprehensive episodic care bundles.

Condition-based care models are organized along specific conditions or disease lines that are further categorized based on complexity. Conditions can be categorized into independent conditions; preference-sensitive conditions; conditions with episodic manifestations; progressive, degenerative conditions; complex episodic conditions; and system conditions. Different segments of the population will be impacted by different categories of conditions. An example of an independent condition would be hyperlipidemia. Any portion of the population can have this condition and treatment should follow evidence-based medicine guidelines.

Preference-sensitive conditions may similarly impact individuals across the population spectrum but may be improved through shared decision-making care models in addition to evidence-based medicine guidelines. An example of such a condition would be low back pain.

Conditions with episodic manifestations benefit from early identification and effective exacerbation control and may have improved outcomes from incorporation of psychosocial services integration. Examples include irritable bowel syndrome and migraine headache.

Progressive, degenerative conditions may best be served by an integrated progressive condition management care model that incorporates the patient's changing needs as the condition progresses over time. Examples include care models designed from progressive chronic kidney disease and multiple sclerosis.

Somewhat similar are care models designed for complex episodic conditions, such as can be seen with class IV congestive heart failure patients, cystic fibrosis patients, and chronic obstructive pulmonary disease patients. Integrated complex condition management can decrease symptoms, decrease hospitalizations, and improve quality of life, although may not alter the course of the condition.

Finally, systemic conditions, such as cancer, may be best managed by models of care that integrate evidence-based medical care with effective social services designed to treat from a "whole-person" point of view. Figure 4-7 illustrates segmentation of patients by conditions, episodes of care, and population.

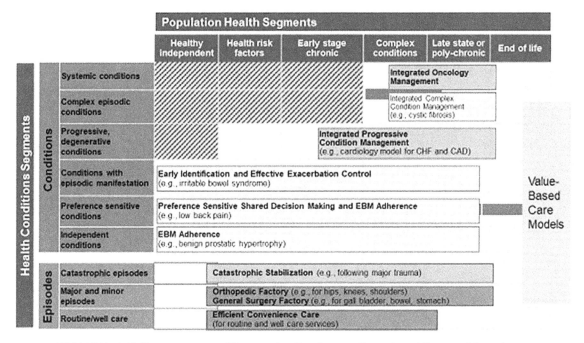

**FIGURE 4-7.** Segmentation of Patients by Conditions, Episodes of Care, and Population

## Development of Care Models

The real solution to improving cost and quality in the healthcare delivery system lies in designing care models that improve outcomes for patients. Although well-designed payment reform will incentivize improved care, the core transformation must occur at the clinical level, not merely at the reimbursement level. The process for developing new models of care is a collaborative process requiring that clinicians and administrative leaders work together to develop and execute changes in clinical processes with high positive impact.

The care transformation process consists of four phases that can be implemented in an iterative fashion in order to accelerate change at the system level. The transformation process begins with strategy development, followed by re-contracting with payers to ensure appropriate financial alignment with care models developed and subsequently implemented.

The four phases for care model transformation are:

1. Selecting the care models.
   - Defining the clinical specialties and programs designed to drive cost and quality improvements.
   - Building the design and implementation roadmap.
2. Designing care models one-by-one.
   - Assessing current fact base by care model, including specialty footprint, issues, and primary opportunities.

- Partnering with clinical leadership through design sessions defining major activities, partnerships, and resources, etc., to develop optimal clinical care delivery.

3. Implementing planning and organizational change.
   - Partnering with office managers, clinical leadership, and corporate cost/quality leadership to build out new policies and procedures.
   - Building new payer relationships to increase risk-sharing.
   - Defining new technology and operational requirements to enable care models (e.g., reimbursement platforms, compensation models, reporting staff).

4. Maintaining and continuously improving the care model.
   - Monitoring progress of implementation.
   - Supporting and driving organizational transformation in support of new clinical models.
   - Identifying opportunities for future phases of the clinical model design.

### Phase 1: Selecting the Care Models

Care models can be prioritized based on the organization's current capabilities and the likelihood of high-impact redesigned models of care will have on the total cost and quality of care. Criteria must include organizational expertise in currently delivering high-quality care in the area and the likelihood that a care model redesign will remain durable in the long term. Carefully modeling the likely impact of care model implementation on current fee-for-service business is a crucial planning step.

Expertise of strategic partners or even current competitors outside the organization can broaden the possibility for more comprehensive care model solutions. For example, a community oncology program may benefit from a strategic partnership with a comprehensive cancer center in order to incorporate broader capabilities into an oncology care model.

Understanding the speed with which a new model of care can be implemented and have impact and the magnitude of the impact is essential to prioritizing development of an institutional care model. With this knowledge, the design and implementation roadmap can be completed prior to designing individual care models one-by-one. Carefully modeling the likely impact of care model implementation on current fee-for-service business is an important additional planning step (see Table 4-10).

### Phase 2: Designing Care Models One-by-One

The care model transformation begins with an assessment of the current state of care delivery. The patient population that will be served by the care model and the context for the care model implementation in both the market and the organization must be understood by defining and evaluating the patient population, assessing the patient population cost profile, evaluating market activity in the scope of the care model, and assessing existing practice and group resources and capabilities.

**TABLE 4-10.** Care Model Transformation Phase 1 Selection Criteria

| CRITERIA | ADDITIONAL CONSIDERATIONS |
|---|---|
| The organization currently has expertise in delivering high-quality care in this area. | Is it possible to gain expertise from partners in important areas? |
| The care model represents a substantial opportunity for cost-of-care reductions. | Can low-opportunity low-risk areas serve as testing grounds? |
| The care model is likely to remain durable in the long run. | Does the model hold value in a more risk-ownership structure? |
| The regional and national competition is unlikely to be overwhelming. | Are there partnership opportunities with potential competition? |
| The care model is commercialized. | Will funding source interest in this area evolve with time? |

Practice readiness assessments, asset overviews, and patient demographics and footprints also should be assessed. Critical questions include who the patients in the system are (by geographic and demographic profile), what is available outside the physician/hospital system (community assets, competitors), and what the provider organization is currently doing (quality programs, practice pattern assessments). Figure 4-8 and Table 4-11 outline Phase 2 components.

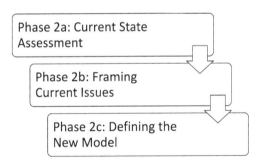

**FIGURE 4-8.** Care Model Transformation Phase 2: Designing Care Models One-By-One

**TABLE 4-11.** Phase 2A Work Plan

| ACTIVITY | ACTIVITY SUB-COMPONENTS | DESIRED OUTPUT | ANALYSIS AND DATA SOURCES |
|---|---|---|---|
| **A. Define and evaluate patient population.** | A1. Define criteria for inclusion in the care model. | Care model admission criteria | Information about patient population is obtained primarily from PM and EMR systems. |
| | A2. Establish number of patients eligible for the care model. | Size of patient population | Data may also be accessed through data management tools such as Epic Healthy Planet©, Lightbeam©, and Optum©. |
| | A3. Evaluate target patient population demographics. | Distribution of patients by location, age, sex | Patient data can then be integrated with a range of other data sources. |
| | A4. Assess target patient population disease burden. | Summary of key patient diseases and risk factors | |
| **B. Assess patient population cost profile.** | B1. Evaluate baseline utilization patterns of target population. | Average number of visits and procedures for the target population | Some information about population costs is derived from PM and EMR data, but this reflects practice cost data only. |
| | B2. Understand baseline cost of care for the target population. | Estimated cost of care for the patient population by site, provider, and service type | A full view of patient costs relies on claims data, where information on total patient spend is available. |
| **C. Evaluate market activity.** | C1. Establish competitor footprint. | Summary of main competitor locations | Information about practice patient population is derived from marketing data and EMR data. |
| | C2. Compare assets in integrating care. | Summary of practice and competitor capabilities | Base of practice data can then be compared to competitor data from other sources, such as Crimson©. |
| | C3. Determine areas for partnership, if appropriate. | Summary of community partner resources for potential use in the care model | |

**TABLE 4-11.** Phase 2A Work Plan (continued)

| ACTIVITY | ACTIVITY SUB-COMPONENTS | DESIRED OUTPUT | ANALYSIS AND DATA SOURCES |
|---|---|---|---|
| D. Assess existing practice/ group resources and capabilities. | D1. Compare practice locations, staff, and patient base. | Number of target patients seen by each provider | Information about patients served by each practice is primarily derived from PM and EMR data. |
| | D2. Plan care model roll-out by location | Confirmed pilot locations and plan for further roll-out | Other information on practices should be derived through discussions with leaders with knowledge of practice staff and practice assessments. |
| | D3. Conduct a practice site visit for implementation locations. | Summary of practice findings (per practice assessment tool) | |
| | D4. Gather existing practice information. | Compilation of key practice materials that may be impacted by care model design | |

Once the assessment of the current state is completed (one to two weeks), then a one- to two-week timeframe is used to define what the problems are in the current clinical model and which of those problems have the greatest opportunities to be improved on. The feasibility of addressing these problems must be quantified in terms of cost of the problem and potential savings over time.

For example, hospital admissions for class IV heart failure patients cost on average $200,000 per patient per year. Implementing an improved care model for patients with this condition could have an impact in the millions of dollars, depending on the size of the population the system serves. Table 4-12 outlines the Phase 2b work plan.

**TABLE 4-12.** Phase 2B Work Plan

| ACTIVITY | ACTIVITY SUB-COMPONENTS | DESIRED OUTPUT | ANALYSIS AND DATA SOURCES |
|---|---|---|---|
| **A. Define issues in current system.** | A1. Assess "hassles" for target patient group. | List of patient problems being addressed in model | Information about patient and caregiver hassles can be derived from patient focus groups, clinical experience, and literature/research. |
| | A2. Assess "hassles" for physicians/groups leading transformation. | List of provider problems being addressed in model | Provider hassles can be derived from provider focus groups or clinical experience. |
| | A3. Determine over-and underutilization of services for target patient group. | List of areas of utilization being impacted by model | Over- and underutilization can be determined by clinical studies and expertise. |
| **B. Identify interventions for improvement and potential savings.** | B1. Define interventions to address hassles and utilization issues identified in Step A. | Summary of care model clinical interventions | The first step of analysis is to identify cost savings associated with interventions through journal articles or other market examples. |
| | B2. Research potential savings associated with interventions. | Catalog of potential care model savings | The next step is to understand the baseline spend to which saving would apply; ideally, this uses claims data, which provides a full picture of patient costs. |
| **C. Size the savings opportunity within the local market context.** | C1. Evaluate and adapt potential savings for target patient group, including any local market factors. | Summary of expected care model savings | Estimating expected savings over time involves assessing the population that will be impacted and how quickly the group can reach full efficiency. |
| | C2. Determine ramp-up and expected timeline to achieve projected savings. | Timeline for care model roll-out and implementation | Number of patients participating can be estimated by the number of groups/providers transforming. |
| | C3. Project expected savings by site of service and intervention type over time. | Summary of total expected care model over 3–5-year implementation timeline | Efficacy can be estimated based on time to impact for savings. |

After the issues have been adequately framed, a four-week period of time is used to define a new model of care in which patient care is addressed in a more integrated and holistic fashion, including defining the capabilities required to support the new models and defining the new roles created to implement and manage the new models. The specific services to be added to improve the quality and cost of care should be explicitly defined. Table 4-13 outlines the Phase 2c work plan.

**TABLE 4-13.** Phase 2C Work Plan

| ACTIVITY | ACTIVITY SUB-COMPONENTS | DESIRED OUTPUT | ANALYSIS AND DATA SOURCES |
|---|---|---|---|
| **A. Establish a guiding framework for the care model.** | A1. Evaluate aspects of operations that should be impacted by clinical transformation. | Summary of design components | Framework should be based primarily on clinical expertise and market examples of success. |
| | A2. Synthesize findings into a guiding framework. | Guiding framework | Framework should also address the issues identified as part of Phase 2b. |
| **B. Define the patient experience.** | B1. Define desired patient experience across all interactions with the care team. | Summary of patient experience | Definition of the patient experience can rely on clinical expertise, market examples, case studies, and patient focus group feedback. |
| | B2. Evaluate the care team and capability requirements associated with creating the desired patient experience. | Summary of care team responsibilities and capability requirements | Patient experience should encompass all touch points between the patient and the care team. |
| **C. Define the care team needs.** | C1. Define the members of the care team. | List of required care team members | Patient experience should address the patient and caregiver hassles identified as a part of Phase 2b. |
| | C2. Determine the appropriate ratio of care team members to patients in the care model. | Summary of care team number to patient ratios | Care team requirements can be estimated based on the roles required to create the patient experience. |
| | C3. Calculate the care team staff requirements based on number of patients and staff ratios. | Summary of total staff required for the model | Staff ratios can be based on comparable market examples and expected utilization of different services. |

*Continued on next page*

**TABLE 4-13.** Phase 2C Work Plan (continued)

| ACTIVITY | ACTIVITY SUB-COMPONENTS | DESIRED OUTPUT | ANALYSIS AND DATA SOURCES |
|---|---|---|---|
| D. Evaluate the ancillary service team needs. | D1. Determine which ancillary services should be offered as a part of the care model. | List of ancillary services | Ancillary services encompass services for patient needs not covered by the care team. |
| | D2. Create criteria to determine which patients should receive ancillary services. | List of eligibility criteria for each service | List of ancillary services required and eligibility criteria can be generated based on clinical expertise. |
| | D3. Determine the demand for ancillary services for the target patient population. | Confirmed pilot locations and plan for further roll-out | Number of patients expected to qualify for services can be determined through analysis of PM and EMR data. |
| | D4. Calculate the expected cost of obtaining required ancillary services. | Summary of practice findings (per practice assessment tool) | |
| | D5. Based on cost and impact, finalize the type and quantity of ancillary services to be provided. | Compilation of key practice materials that may be impacted by care model design | |

## Phase 3: Detailing Implementation Activity

The objectives of Phase 3 are to prepare to launch the care model and establish processes for future-state clinical operations by creating care model policies and procedures, preparing office space for clinic launch, hiring new staff based on care model needs, contracting with ancillary service providers, crafting care model marketing and communication, preparing information systems for new operations, and revising physician compensation if needed.

This phase may take up to 16 weeks to complete, due to the complexity of facility and human resources needs. However, once office workflows, policies and procedures, and compensation models are developed for one care model, standardization and customization with additional care models may be implemented more efficiently. Clinical workflow analyses, infrastructure build-out plans, and physician compensation changes cannot be implemented overnight, so rapid change process work must nonetheless consider basic change management principles in order to be successful, with carefully designed internal and external communication plans. Table 4-14 outlines the Phase 3 work plan.

TABLE 4-14. Phase 3 Work Plan

| ACTIVITY | ACTIVITY SUB-COMPONENTS | DESIRED OUTPUT | ANALYSIS AND DATA SOURCES |
|---|---|---|---|
| **A. Create care model policies and procedures.** | A1. Define scope of policy and procedure manual. | Policy and procedure manual table of contents | Policy and procedure manual should correspond to the care model parameters defined as part of Phases 2a-c. |
| | A2. Convene a working team to develop policies and procedures. | Working team meetings | Manual table of contents can be based on the steps of the patient experience. |
| | A3. Create draft policy and procedure manual for review with providers and other relevant stakeholders. | Draft policy and procedure manual | Minimal additional analysis should be required to create the policy and procedure manual. |
| | A4. Finalize policy and procedure manual with expectation of ongoing revisions/updates. | Final policy and procedure manual | |
| **B. Prepare office space for clinic launch.** | B1. Conduct evaluation of existing space. | Summary of site visit evaluation of available space | Assessment of existing space can be based on the practice site visit findings (Phase 2a). |
| | B2. Determine additional space requirements associated with care model implementation. | Summary of total new space requirements | Total space requirements can be based on the number of new staff required as part of the care model, in addition to any new spaces required (e.g., patient education room). |
| | B3. Assess options to accommodate new space requirements. | Revised floor plans/office layout | Most new staff will require private workspaces, although some part-time staff could use shared spaces. |
| | B4. Proceed with space renovation, if needed. | Construction bids, if needed | |
| **C. Hire new staff based on care model needs.** | C1. Determine the total number and type of new staff required. | List of new staff required, with job descriptions as needed | Total new staff requirements can be based on the number of care team members required as part of the care model, in addition to any ancillary services that will be offered by the practice (e.g., nutrition). |
| | C2. Develop plan to hire new staff. | Overview of hiring process with accountabilities and timelines | Most new staff can be recruited through existing channels with minor modifications to existing job descriptions. |
| | C3. Recruit new staff. | New staff | |
| | C4. Train and onboard new staff. | Trained staff | |

*Continued on next page*

**TABLE 4-14.** Phase 3 Work Plan (continued)

| ACTIVITY | ACTIVITY SUB-COMPONENTS | DESIRED OUTPUT | ANALYSIS AND DATA SOURCES |
|---|---|---|---|
| **D. Contract with ancillary service providers.** | D1. Based on ancillary service requirements, determine total needs and plan to develop partnerships. | List of ancillary service requirements with timelines and accountabilities for forming partnerships | External ancillary services providers should be tracked and evaluated using standardized, transparent screening forms. |
| | D2. Create ancillary service provider evaluation. | Vendor evaluation form | Evaluation should include the type of services provided as well as the types of outcomes and performance metrics being tracked by the vendor. |
| | D3. Evaluate and contract with service providers. | Vendor cross-comparison results | |
| **E. Craft care model marketing and communication.** | E1. Define total marketing requirements. | List of marketing requirements | Marketing needs should include: <br>• Patient-facing collateral. <br>• Scripts (e.g., care model introduction). <br>• External communication pieces. |
| | E2. Create a plan to develop marketing materials. | Timeline and accountabilities for marketing material development | Marketing design should also include a plan to socialize materials with practices, especially for scripts. |
| | E3. Create draft marketing materials. | Draft marketing materials | |
| | E4. Finalize marketing materials. | Final marketing materials | |
| | E5. Produce marketing materials. | Marketing materials for distribution | |
| | E6. Begin marketing to patients. | | |

**TABLE 4-14.** Phase 3 Work Plan (continued)

| ACTIVITY | ACTIVITY SUB-COMPONENTS | DESIRED OUTPUT | ANALYSIS AND DATA SOURCES |
|---|---|---|---|
| **F. Prepare IT systems for new operations.** | F1. Prepare practice IT systems for care model launch (including templates, notes, appointments in PM system, etc.). | PM and EMR prepped for model operation | IT will be involved during planning phase so they will be prepared to lead the charge of IT preparations for care model launch, in combination with guidance from office managers and health navigator supervisor. |
| | F2. Develop IT support for care coordination and navigation. | Care-coordination technology solution | Practice will likely not have an existing base of templates and forms that can be used and will require support to develop these tools. |
| | F3. Create IT support for key care model documents (e.g., patient care plan). | Electronic site for documents | |
| | F4. Determine method to flag enrolled patients in EMR. | Patient registries of flags in EMR | |
| **G. Revise physician compensation as needed.** | G1. Evaluate impact of care model on participating physician compensation. | Summary of compensation impact | Due to changes in clinic operation associated with many care models, it may be necessary to revise physician compensation. |
| | G2. Develop plan to align physician compensation appropriately to transformation goals. | Summary of proposed compensation model | In some cases, productivity will decrease as a part of the model and physician compensation should not decrease as a result of transformation-related productivity changes. |
| | G3. Approve revised compensation through standard practice processes (e.g., compensation committee, etc.). | | Analysis should tie any proposed changes to compensation to total cash flows and gain-share revenue. |

## Phase 4: Measures and Continuous Improvement

The objectives of the fourth phase of care model transformation are to track the impact and outcomes of the redesigned model of care and use the classic techniques of continued quality improvement to create and implement the culture and processes for continuous improvement. Internal performance reporting and tracking of processes, people, vendors, and strategic partners will necessarily become part of the transformation efforts at the cultural level and will help facilitate year-over-year improvement in quality and cost.

Specifically measuring outcomes rather than simply assessing processes will be essential to performance improvement. Transparency is a cultural expectation that will accelerate effective performance management. Table 4-15 outlines the Phase 4 work plan.

**TABLE 4-15.** Phase 4 Work Plan

| ACTIVITY | ACTIVITY SUB-COMPONENTS | DESIRED OUTPUT |
|---|---|---|
| **A. Create internal performance reporting and tracking processes.** | A1. Define the audiences for performance reports. | List of audiences for performance dashboards |
| | A2. Identify key areas to be tracked and measured. | List of major questions answered by dashboards |
| | A3. Define metrics within each key area. | List of metrics to be reported in dashboards |
| | A4. Create dashboard for metric tracking and reporting. | |
| | A5. Collaborate with clinical data analytics team to establish reporting mechanisms. | |
| | A6. Create clinical data analytics processes to report data to required audiences in required timeframe. | Performance management dashboards |
| | A7. Conduct ongoing optimization to ensure reports meet needs. | Report on effectiveness/relevance of dashboards |
| **B. Establish process for continuous improvement.** | B1. Define team to intervene on improvement opportunities. | |
| | B2. Create process to track continuous improvement and measure impact. | Definition of continuous improvement process |
| **C. Track performance of vendors and partners.** | C1. Based on ancillary service partnerships, define metrics to be tracked over time. | Definition of continuous improvement process |
| | C2. Define interventions for low-performing vendors/partners. | List of performance metrics by vendor/partner |
| | C3. Conduct ongoing vendor/partner performance tracking. | Definition of intervention process |

## Information Integration

*"Western societies are moving towards a society of networks, i.e., a society, in which the formal, vertically integrated organization that has dominated the 20th century is replaced or at least complemented by consciously created and goal directed networks."* —Jörg Raab and Patrick Kenis[84]

Central to population health management is the ability to have actionable, integrated information from across the spectrum of community and care settings. However, healthcare information systems have by and large been designed for the functions of the fee-for-service payment system: transaction based, focused on documentation and coding for billing purposes, and organized at the individual provider or facility level.

Although the 2009 HITECH act, which provided stimulus money and subsequent penalties for healthcare providers through the Meaningful Use program, has essentially fulfilled its intended aim of converting the vast majority of healthcare providers from paper to electronic health records, this regulatory market changer has not led to health information exchange and interoperability. Consequently, the technological innovations necessary to adequately manage populations are still under development in a relatively immature market. It is therefore necessary for healthcare delivery systems to take a functional assessment approach to understanding the capabilities and investments needed for adequate health information technology for successful population health management.[85]

Healthcare delivery systems have used the HIMSS EMRAM© assessment model through the years to determine their level of adoption of information technology and plan their information technology investments. The systems are assessed on a functional basis into eight stages (stages 0–7) based on their adoption of electronic health records. These eight stages rate the level of a facility's EMR capabilities. Table 4-16 provides HIMSS Analytics' descriptive summary of each stage, from most basic to advanced.[86]

**TABLE 4-16.** HIMSS Health Information System EMRAM© Assessment Stages

| Stage 0 | The "3 key ancillaries," radiology, laboratory, and pharmacy departments, have not been installed. |
| --- | --- |
| Stage 1 | The 3 key ancillaries have been installed at the organization. |
| Stage 2 | The organization is able to submit data to a clinical data repository (CDR) from key ancillary departments. The data are then available for viewing by medical staff. The CDR must have a controlled medical vocabulary, clinical decision support (CDS), and may have image viewing capabilities. |
| Stage 3 | The organization has installed clinical documentation flow sheets, a clinical decision support system has been executed, and there is image viewing accessibility. |
| Stage 4 | Computerized physician order entry (CPOE) has been implemented. CDS have been modified to allow evidence-based medicine (EBM) practices. |
| Stage 5 | Implementation of "closed loop medication administration environment" has occurred in a minimum of one patient service department. Auto-identification technologies have been synced with the CPOE and pharmaceutical department. |
| Stage 6 | Structured templates are used in a minimum of one patient service department. The radiology PACS system is in use, allowing providers to view all medical images through a "intranet or secure-network." |
| Stage 7 | The organization has achieved the highest level of integration and functions in a paperless environment. It has full sharing capabilities with other healthcare facilities and Health Information Exchanges (HIEs).[87] |

The inpatient-focused, facility-based orientation of the HIMSS stages illustrates the inadequacy of its evaluation criteria for the purposes of population health management.

From a clinical approach, the evolution of health information technology has developed to facilitate operational and business processes, with clinical information designed and collected based on these processes.

The first stage of health information technology is the systems designed around the operations of revenue cycle management. Practice management systems and financial management systems are focused on billing, collecting, scheduling, and coding and are mature technology that has been an essential part of healthcare management for more than 40 years.

Clinical management information systems are less-mature technology. The widespread adoption of electronic health records has only occurred since the HITECH act, and many health systems have yet to achieve stage 7 HIMSS criteria. The tools of clinical decision support and comparative effectiveness research are not yet embedded in clinical process.

If population health management is the next stage of health information maturation, it is in its infancy. The next stage of development, which would include integration of consumer health information with healthcare delivery information systems, is still on the horizon. A fifth stage, where big data and genomic information are integrated to provide personalized medicine, is theoretical at best.

John Cuddeback developed an exceptional framework for understanding what clinical information integration might look like as this part of the health delivery system further matures (see Figure 4-9).

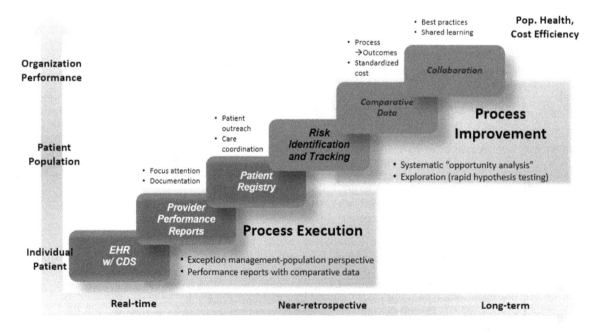

**FIGURE 4-9.** Cuddeback's Clinical Information Integration Framework

Cuddeback's progression from the individual patient to population health focuses on process execution and subsequent process improvement at the system level.[88]

In 2013, the Certified Commission of Health Information Technology (CCHIT) developed and made publicly available a health IT framework and glidepath for accountable care. The framework was designed to be a starting point for provider groups developing HIT roadmaps, for payers looking to assess or complement the HIT capabilities of their provider partners, and for HIT developers designing products to fill gaps in currently available technology.

The commission delineated seven key processes required to meet the aims of high-quality care, cost efficiency, and customer loyalty; defined the functions within each process; and identified HIT capabilities to support each function.[89] Despite the fact that the document is more than seven years old, its process and functional framework remains contemporary with respect to assessing delivery system population health integration capabilities. Although its HIT glidepath for supporting healthcare transformation is outdated with respect to the technology used illustratively for the transitional and transformational states, the overall categories of clinical culture, cost control, financial risk, patient influence, and quality control remain relevant categories from which to assess population health management integration. The framework is outlined in Figure 4-10.

**The CCHIT Health Information Technology Framework for Accountable Care: An Infrastructure to Support Health Care Transformation**

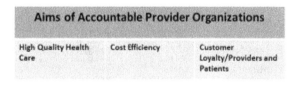

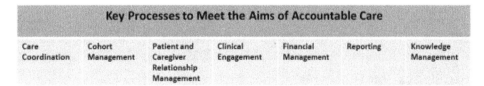

**FIGURE 4-10.** CCHIT Health Information Technology Framework for Accountable Care

Two approaches are typically taken in institutional health information technology investment. The first is a "best-in-class" approach in which the function required to be served by a technological solution is explicitly defined and then technology is sought that best meets the functional requirements. The other approach is an integrated solutions approach where technology is sought with a broader range of functionality.

In the best-in-class approach, leading-edge functionality in core focus areas may be important for building differentiated capabilities that rely heavily on underlying technology. These vendors are typically smaller companies with shorter development cycles and more likely to have an interest in strategic partnerships in new markets. However, the lack of integration of these types of solutions can increase the overall complexity and cost of the technology environment.

In contrast, integrated solutions often offer a broad range of functionality with lower maintenance costs, less complexity in the technology environment, and fewer vendors to manage. These types of solutions often trade off the best-in-class offering for a specific capability in exchange for a broader range of capabilities.

Table 4-17 outlines CCHIT key functions and processes necessary to meet the goals of ACOs.

**TABLE 4-17.** CCHIT Key Functions and Processes to Meet The Goals Of ACOs

| Care Coordination | Cohort Management | Patient and Caregiver Relationship Management | Clinical Engagement | Financial Management | Reporting | Knowledge Management |
|---|---|---|---|---|---|---|
| • Access real time health insurance coverage information<br>• Establish rapier relationships<br>• Establish provider relationships<br>• Share clinical data during transitions of care<br>• Identify best setting for care<br>• Identify social and community supports<br>• Manage referrals<br>• Patient-centric medication management<br>• Clinical information reconciliation. | • Identify cohort from within entire patient population<br>• Monitor individual patients<br>• Clinical Decision Support<br>• Patient engagement within cohort<br>• Engage preferred providers and clinicals in care teams<br>• Share care management plan<br>• Interventions<br>• Follow up<br>• Monitor cohort | • Basic information services<br>• Administrative simplification for patient s<br>• Patient educational services<br>• Patient communication<br>• Patient engagement in care<br>• Patient assumption of care responsibilities<br>• Monitor patient goals and outcomes<br>• Patient experience of care surveys. | • User friendly, timely and actionable Clinical Decision Support<br>• Standard clinical assessment tools<br>• Wall-defined care teams<br>• Communication within organization<br>• Communication external to organization<br>• Administrative simplification for providers<br>• Usability of HIT<br>• Comprehensive educations systems for clinicians Community-based resources<br>• Public Health Information<br>• Research protocol information | • Administrative simplification for operations<br>• Normalized and Integrated data<br>• Health assessment of entire patient population<br>• Patient attribution algorithms<br>• Performance reports<br>• Risk sharing analytics<br>• Payer contract management<br>• Provider contract management<br>• Cost accounting Reimbursement systems for other than fee-for-service<br>• Billing for revenue outside of risk contracts<br>• Financial management for patient s | • Retrieve Data specific to measures<br>• Story quality metric data<br>• Calculate quality measures<br>• Report quality metrics for internal use<br>• Report measures to external designated entities<br>• Report data required for syndromic surveillance<br>• Public Health reporting<br>• Registry reporting<br>• Report resource consumption for internal use<br>• Report adverse events to Patient Safety Organization | • User friendly timely and actionable clinical decision Support<br>• Personalize patient specific information<br>• Create and share clinical knowledge<br>• Create and share process improvement knowledge<br>• Support comparative effectiveness research |

Because the current population health management information technology is an immature market, determining technical investment and selecting vendors must be a process that will evolve over time, with many start-up companies being acquired by consolidators or going out of business as the market matures. Therefore, the information technology strategy for a healthcare integrated delivery system should be built around a plan to substitute improved technological solutions as the industry evolves.

Careful attention to the length of vendor contracts, data ownership, and committed capital must be part of the overall population health management strategic investment plan. By maintaining a focus on functional capabilities facilitated by technology rather than the specific technology itself, healthcare organizations can maintain more flexibility during the transformation process and avoid "vendor capture" that erodes operating margins and competitive advantage in an IT market that thus far remains insufficient for the functional capabilities expected of it.

At the institutional level, IT governance is a crucial component in change management. The high capital cost of information technology makes the decision making around who determines resource investment a crucial component of an effective investment plan. In many organizations, decisions surrounding IT management are not clear, often leading to poor interoperability, duplication, and higher capital costs than would be possible with improved IT governance policies. Peter Weill and Jeanne W. Ross at MIT's Sloan Center for Information Systems Research created a framework around IT governance (Figure 4-11) that is a useful guideline for IT management decision-making policy.[90] Using this framework while implementing population health management capabilities can improve the processes needed to achieve successful information integration.

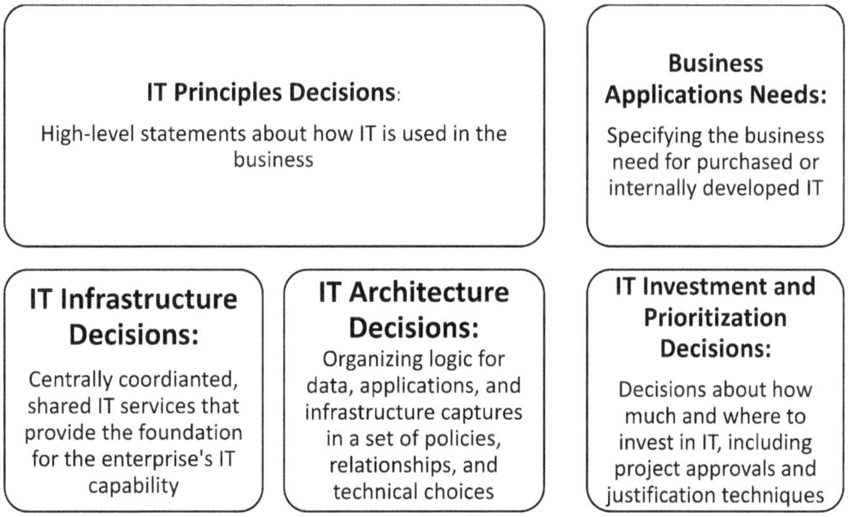

**IT Principles Decisions**:
High-level statements about how IT is used in the business

**Business Applications Needs:**
Specifying the business need for purchased or internally developed IT

**IT Infrastructure Decisions:**
Centrally coordianted, shared IT services that provide the foundation for the enterprise's IT capability

**IT Architecture Decisions:**
Organizing logic for data, applications, and infrastructure captures in a set of policies, relationships, and technical choices

**IT Investment and Prioritization Decisions:**
Decisions about how much and where to invest in IT, including project approvals and justification techniques

**FIGURE 4-11.** Key IT Governance Decisions

The IT governance can then be organized around these principles to determine who has input and who has decision-making authority within the institution's governance structure.

Analytics can be embedded into business processes in three basic ways:

1. *Automated decision applications.* The heuristics used may vary, depending on whether the application is an evidence-based clinical process or a financial planning process, but the ability for data-informed decisions to be made in certain circumstances with minimal human intervention can drive efficiency at an organizational and population health level.

2. *Business applications for operational and tactical decision making.* Analytical managers can rely on analytical applications that are integrated directly into enterprise systems for tasks such as supply chain optimization, clinical effectiveness analysis, and financial forecasting.

3. *Information workflow, project management, collaboration, and personal productivity tools.* Healthcare technology will continue to evolve toward consumer-centric models such as wearable devices with patient-generated data. The use of common tools such as Microsoft Office or Prezi as personal productivity tools will need to take into account the open architecture of the consumer-driven healthcare environment of 2020, where big data, genomics-informed personalized medicine, and patient communication applications will require analytic capabilities to manage new sources of information in way that will maximize organizational effectiveness.[91]

# CHAPTER FIVE

# Value-Based Payment Models

## CATEGORIES OF PAYMENT MODELS

Payment for healthcare services in the United States is complex on many different levels. First, different types of payers cover different parts of the population. Government payers include Medicaid, Medicare, the Indian Health Services program, the Department of Defense TRICARE programs, the Veterans Health Administration, and, sometimes, public health. Individuals may pay for medical care directly. Individuals may have an individual insurance policy that covers them or them and their family, and may choose different benefits designs with different deductibles, copays, covered services, prices, and subsidies through the ACA.

Employers may offer insurance as a benefit through a fully insured commercial product or self-insure and use a third-party administrator to manage the benefits. Employers may offer variously designed benefits based on their size and market competition for employees and minimal federal requirements governed by the ERISA laws and the ACA. These payers must then contract with providers of the healthcare services in a way that meets the needs of the people to be covered as well as policy goals, in the case of government payers, and business goals in the case of employers.

For all these payers, achieving high quality at a fair price is a goal that increasingly is putting focus on the types of payment models with which they contract with service providers. Value-based payment models are being developed within several broad categories and adapted by payers to meet their specific objections:

1. **Enhanced fee-for-service**: Adding new codes to pay for high-value services previously underutilized due to lack of payment, such as transitional care codes paid to primary care physicians who see patients discharged from the hospital within 14 days, as that is associated with improved outcomes and fewer readmissions.
2. **Pay-for-performance**: Paying a bonus to a healthcare provider for meeting certain quality, cost, or utilization goals. Federal efforts include the Meaningful Use payments that were part of the HITECH act and MIPS quality measures, and private efforts such as efficiency bonuses to providers who meet certain generic prescribing rates and lower-cost site-of-service choices.

3. **Bundled payments**: Providing a single payment for a bundle of services meant to treat a certain condition as opposed to paying for each service individually.
4. **Care-coordination payments**: Paying a monthly episode-based payment to coordinate services for patients around conditions or episodes of care.
5. **Share-savings payments**: Providing services in a fee-for-service arrangement and then sharing in any savings generated for efficient provision of care based on pre-established benchmarks.
6. **Shared-risk payments**: Providing services in a fee-for-service arrangement and then sharing in any savings or losses generated based on pre-established benchmarks.
7. **Population-based payments**: Transmitting a per-member per-month payment for services upfront irrespective of the amount of services provided. The provider is responsible for providing that service for the entire population for which they are contracted.

## PAYMENT MODEL REDESIGN

Value-based payments change everything in healthcare. Corporate strategy, financial incentives, access, quality, profitability, and operations are all affected. Understanding how to transition an organization from fee-for-service to fee-for-value requires paying attention to how value-based payments will affect each aspect of the organization and developing tactics to make the transition successfully. It also requires new skills at the contracting level, as normative approaches to fee-for-service contracting are insufficient and in some situations counter-productive in the new payment models.

Traditionally, fee-for-service has been perceived to be low risk for providers compared to capitated models of reimbursement. Efficient provision of service at the unit level combined with driving volume at the unit level and investing in capacity to provide more volume created adequate margin for most health organizations that were able to develop operational efficiencies. Whether fee-for-service will continue to be considered low risk is unclear because as volume of services continues to increase, both private and governmental payers are reducing fees through their leveraged market power for providers who are unable to demonstrate cost-effective, high-quality care.

The MIPS program under MACRA, for example, has essentially moved physician payment to a pay-for-performance-based fee-for-service model across the board, with penalties continuing to increase annually for poor performers. As providers learn to take on more performance risk at the level of the service they provide, it will behoove them to seek contracts that permit them to manage the total cost of care through global payments, so long as they have integrated patient care delivery systems and payment administration capabilities that will permit them to have access to the total premium dollar.

Global payment fosters new business relationships and interdependencies because it forces improved patient management at each point along a continuum of care. In a capitated environment, collaboration among providers rather than adversarial competition is a more effective management strategy so long as incentives can be adequately aligned.[92] Figure 5-1 presents a view of the transition to value-based care.

*In the provider context, the transition to value will unfold as different journeys with differing timelines.*

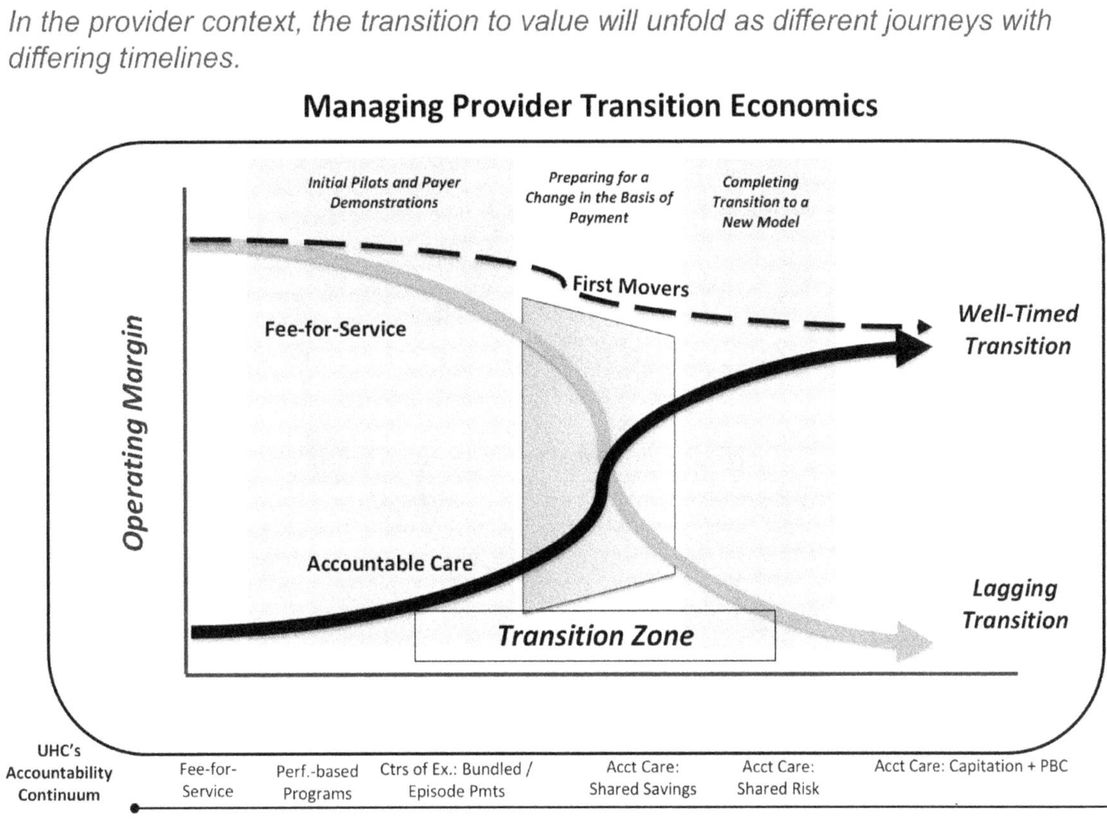

**FIGURE 5-1.** Provider View of Transition to Value-Based Care

When developing strategies for value-based contracting, an emphasis on understanding the total cost of care at a population level rather than a focus on the revenues/expenses of providing specific components of care at the institutional or provider level is crucial. For the population at large, healthcare costs have been consistent through the years in terms of category, although recently drug costs are rising faster than other areas[93] (see Figure 5-2).

The specific population in a contract varies greatly with respect to cost, however.

Payers design their benefits based on highly differentiated customer bases that must be considered in value-based payment negotiation in ways that are not directly apparent in traditional fee-for-service. Understanding the impact of network requirements, benefits requirements, and expect payer profit margin is crucial in value contracting. Payers have a complex customer base and view performance differently according to these customer bases (see Table 5-1).

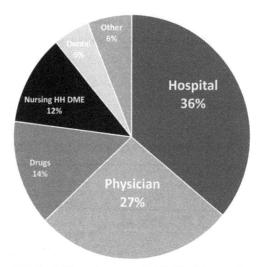

**FIGURE 5-2.** Distribution of U.S. Healthcare Spending

**TABLE 5-1.** Payer Perspective of Performance in Relationship to Customer Base

|  | Individual | Medicare Advantage | Small Group | Fully-insured Large Group | Administrative Services Only/Self-insured |
|---|---|---|---|---|---|
| Percentage of Lives | <10% | <10% | 20% | 20% | 45% |
| Percentage of Revenues | 5% | 40% | 15% | 35% | <5% |
| Channel | Exchange or Direct | Direct or Broker | Broker | Broker or Consultant | Consultant |
| Network Considerations | Want "their" doctors in | Must meet CMS Network Adequacy Requirements | Prefer Broad Network but will Trade Access for Price | Broad Access Network | Network Discount

Nationwide Network |
| Benefit Considerations | Standard | Standard | Less Important | More Important | Highly Customized |

In value-based contracting, it is helpful to follow the dollars through the system from a payer's point of view. From this perspective, pricing, underwriting, product development, and benefit design all occur prior to provider contracting, with medical trend serving as a lagging measure to manage future healthcare premium pricing and expense control strategies. Table 5-2 and Table 5-3 illustrate how payers may view various insurance market segments and the healthcare value chain, respectively.

As providers move from fee-for-service to performance payments and then on to shared savings, risk sharing, and finally taking responsibility for the total cost of care,

TABLE 5-2. How Payers View the Various Insurance Market Segments

| Market Segment | Population in Millions | Percent | Utilization | Provider Profit | Insurer Profit Low |
|---|---|---|---|---|---|
| Group | 165 (20% small group/80% large group) | 50% | Low | High | Small Group High, Large Group Small |
| Individual | 20 | 6% | Medium | High | Loss |
| Medicaid | 45 | 13% | Medium | Loss | N/A |
| Medicare | 50 | 15% | High | Neutral to Slight Loss | Positive for Medicare Advantage |
| Other (Tricare/Indian/VA) | 10 | 3% | Low | Neutral | N/A |
| Uninsured | 45 | 113% | Low | Loss | N/A |

TABLE 5-3. View of the Healthcare Value Chain from One Payer's Perspective

| | |
|---|---|
| **Employer/Individual/Government:** What they want and will pay | **Provider Contracting:** Volume revenue model, bridging economics |
| **Benefit Design:** Behavior economics, deductible leveraging | **Clinical Services:** Mix, charge masters, pricing strategies, variation |
| **Product Development:** What is worth including, health and wellness | **Payments:** Allowed versus paid, member liability |
| **Pricing and Underwriting:** Premium, community rating, blind spots | **Medical Expense Trend:** Predictability, sustainability |
| **Network Configuration:** Open Access, narrow networks, ACOs, leakage, cost, adequacy | **Health Plan Profitability:** Nonprofit vs. for-profit, community steward |

the capabilities of current payers must be integrated into provider capabilities or bought through vendors or payer partnerships.

The types of payer management capabilities available are differentiated by contract type. Commercial populations vary considerably in terms of cost from Medicare populations, and total spending and type of spending vary accordingly. Providers taking on value-based contracts must develop strategies for the different types of contracts, including the individual commercial market, the public exchange market, the small-group commercial market, the large-group commercial market, the self-insured employer market, the Medicare Advantage market, the Medicaid market, and traditional Medicare value-based payment market.

Understanding what contributes to the total cost of care as well as the medical spend trend is crucial to managing costs. An increase in medical trend is the increase in medical costs per patient from one time period to another. The causes of trend increase can be difficult to analyze; a patient may go to the doctor more frequently than past trend, or the benefit design may increase patient share of cost and lower utilization.

Medical trend is the result of four components:

1. The cost per service (including severity).
2. The number of services (utilization/frequency).
3. The interaction between cost and utilization (mix of services).
4. The influence of the benefit plan (leveraging).

From a health plan point of view, cost per service is a prominent driver of overall trend, more so than utilization, which is one reason leveraging through high deductibles and copays is used to decrease demand for services and push providers to lower fees.

Pharmacy costs are becoming an increasingly strong driver of medical trend and, as the population ages and healthy lifestyles decrease, the number of high-cost cases increases. Migration to high-cost providers and the increase in provider-sensitive conditions (specifically spine, orthopedics, cardiac care, and cancer) have a significant impact on medical spend. Providers taking risk for the total cost of care have substantial opportunity by controlling migration to high-cost providers and providing evidence-based care for provider-sensitive conditions and drug use.

Questions organizations must be prepared to ask when migrating to value-based contracts are directly related to these factors:

- How will the healthcare value chain work?
- What is the synergy for our organization between clinical, operating, and business models?
- How is health risk being managed?
- Can we commit to medical trend strategic targets?
- What is happening to leakage/keepage?
- What is narrow versus open access?
- How will development of a CIN and strategic partnerships help us along the journey to value-based payments and will we use it that way?
- Are we truly ready to compete and risk losing based on price and total cost of care?

Integrating value-based payment models with care model redesign can help focus resources based on characteristics of the population being served by a specific type of contract. For a Medicaid population, focus on pregnancy and neonatal services has a high impact, as do models designed around the complex social needs of the dual-eligible population.

For a Medicare Advantage or MSSP contract, care models focused on the frail elderly and those with complex chronic conditions can have high impact. For the individual commercial market, convenience care, prevention, and chronic care management will have significant impact. For commercial populations, cancer costs and episodic care for trauma can be a focus.

In each case, understanding the population being served and what needs to focus on to have maximum impact can be a starting point for developing successful care models that can be tied directly to payment models that provide adequate resources to cover high-value care in forms typically not paid well under traditional fee-for-service models. Figure 5.3 illustrates an example of a population and how the math is calculated.

| | # of Lives | $PMPY | Total Spend |
|---|---|---|---|
| Medicare | 42,000 | $11,000 | $462M |
| Medicaid | 60,000 | $2000 | $120M |
| Commercial | 153,000 | $2,800 | $428M |
| Uninsured | 45,000 | $500 | $23M |
| Total | 300,000 | $3,440 | $1,003M |

5% Savings on Medicare Populations =$23,000,000=2,300 Less admissions (165 Decline)

| | Per Capita | Total Spend |
|---|---|---|
| Hospital | $1,250 | $375M |
| Physicians | $940 | $280M |
| Drugs | $480 | $144M |
| Dental | $170 | $50M |
| NH,HH, and DME | $400 | $120M |
| Other | $200 | $61M |
| Total | $3,400 | $1,033M |

What % of Spend is Outside of Your System?

**FIGURE 5-3.** Healthcare Population Math from the Payer's Perspective

## DESIGN CONSIDERATIONS IN VALUE-BASED PAYMENT MODELS

When payers design value-based payment models, they design performance measures around specific objectives—a process that inherently involves tradeoffs. Dimensions of program design include penalties and bonuses, quality measures, quality benchmarking, cost measures, cost benchmarking, attribution, and risk adjustment.

With respect to performance bonuses or penalties, Daniel Kahneman's Prospect Theory, based on extensive psychosocial science research, indicates that humans place more value on losses than on equivalent gains, and therefore penalties may have a stronger impact than bonuses in pay-for-performance programs.[94] Bonus programs, in general, may be less economical because essentially one is paying high performers to motivate change among low performers.

The decision to have a broad array of quality measures or focus on a few depends on whether the objective is to promote system-wide intervention or focus more narrowly on critical issues that need to be addressed.

Quality benchmarks may be set relative to past performance, against an absolute benchmark, or against competitors. Benchmarks based on relative performance give payers some certainty; benchmarks based on absolute performance give providers more certainty by establishing concrete targets. Low baseline performers may benefit from rewarding improvement, but transparency surrounding financial performance based on improvement alone in a comparator model set against a cohort may rouse controversy if low-performing but improving performers are awarded more than consistently high performers.

Measuring costs of care for payers and designing performance-based reimbursement around it has its own design constraints. What is important for payers as they design budgets (federal/state governmental payers, self-insured employers) or premiums (commercial payers) is the total cost of care per capita. But contracting with specific providers requires an understanding of what costs the providers have agency to control. Total cost of care is how the Medicare Shared Savings Program is designed.

On the other hand, bundled payments for joint replacement are designed around costs of a single episode of care with associated services bundled together into one payment. Some payers exclude drug benefits cost from provider performance while others include it. Some performance measures are surrogates from costs, such as readmission reduction rate performance standards.

Measures of cost at the level of an episode of care, condition-specific, or population-based are designed very differently but have some of the same tradeoffs as quality measures. Broader cost measures may promote broader care redesign but may be too broad to be actionable. Condition-specific measures may focus efforts more practically but may lack the capacity to motivate broader redesign. Certain specialties may be best aligned to chronic care (endocrinologists) or episodic care (most surgical specialties) design models, whereas some specialties may be more mixed such as cardiology which would be chronic care-focused with some patients (CHF) and episode-focused with others (TAVR).

Cost benchmarking has significant tradeoffs depending on how the spending benchmark is set. Measuring providers against their own historical spending may give baseline higher spenders the easiest task. Assuming high-cost providers may benefit from attacking the opportunities of "low-hanging fruit," more efficient providers may be hurt. In benchmarking against oneself, risk-adjustment is less important, assuming that the patient population being served does not change substantially over time.

Evaluating providers against others sets up the opposite dynamic. The most efficient providers at baseline will do better. It will be crucial in this model to make accurate risk-adjustment measures, however, as often the most complex, high-risk patients are cared for by the best providers. But unless costs are risk adjusted to consider the naturally higher costs in such populations, those caring for the sickest patients will be penalized.

# CHAPTER SIX

# Optimizing Value

The move to value begins with assessing organizational readiness and then proceeds to implementing a change strategy focused on patient care model redesign, clinical and information integration, and value-based contracting and the adequate investment in resources to be successful in a well-timed transition. But ongoing operational success requires synthesis of the new way of providing care as it relates to the needs of the larger community and ongoing market forces that will continue to drive change in how healthcare services are delivered.

The pace of change for healthcare will continue to accelerate as traditional healthcare providers face consumers empowered with personalized smart technology able to immediately access services that meet their needs in ways that bypass traditional healthcare facilities and are available at lower costs.

The influence of big data and genomics will be a third wave of radical change to affect the healthcare industry. To adapt, organizations must become flexible and learn to assess their capabilities and strategic options from nontraditional perspectives. By focusing on the mission, vision, and values of the organization rather than the current strategies for fulfilling them, they can generate fresh perspectives on how the organization can continue to evolve.

## SOCIAL DETERMINANTS OF HEALTH

A person's social circumstances play a profound role in determining health status and outcomes from medical interventions, including socioeconomic status, educational attainment, housing status, food security, family and social network, and access to transportation. Researchers and clinicians agree that if a patient cannot afford a treatment or has limited access to health resources, clinical effectiveness of care decreases, costs go up, and morbidity and mortality rates increase.

However, simply recognizing these factors without addressing them head-on is not adequate. CMS is changing its policies to allow Medicare Advantage plans to cover certain services that would address beneficiary social health, such as permitting payment for transportation services or nutritious food—services that have not been covered under inducement regulations that have been part of fee-for-service Medicare for a generation.

Organizations must design programs that are evidence-based to begin the hard work of addressing social risk factors. Often, this means creating partnerships outside of traditional healthcare service providers, including faith-based organizations, community organizations, the educational system, local governments, and employers. Not-for-profit health systems have a fiduciary responsibility to serve their communities and may benefit from using their required community needs assessments to rethink their traditional role in providing sick care services. Payers are beginning to think about designing benefits that consider social determinants, such as risk-adjusting payments for providers who serve patients with high social needs.

## STRATEGIC PARTNERSHIPS

Healthcare delivery systems will need to seek out and nurture strategic partnerships in order to be successful going forward. However, the nature of these partnerships may be quite different than traditional partnerships. Healthcare organizations tend to think about strategic partnerships within the context of the customary members of the healthcare industry: acute care centers, primary care and specialist providers, skilled nursing facilities, pharma and technology industry vendors, and payers.

These strategic partnerships will continue to be important, and identifying which partners can add value through collaborative relationships across the industry will be an ongoing need in the move to value for the entire healthcare industry. However, it is important to understand that strategic partnerships in the value world extend beyond traditional health system providers and include safety-net community service organizations, churches, agriculture extension agents, town and county governments, food suppliers, transportation services, housing authorities, and other members of both the official and unofficial community social network. This may be new territory for many in the healthcare industry.

## COMMUNITY ECOSYSTEMS AND REINVESTMENT

One principle of system theory that must be reemphasized is that system boundaries are artificially imposed. Understanding that there is continuity between what we traditionally consider the healthcare ecosystem and what extends beyond it helps to break down artificial barriers that appear to limit healthcare industry solutions.

Some nontraditional community sectors that are approaching healthcare solutions are beginning to do work that bypasses the dominance of traditional healthcare providers. For example, philanthropist Ester Dyson established HICCUP, an organization focused on creating a financial market for healthier communities where improvements in health outcomes are monetized and reinvested back into community improvement projects. In Greensboro, North Carolina, an African-American church established a Health Faith Summit and subsequently a Mental Health Faith Summit in order to develop community-focused approaches to integrated community health improvement. The Medicaring project is a proposed payment model in which a not-for-profit community organization receives lump-sum payment from Medicare to provide integrated community-based healthcare to the frail elderly population and pays traditional healthcare providers for services.

Each of these examples illustrates efforts by non-healthcare delivery system members of the community to organize healthcare into a more integrated community ecosystem. The large palatial facilities, resplendent with works of art and architectural marvel, that house our current healthcare services may appear to be capital-rich juggernauts compared to these community-based approaches, but Clay Christensen's lessons on disruptive innovation emphasize that the simple "good enough" solutions often overtake market leaders by providing simpler solutions to the market in the face of the complexity of the current healthcare system options.

The move to value-based payments and consumer-driven market forces will disenfranchise traditional healthcare system hierarchies. Those healthcare organizations that recognize this and embrace new nontraditional strategic partnerships can continue to be relevant in meeting community need and in meeting their mission in a healthcare market landscape that no longer is based on fee-for-service paradigms.

Adrian Slywotzky and Michael Porter developed discrete interpretations of the economic concept of value migration.[95] Interestingly, both have focused their attention in the past few years on how value migration is relevant in healthcare and especially on understanding accordance and difference with value migration in other industries.[96] Slywotzky emphasizes that profit is the outcome of smart business design based on reinventing oneself to focus on what is important to the customer (patient) and understanding how customers (patients) are changing.

Competing on uniqueness rather than on being the "best" deemphasizes market share, competition by imitation, and the zero-sum game no one can win. Instead, meeting diverse needs of targeted customers (patients) allows competition through innovation and multiple winners with positive sum gains. This replaces the rather Hobbesian assumptions of competition in a "nasty, brutish, and short" healthcare organizational life. Essential healthcare industry core values are affirmed in a value migration based on meeting the diverse needs of our patients. New business design alternatives interact with changing patient priorities and dynamic patient decision patterns. The result for healthcare systems that move successfully to value-based payment models will be mission-affirming sustainability.

# CHAPTER SEVEN

# Frontline Strategies From Subspecialists

Each of the specialty-specific value-optimizing strategies that follow are the culmination of national research and input from practicing subspecialists or community health partners. They are strategies that have proven successful in the field. The authors were extensively involved in these projects, sponsored by the multispecialty Toward Accountable Care Consortium, and the effort revealed one recurring gap, short of MACRA: lack of *bona fide* metrics associated with the desired outcomes or behavior each strategy suggested.

# ANESTHESIOLOGISTS

I.    **Why and How You May Want to Utilize Anesthesiologists in Your CIN/ACO**

A.    **Perioperative Process Improvement**—ACOs can use anesthesiologists to lead perioperative process improvement. This includes primary care coordination to have the patient's diagnosis and preparation optimized, and all relevant data from the medical home presented preoperatively. The anesthesiologist can be part of the perioperative team to schedule the surgery and the transition of the patient from the outpatient to the inpatient setting.

Once in the perioperative setting, the anesthesiologist can lead development of pre-, intra-, and post-operative protocols. Members of the Accountable Care Workgroup of the North Carolina Society of Anesthesiologists suggest several possible evidence-based best practice protocol steps to improve the perioperative process:

- Develop preoperative screening criteria for specific procedures and/or complex patients (*e.g.*, morbidly obese; ESRD or HD).
- Monitor and minimize anesthesiologist-related delays.
- Monitor and minimize surgeon-controlled delays.
- Enable and incentivize anesthesiologist frontline leadership in through-put.
- Ensure SCIP initiatives are met.
- Implement post-operative pain control protocols and best practices.
- Facilitate optimal referrals without unnecessary costs or delays.
- Implement health information technology, including real-time critical information and decision support for best practices, which follows patient across care settings, "hardwires" ACO initiatives, and support.
- Coordinate to avoid duplication of tests, delays, insufficient referrals, or compromised actions.
- Identify and correct delays in surgery due to equipment malfunction.
- Use localized systems analysis to implement meaningful start time and improve through-put.

B.    **Inpatient Link to Medical Home**—Primary care/medical home initiatives have been the first ACO activities implemented in many areas. As the reach of these initiatives extends to the inpatient setting, anesthesiologists can be utilized in leadership roles, particularly for patients who will be having surgery. They are comfortable with systems, technology, protocols, clinical management, and working with diverse healthcare providers. Their role in the preoperative evaluation and handoff from the Medical Home present opportunities to become involved, if not lead. Is there a recurring frustrating type of surgical or pain procedure? Are there patterns causing frequent delays, errors, bad results, and/or gaps in care?

*Strategic Note:* The value of anesthesiologists is amplified if they help create the outpatient/inpatient bridge. Their role in preoperative assessment positions prepares them well for this role.

C. **High-Impact Avoidable Adverse Events**—In 1999, the Institute of Medicine published its landmark study "To Err is Human," reporting that as many as 98,000 people die each year in hospitals as a result of medical errors that could have been prevented.[97] As follow-up, the Office of Inspector General (OIG) of the Department of Health and Human Services undertook a study entitled "Adverse Events in Hospitals," issued in November 2010.[98] This analysis surveyed the adverse events of Medicare patients that were avoidable and ranked them according to the greatest harm.

   In Winter 2010/2011, the NCSA Accountable Care Workgroup reviewed these results and prioritized the avoidable adverse events over which anesthesiologists might exert the greatest influence. ACOs are targeting these areas for the obvious health policy reasons, but also because the OIG recommended that "CMS look for opportunities to hold hospitals accountable for adoption of evidence-based practice guidelines," and CMS commented that it will "aggressively pursue" lowering the incidence of these adverse events.

D. **Complex Obese Patient Pilot (COPP) Case Study**—The COPP is an example of an initiative that can be supported by anesthesiologists. The project was effective as a case study in that: (a) it meets most of the categories recommended for ACO targeting; (b) it scores high using on the local project selection criteria; and (c) when reviewing this against the recommended anesthesiologist ACO initiatives above, it is clear that anesthesiologists can contribute in multiple ways.

### What Is the Complex Obese Patient Project (COPP)?

COPP is a replicable shared savings pilot project focusing on the complex obese patient population using best practices across the continuum, from diagnosis to discharge, created by a multidisciplinary team with the goal of increasing quality, patient satisfaction, and savings for this patient population. Initial thinking identified potential opportunities for (1) better information at the primary care diagnosis and treatment design phase, (2) better information flow along the entire continuum of care, (3) improved transition from the outpatient to the inpatient setting, (4) improved perioperative processes and outcomes, and (5) improved post-op follow up.

   To align incentives to create the highest quality at the lowest overall cost, an important feature of COPP would be a shared savings payment component, which would be in addition to fee-for-service payments.

### Why COPP Now?

- It targets some clear disconnects in our current fragmented system. Significant savings are anticipated in high-yield areas of prevention, chronic disease management, care transitioning, and process improvement.

- Champions from different specialties and hospital administration have been identified.
- Tackling the obesity epidemic and the cost impact of the "super-utilizers" are in the national health policy forefront.[99] It tackles this group, which is roughly 5% of the typical patient population but consumes over 50% of that population's total healthcare expenditures.
- A small pilot with champions and likely high-impact initiatives may be appropriate to spark a "spiral of success" in working together in the future to achieve greater value in healthcare. The prospects are reasonably high for there to be a meaningful shared savings pool. If this happens, it will be much easier to generate buy-in for additional successful projects.

**Executive Summary**

- **Diagnosis and Treatment Planning.** The primary care physician, preferably in the medical home model, will have better access to relevant data and evidence-based best practices. A complex obese patient comprehensive data template will facilitate intake and later handoffs. This will build on existing hospital diabetes and other initiatives. A multidisciplinary Complex Obese Patient Support (COPS) team (nutritionist, mental health professional, orthopedic pain management specialist, clinical pharmacist, case navigator, etc.) will provide real or virtual access to specialized expertise for optimum diagnosis and treatment planning.[100]
- **Wellness/Lifestyle Management.** Includes continued access to the COPS team to manage and identify co-morbidities and weight-loss techniques; tools for patient education and engagement; and relevant decision support and clinical data that follows the patient through virtual-provider workstation.
- **Surgery.**
  - **Non-Weight-Loss Surgery.** These are often challenging surgical candidates with many medications, co-morbidities, sleep apnea, and other high-risk issues. However, they often require surgeries due to poor health status. The multispecialist team will have best practices for presurgical evaluation, data transfer, anesthesia-specific pre-op, cardiac evaluation, OSA screening, HTN screening, upper GI if appropriate, patient education, airway assessment, and possible need for tracheotomy, etc. There will be enhanced transition coordination with the medical home. The surgery will follow optimum perioperative process best practices and use the virtual-data workstation. Post-op and post-discharge, the patient is transitioned back to the medical home. The physicians have met several times to map out preliminary pathways from the initial visit to three years post-surgery follow-up.

- **Weight-Loss Surgery.** Recommended only if the patient is unsuccessful losing weight by all other measures after a six-month + period, the patient is otherwise a proper candidate (*i.e.*, BMI and health status), and the surgery otherwise comports with evidence-based best practices. A special post-weight-loss-surgery patient follow-up protocol will be managed by the medical home physician with ongoing support from the COPS team. Currently, the surgeon usually provides medical and lifestyle management for these patients for up to three years.

- **Reporting/Shared Savings.** Appropriate quality, patient satisfaction, and cost-effectiveness performance metrics will be established using nationally recognized benchmarks. If the quality and satisfaction standards are met, and there are savings for this patient population enrolled with a particular payer, 50% of those savings would be distributed to care providers roughly in proportion to their relative estimated contributions to the savings pool. Financial predictive modeling is anticipated.

## Preliminary "SWOT" Analysis

- **Strengths**—Chances for success are high. COPP targets four of the top five recommended areas for collaborative care: prevention/wellness, chronic disease management, transitions across fragmented parts of system, and multispecialty complex patient management. It would not likely impact the fifth area: reduced hospitalizations. Natural collaboration and transition opportunities.

- **Weaknesses**—Physicians lose some independence. The hospital loses some control. Participants already are too busy. Do I trust my partners enough? Do we have an interested payer? Will this cost money? Will I lose volume?

- **Opportunities**—Low-risk pilot. It is a good way to begin building culture and skills. There are existing champions (primary care, anesthesia, surgical, other). It could build market share. There is great potential ROI documentation for bariatric surgery. It's politically consistent with health policy objectives, image, and community benefit.

- **Threats**—I might not get fair credit. The data and/or the money will be manipulated. It's still in the fee-for-service environment. This is too early to create a precedent that might reduce hospitalization and surgical volumes even though this one won't. I have other priorities. I'm wary of shared-savings methods. On the other hand, what is the threat of not doing this? Do we risk being unprepared when the transition hits the tipping point of value-based reimbursement?

E.  **Other**—Please see *The Accountable Care Manual for Anesthesiologists*, which may be downloaded at www.ncmedsoc.org/physician-resources/accountable-care/aco-toolkits.

F.  **PCSP Standards**—The NCQA Patient-Centered Specialty Practice standards regarding care team and patient coordination are recommended generally for all specialists, including anesthesiologists.

II.  **Metrics**

A.  **Overview**—After determining the initiatives involving this specialty that are most appropriate for your CIN/ACO, to incentivize the desired behavior and outcomes, it is recommended that clinically valid metrics track adherence to the chosen activities and accomplishment of the desired results. Use the available array of measures from various sources as a "menu" from which to start, and then tailor, prioritize, and weight them to fit your incentivization goals.

B.  **Initiative—Perioperative Process Improvement**

- General
  - Measure overall improvements in operating room through-put (*i.e.*, "wheels in, wheels out").
  - Measure reduction in anesthesiologist delays.
  - Measure shorter recovery time trend.
  - Measure improved primary care and specialist coordination to avoid duplication of tests, delays, inefficient referrals, or compromised outcomes.
  - Preoperative screening criteria by diagnosis.
- Specific Protocol Compliance Measurement
  - Reduce surgeon-controlled delay; targeted cases with greatest time variability by surgeon.
  - Measure anesthesiologist frontline leadership.
  - Post-operative pain control process.
  - Intake process for efficient referrals—active communications with primary care physician.

C.  **Inpatient Link to Medical Home**—Performance metrics would address success in facilitating specialist input to assist medical home physician in diagnosis; better admission and discharge communications and coordination; protocols to smooth transitions; and collecting and delivering relevant clinical data to the caregiver at the point of care across the continuum.

D.  **Adverse Events in Hospital**—These "efficiencies" or savings, if you will, largely stem from better quality and cost savings through avoided errors. Efficiency performance metrics will, at best, be incidental to the quality protocols and metrics.

E.  **MACRA's Quality Payment Program MIPS Measures Relevant to Anesthesiology** (see Table 7-1).

TABLE 7-1. Relevant Anesthesia MIPS Quality Measures

| MEASURE NAME | MEASURE DESCRIPTION |
|---|---|
| Anesthesiology Smoking Abstinence | The percentage of current smokers who abstain from cigarettes prior to anesthesia on the day of elective surgery or procedure. |
| Coronary Artery Bypass Graft (CABG): Preoperative Beta-Blocker in Patients with Isolated CABG Surgery | Percentage of isolated CABG surgeries for patients aged 18 years and older who received a beta-blocker within 24 hours prior to surgical incision. |
| Documentation of Current Medications in the Medical Record | Percentage of visits for patients aged 18 years and older for which the eligible professional attests to documenting a list of current medications using all immediate resources available on the date of the encounter. This list must include ALL known prescriptions, over-the-counters, herbals, and vitamin/mineral/dietary (nutritional) supplements AND must contain the medications' name, dosage, frequency and route of administration. |
| Perioperative Temperature Management | Percentage of patients, regardless of age, who undergo surgical or therapeutic procedures under general or neuraxial anesthesia of 60 minutes duration or longer for whom at least one body temperature greater than or equal to 35.5 degrees Celsius (or 95.9 degrees Fahrenheit) was recorded within the 30 minutes immediately before or the 15 minutes immediately after anesthesia end time. |
| Post-Anesthetic Transfer of Care Measure: Procedure Room to a Post Anesthesia Care Unit (PACU) | Percentage of patients, regardless of age, who are under the care of an anesthesia practitioner and are admitted to a PACU in which a post-anesthetic formal transfer of care protocol or checklist which includes the key transfer of care elements is utilized. |
| Post-Anesthetic Transfer of Care: Use of Checklist or Protocol for Direct Transfer of Care from Procedure Room to Intensive Care Unit (ICU) | Percentage of patients, regardless of age, who undergo a procedure under anesthesia and are admitted to an Intensive Care Unit (ICU) directly from the anesthetizing location, who have a documented use of a checklist or protocol for the transfer of care from the responsible anesthesia practitioner to the responsible ICU team or team member. |
| Prevention of Central Venous Catheter (CVC)-Related Bloodstream Infections | Percentage of patients, regardless of age, who undergo central venous catheter (CVC) insertion for whom CVC was inserted with all elements of maximal sterile barrier technique, hand hygiene, skin preparation and, if ultrasound is used, sterile ultrasound techniques followed. |
| Prevention of Post-Operative Nausea and Vomiting (PONV) - Combination Therapy | Percentage of patients, aged 18 years and older, who undergo a procedure under an inhalational general anesthetic, AND who have three or more risk factors for post-operative nausea and vomiting (PONV), who receive combination therapy consisting of at least two prophylactic pharmacologic antiemetic agents of different classes preoperatively or intraoperatively. |
| Preventive Care and Screening: Screening for High Blood Pressure and Follow-Up Documented | Percentage of patients aged 18 years and older seen during the reporting period who were screened for high blood pressure AND a recommended follow-up plan is documented based on the current blood pressure (BP) reading as indicated. |

# CARDIOLOGISTS

I.    **Why and How You May Want to Utilize Cardiologists in Your CIN/ACO**

   A.  **Significant Coronary Costs That Can Be Impacted Through Integrated Population Health**—According to the American Heart Association, coronary heart disease alone costs the United States $108.9 billion each year when medical costs and lost productivity are considered.[101] Yet only 27% of Americans recognize all the symptoms of a heart attack. The Advisory Board Company, a consultancy, reports that since 97% of the highest-cost Medicare patients have at least one cardiovascular condition, cardiovascular (CV) care-management strategy should extend beyond the cardiology service line and across every hospital institution.[102]

   In addition to these high costs, an ACO is in position to inflect substantial reductions in cost while improving quality. For example, as Grace Terrell, MD, noted from experiences in her practice, "the Heart Function Clinic in High Point, North Carolina, caused a 69% decrease in hospital admissions for heart failure and 75% reduction in emergency department utilization for heart issues. Patient care was better, the cardiologists and patients were happier, and the savings were substantial."

   Payers are recognizing cardiologists who demonstrate this leadership through preferential reimbursement and steerage. In recognition of the potential for high-value cardiologists' contributions, Blue Cross and Blue Shield of North Carolina has introduced its Tiered Network and cardiology practices exceeding both quality and cost thresholds are included in their preferred "skinny" network called Tier 1.[103] Data show that there is considerable county-to-county variability in risk-adjusted congestive heart failure mortality, illustrating the substantial savings from reduced variability of care. That 18 out of 48 episodes of care eligible for the Medicare bundled payment initiative relate to cardiovascular care suggests much available "low-hanging fruit" for cardiologists in value-based payment.

   B.  **Recommended ACO Initiatives for Cardiologists**—The Cardiology Accountable Care Workgroup found that there are a number of high-impact readily achievable cardiology team contributions to quality and patient population savings, heretofore not feasible under the fee-for-service system. The cardiologists' potential to add value in integrated care is underscored by some telling statistics:

   • Only 1.1% of the population meets all seven of the American Heart Association's metrics for ideal health (smoking, BMI, exercise, diet, cholesterol, blood pressure, and HbA1c).[104]

   • Cardiac-related procedures are 3 of the top 10 drivers of avoidable inpatient admissions.[105]

- ACO-like systems of care for acute ST elevation myocardial infarction (STEMI), stroke, and cardiac arrest have translated into measured quality improvement and cost reductions.[106]

For a graphic regarding cardiovascular care-management strategy see: http://www.tac-consortium.org/wp-content/uploads/2014/02/27890_CR_CV_Infographic_Final.jpg.

The most promising and replicable initiatives follow:

There was consensus among the Cardiology Accountable Care Workgroup that avoiding unnecessary hospitalizations presented the proverbial "low-hanging fruit." They noted that the American Heart Association's seven ideal health metrics and tools are easy to use and can produce significant savings. As noted, the cardiologist-led Heart Function Clinic reduced admissions by 69%.

C. **Cardiologist and Primary Care Partnership**—One cardiologist noted that her greatest contribution to value may be as leader of a cardiac care team where "patients I never saw got the right cardiac care." The care team needs to coordinate, know their roles, practice to the top of their licenses, and be supervised by a cardiologist. "Supervision" is a carefully chosen role, as cardiologists need to rationalize how they spend their time. They need to delegate, coordinate, and supervise, to avoid managing multiple uncoordinated tasks related to a patient's care. One Workgroup member noted that it is inevitable to "make mistakes when you get overwhelmed," by constantly getting pinged to perform unrelated delegable patient care tasks.

The team should include primary care medical homes and community public health partners. One Workgroup member noted that if supported by evidence-based best practices, "primary care physicians need to measure [such things as] hypertension without a cardiologist." Clear data feedback algorithms, standing protocols, referral guidelines, and periodic team service-line meetings will all benefit team coordination.

This type of cardiologist/primary care partnership teaming to prevent acute cardiac events will significantly improve health status while reducing hospital admissions. This is becoming the classic ACO initiative involving many specialists, not just cardiologists. It would not be feasible under the siloed and fragmented fee-for-service model.

The cardiologists at Cornerstone Health Care ACO based in High Point, North Carolina, developed a multidisciplinary Heart Function Clinic. It is a cardiologist-led collaboration including specially trained nurses, psychologists, cardiologists, dieticians, and frequently their home health and nursing home providers. It is comprehensive and proactive with frequent office visits and telephone outreach to patients. It has generated the previously mentioned 69% reduction in admissions and 75% reduction in emergency department utilization for heart issues.

The cardiologists at Piedmont Heart in Atlanta collaborated with Piedmont Healthcare to create integrated multidisciplinary teams. "Most CV physicians divide their time among making clinic visits, performing office-and-hospital-based procedures, reviewing diagnostic study results, and rounding on patients. That fragmented approach preserves the individual physician 'ownership' of the patient, but it often results in inefficient time usage and does not encourage physicians to 'play to their strengths' and work as an integrated team. . . . [which] allows a physician to focus attention on one or two activities rather than trying to manage multiple uncoordinated tasks related to a patient's care."[107] Physician extenders are utilized extensively to the full breadth of their licenses, further relieving cardiologists of distracting tasks.

In another example, the heart and vascular institute at Summa Health System in Akron, Ohio, involves not only cardiologists but also primary care physicians and radiologists in a performance-based clinical co-management agreement.[108] The Advisory Board Company urges cardiologists to "work collaboratively with PCPs to manage care; perform appropriate procedures only when necessary,"[109] and notes that coordinating with PCPs will ease the manpower concerns in coming years as the number of elderly and chronic patients grows."[110] The consulting company also recommends better referral patterns to streamline care processes.[111]

D. **Emergency Department Triage and Diversion**—Too often, the emergency physician is uncertain regarding a patient's chest pain, and that patient gets admitted to the hospital unnecessarily. Sometimes, the admission is a default measure simply because no physician is available to take responsibility for that patient. In the current fragmented system, the process of transition from emergency department to cardiologist to discharge planning is complex and uncoordinated, leading to substantial inefficiencies. An ACO savings strategy is for the highest-trained cardiovascular-trained physician (cardiologist) to be involved in the decision making and to take responsibility. Education, telemedicine access, protocols, and other alternatives to live presence suggest themselves to accomplish these objectives.

**Example:** ED Availability = Value. One ACO embeds a cardiologist in the hospital's emergency department to provide immediate access. The cardiologist does other things but is instantly available. This reversal from the traditional fee-for-service practice of the emergency department contacting the cardiologist only for the highest acuity patients has generated surprisingly strong results. The key is getting an accurate *early* diagnosis, as the ACO's cardiologist stated, "before a lot of money has been spent." This early input allows acuity tracking to triage the low-risk patients instead of admitting them, quicker cath lab access, and avoids unnecessary CT scans and admissions. He noted another benefit in that with CT angiograms, the patient occasionally gets lots of contrast and goes into renal failure. And, once the patient has been stabilized and is ready for discharge in lieu of admission, if a physician is available to assume responsibility, an expensive admission is avoided simply by that ACO cardiologist's presence.

Obviously, a patient in an ACO with a non-acute problem should not go to the emergency department at all. A functioning primary care team, also with access to the cardiologist described above, should move this patient to the appropriate cardiac care provider without resorting by default to the local emergency department. An ACO patient should have, in hand, an appointment with their medical home physician upon discharge.

E. **Define and Develop Clinical Pathways**—More clinically credible, evidence-based best practices are emerging for cardiac care. Standardized observance of them would produce meaningful savings. Members of the Cardiology Accountable Care Workgroup felt, and research supports, that reduction in variation regarding guidelines for lipid and hypertrophy management would be particularly cost-effective. The cardiologists could lead in selecting the most appropriate and impactful best practices, interpret and remediate variation issues, and communicate and educate to effectively change behavior in outliers. Outlier physicians must find the benchmarks and processes credible, trust the data, and accept the feedback in order to reduce treatment variability. When that happens and the identities and data of physicians are shared, that is when one finds behavior change in an ACO.

F. **Organize by Disease State or Condition**—Instead of the fragmentation of provider grouping by provider specialty or hospital department, organize the multidisciplinary care team around the patient disease state or condition. Candidates for such grouping are led by arrhythmia, acute myocardial infarction, chest pain, coronary therapeutics, general and preventive cardiology structural and valvular heart disease, and vascular. Advantages include fast-tracking subspecialty depth and expertise, reduced variation in the care provided, better workflows, and ease in selection and monitoring of clinically valid metrics. It is easier to bring cardiologists of similar subspecialties together to identify best practices and metrics. A cardiovascular center for women could target cardiovascular disease in women.

In the *Journal of Vascular Surgery*, Dr. Phillip Goodman notes that "vascular surgeons will need to continue to expand the role we play in improving the vascular health of populations at risk beyond our current procedurally-based efforts toward disease-based care."[112] It is a good example of the new model of accountable care: integrated services across the care continuum would include evaluation, risk factor modification, nutrition counseling, exercise programs, and structured individualized medical plans, with the cardiologist expertise leveraged through allied providers and administrative support.

For example, Piedmont Heart in Atlanta determined, "Rather than organize by functional departments, like a traditional hospital organizational structure, Piedmont Heart physicians organized themselves along a continuum of patient care by disease state or condition." This has resulted in subspecialty depth and expertise, as each physician picks a "major," thus reducing variation in care.[113]

G. **Harnessing Pharmacy and Supply Costs**—Often the first initiative in cardiology accountable care, hospital co-management arrangements, or bundled payment projects, is to agree to a common set of devices, supplies, and drugs, and negotiate a better volume discount rate. This will, of course, fail unless led by practicing cardiologists, and the savings incentives flow to all participating cardiologists. The Cardiology Accountable Care Workgroup noted savings and quality improvements through such things as Coumadin Clinics and active anticoagulation management safely reducing utilization of some very expensive drugs. Group sessions of patients using the same retail drug are proving cost-effective. Multiple patients come in and meet with a provider, initially a cardiologist, but then the patient is tracked by a non-physician.

H. **Identifying and Managing High-Risk Patients**—Ten percent of cardiology patients consume 50% of the cardiology dollars. ACO business intelligence can now pull data from disparate sources to reveal the cohort of incipient future high-risk/high-cost "super-utilizer" patient with multiple co-morbidities in addition to cardiac issues. Analytics can assist in structuring multidisciplinary continuity of care workflow and coordination. Special focus can be placed on this vulnerable cohort for discharge planning, post-discharge follow-up, self-management, and engagement tools. Again, the cardiologist should lead the design of this initiative and supervise the care management but should not do all the work. So, on the post-acute end of cardiac care, as noted for the preventive end of the spectrum, the cardiologists' greatest value contribution may be for the patient she never sees.

I. **Selection of Optimum Site of Service**—This is an obvious result of adhering to evidence-based best practices in the accountable care era. But it has historically not often been within the purview of the treating cardiologist, so it is mentioned here as a separate initiative. Provision of care of equal or better quality at a lower cost is fundamental to value-based care. It is, however, going to be one of the most wrenching of the "disruptive innovations" necessary to transform our current healthcare delivery system. It is inevitable.

J. **Leverage Impact Through Technology**—The above recommendations are feasible in large, integrated environments, but what about locations where the cardiologists, emergency physicians, primary care physicians, pharmacists, and other providers are far apart, say in rural areas? While fee-for-service "punished" use of available techniques and tools to allow collaboration—they would not pay for them and it took away from fee-generating opportunities—value-based payment introduces a significant return on investment or ROI. Telephone, email, referral algorithms, web-portals, and multidisciplinary service-line meetings, real or virtual, all help bridge the distance between care team members.

K. **Other**—Please see *The Accountable Care Manual for Cardiologists*, which may be downloaded at www.ncmedsoc.org/physician-resources/accountable-care/aco-toolkits

L. **PCSP Standards**—The NCQA Patient-Centered Specialty Practice standards regarding care team and patient coordination are recommended generally for all specialists, including cardiologists.

II. **Metrics**

A. **Examples of Measures That Serve Multiple Interests in the ACO Include:**
   - Preventive services measures such as influenza and pneumonia vaccination, tobacco cessation counseling.
   - Ambulatory sensitive admissions for CHF and for COPD.
   - Acute care indicators such as aspirin for acute MI.
   - Patient safety and care transition activities such as medication reconciliation, patient receipt of transition records, and fall risk assessment.
   - Utilization and financial measures such as % revisits to ED, pm/pm for ED care, imaging rates (CT, MRI).
   - ED utilization rates.

B. **Examples of Metrics More Focused on Cardiac Care Include:**

   1. **National Cardiovascular Data Registry** (see Table 7-2)

   2. **Blue Cross Blue Shield of North Carolina (BCBSNC) Tiered Network Quality Measures**—Cardiology quality measures include:[115]
      - Beta blockers and (ACEI or ARBs) prescribed after most recent MI.
      - Beta-blocker treatment post-MI.
      - Beta-blocker therapy for those with heart failure.
      - Measurement of LC function for those with heart failure.
      - Lipid-lowering therapy for those with CAD.
      - Lipid profile for those with CAD.
      - Warfarin prescription for those with heart failure and atrial fibrillation.
      - Angioplasty: Potentially avoidable complications.

      MACRA's quality payment program MIPS measure relevant to cardiology are outlined in Table 7-3.

**TABLE 7-2.** NCDR Risk-Adjusted and Composite Measures and Metrics

| REGISTRY | MEASURE/METRIC | |
| --- | --- | --- |
| | **RISK-ADJUSTED** | **COMPOSITE** |
| Cath PCI Registry® | PCI In-Hospital Mortality<br>• All PCI Patients<br>• STEMI Patients<br>• NSTEMI Patients<br>PCI Bleeding<br>PCI 30-Day Readmission | Death, emergency CABG, stroke or repeat target vessel, revascularization<br>Therapy with aspirin, P2Y12 inhibitor, and statin at discharge following PCI in eligible |
| ACTION Registry®-GWTG™ | AMI In-Hospital Mortality<br>AMI Bleeding | Overall Performance<br>• AMI<br>• STEMI<br>• NSTEMI<br>Overall Defect-Free Care |
| ICD Registry™ | Incidence of death or major adverse event | Therapy with ACE/ARB and beta-blocker at discharge following ICD implantation in eligible patients |
| CARE Registry® | | Reported separately for CAS and CEA Patients:<br>• Incidence of stroke or death for symptomatic patients<br>• Incidence of stroke or death for asymptomatic patients<br>• Incidence of stroke, death, or MI for symptomatic patients<br>• Incidence of stroke, death, or MI for asymptomatic patients |

PCI=Percutaneous Coronary Intervention, ICD=Implantable Cardioverter Defibrillator, AMI=Acute Myocardial Infarction, CAS=Carotid Artery Stenting, CEA=Carotid Artery Endarterectomy, STEMI=ST Elevated MI, NSTEMI=Non-ST Elevated MI.[114]

**TABLE 7-3.** Macra's Quality Payment Program MIPS Measures Relevant to Cardiology

| MEASURE NAME | MEASURE DESCRIPTION |
| --- | --- |
| Atrial Fibrillation and Atrial Flutter: Chronic Anticoagulation Therapy | Percentage of patients aged 18 years and older with a diagnosis of nonvalvular AF or atrial flutter whose assessment of the specified thromboembolic risk factors indicate one or more high-risk factors or more than one moderate risk factor, as determined by CHADS2 risk stratification, who are prescribed warfarin OR another oral anticoagulant drug that is FDA approved for the prevention of thromboembolism. |
| Cardiac Stress Imaging Not Meeting Appropriate Use Criteria: Preoperative Evaluation in Low-Risk Surgery Patients | Percentage of stress SPECT, MPI, stress ECHO, CCTA, or CMR performed in low-risk surgery patients 18 years or older for preoperative evaluation during the 12-month reporting period. |
| Cardiac Stress Imaging Not Meeting Appropriate Use Criteria: Routine Testing After PCI | Percentage of all stress SPECT, MPI, stress ECHO, CCTA, and CMR performed in patients aged 18 years and older routinely after PCI, with reference to timing of test after PCI and symptom status. |

**TABLE 7-3.** Macra's Quality Payment Program MIPS Measures Relevant to Cardiology (continued)

| MEASURE NAME | MEASURE DESCRIPTION |
|---|---|
| Cardiac Stress Imaging Not Meeting Appropriate Use Criteria: Testing in Asymptomatic, Low-Risk Patients | Percentage of all stress SPECT, MPI, stress ECHO, CCTA, and CMR performed in asymptomatic, low CHD risk patients 18 years and older for initial detection and risk assessment. |
| Care Plan | Percentage of patients aged 65 years and older who have an advance care plan or surrogate decision maker documented in the medical record or documentation in the medical record that an advance care plan was discussed but the patient did not wish or was not able to name a surrogate decision maker or provide an advance care plan. |
| Closing the Referral Loop: Receipt of Specialist Report | Percentage of patients with referrals, regardless of age, for which the referring provider receives a report from the provider to whom the patient was referred. |
| Controlling High Blood Pressure | Percentage of patients 18-85 years of age who had a diagnosis of hypertension and whose blood pressure was adequately controlled (<140/90mmHg) during the measurement period. |
| CAD: ACE Inhibitor or ARB Therapy - Diabetes or Left Ventricular Systolic Dysfunction (LVEF < 40%) | Percentage of patients aged 18 years and older with a diagnosis of coronary artery disease seen within a 12-month period who also have diabetes OR a current or prior LVEF < 40% who were prescribed ACE inhibitor or ARB therapy. |
| Coronary Artery Disease: Antiplatelet Therapy | Percentage of patients aged 18 years and older with a diagnosis of CAD seen within a 12-month period who were prescribed aspirin or clopidogrel. |
| Coronary Artery Disease: Beta-Blocker Therapy-Prior MI or Left Ventricular Systolic Dysfunction (LVEF <40%) | Percentage of patients aged 18 years and older with a diagnosis of coronary artery disease seen within a 12-month period who also have a prior MI or a current or prior LVEF <40% who were prescribed beta-blocker therapy. |
| Documentation of Current Medications in the Medical Record | Percentage of visits for patients aged 18 years and older for which the eligible professional attests to documenting a list of current medications using all immediate resources available on the date of the encounter. This list must include ALL known prescriptions, over-the-counters, herbals, and vitamin/mineral/dietary (nutritional) supplements AND must contain the medications' name, dosage, frequency and route of administration. |
| Heart Failure F: ACE Inhibitor or ARB Therapy for LVSD | Percentage of patients aged 18 years and older with a diagnosis of HF with a current or prior LVEF < 40% who were prescribed ACE inhibitor or ARB therapy either within a 12-month period when seen in the outpatient setting OR at each hospital discharge. |
| Heart Failure: Beta-Blocker Therapy for LVSD | Percentage of patients aged 18 years and older with a diagnosis of HF) with a current or prior LVEF < 40% who were prescribed beta-blocker therapy either within a 12-month period when seen in the outpatient setting OR at each hospital discharge. |

*Continued on next page*

**TABLE 7-3.** Macra's Quality Payment Program MIPS Measures Relevant to Cardiology (continued)

| MEASURE NAME | MEASURE DESCRIPTION |
|---|---|
| Ischemic Vascular Disease: Use of Aspirin or Another Antiplatelet | Percentage of patients 18 years of age and older who were diagnosed with AMI, CABG or PCI in the 12 months prior to the measurement period, or who had an active diagnosis of IVD during the measurement period, and who had documentation of use of aspirin or another antiplatelet during the measurement period. |
| Preventive Care and Screening: BMI Screening and Follow-Up Plan | Percentage of patients aged 18 years and older with a BMI documented during the current encounter or during the previous six months AND with a BMI outside of normal parameters, a follow-up plan is documented during the encounter or during the previous six months of the current encounter. Normal Parameters: Age 18 years and older BMI ≥ 18.5 and < 25 kg/m². |
| Preventive Care and Screening: Screening for High Blood Pressure and Follow-Up Documented | Percentage of patients aged 18 years and older seen during the reporting period who were screened for high blood pressure AND a recommended follow-up plan is documented based on the current blood pressure reading as indicated |
| Preventive Care and Screening: Tobacco Use: Screening and Cessation Intervention | Percentage of patients aged 18 years and older who were screened for tobacco use one or more times within 24 months AND who received cessation counseling intervention if identified as a tobacco user |
| Preventive Care and Screening: Unhealthy Alcohol Use: Screening & Brief Counseling | Percentage of patients aged 18 years and older who were screened for unhealthy alcohol use using a systematic screening method at least once within the last 24 months AND who received brief counseling if identified as an unhealthy alcohol user |
| Statin Therapy for the Prevention and Treatment of Cardiovascular Disease | Percentage of the following patients-all considered at high risk of cardiovascular events-who were prescribed or were on statin therapy during the measurement period: Adults aged ≥ 21 years who were previously diagnosed with or currently have an active diagnosis of clinical ASCVD; OR Adults aged ≥ 21 years who have ever had a fasting or direct LDL-C level ≥ 190 mg/dL or were previously diagnosed with or currently have an active diagnosis of familial or pure hypercholesterolemia; OR Adults aged 40–75 years with a diagnosis of diabetes with a fasting or direct LDL-C level of 70-189 mg/dL |
| Tobacco Use and Help with Quitting Among Adolescents | The percentage of adolescents 12 to 20 years of age with a primary care visit during the measurement year for whom tobacco use status was documented and received help with quitting if identified as a tobacco user |

AMI = acute myocardial infarction; ACE = angiotensin-converting enzyme; ARB = angiotensin receptor blocker; ASCVD = atherosclerotic cardiovascular disease; AF = atrial fibrillation; BMI = body mass index; CCTA = cardiac computed tomography angiography; CMR = cardiac magnetic resonance; CABG = coronary artery bypass graft; CAD = coronary artery disease; CHD = coronary heart disease; ECHO = echocardiogram; HF = heart failure; IVD = ischemic vascular disease; MPI = myocardial perfusion imaging; LVEF = left ventricular ejection fraction; LVSD = left ventricular systolic dysfunction; LDL-C = low-density lipoprotein cholesterol; MI = myocardial infarction; PCI = percutaneous coronary intervention; SPECT = single-photon emission computed tomography[116]

# CHILD PSYCHIATRISTS

I.   **Why and How You May Want to Utilize Child Psychiatrists in Your CIN/ACO**
The development of CIN/ACOs has largely been focused on adult care initiatives because they have been driven by the Medicare Shared Savings Program, which includes only adults 65 and over. But the movement of state Medicaid programs to value-based payment for integrated population health thrusts pediatric care generally, and pediatric behavioral and mental healthcare specifically, from being an afterthought to the forefront of value-based care innovation and opportunity.

The opportunity arising from this movement regarding increased payer attention to care management for children is leveraged even more for child psychiatry, as the benefits of integration of mental and physical health are also better recognized. However, there is a national shortage of child psychiatrists. The following prioritized strategies for CIN/ACOs are designed to maximize the potential and minimize the provider shortage issue.

A.   **Integrate Physical Health and Mental Health for Children**—"The ACO payment mechanism gives healthcare providers a new opportunity and incentives to rebuild the healthcare system in a way that reverses the separation between primary care and behavioral healthcare.... If ACOs can effectively integrate behavioral health services into their care and connect patients to these services, they may be better positioned to reach both cost and quality benchmarks."[117]

There was no hesitation by the Child Psychiatrists Accountable Care Workgroup to include integration of mental health and pediatric primary care as an obvious and prioritized initiative. In fact, this care model is desirable to improve care delivery and reduce both behavioral and physical healthcare costs in all settings. The Workgroup concurred with the conclusion of a study reported in *Health Affairs* that "ACOs could identify [integration] approaches that other providers may wish to emulate."[118] This model is also referred to as the "pediatric health home" by the American Academy of Child and Adolescent Psychiatry.

First, there is significant unaddressed need that negatively impacts quality of care and medical utilization. For example, looking at depression, by age 18, 20% of youth have experienced at least one episode of major depression, with increased risk for suicide, school failure, substance abuse, nicotine dependence, early pregnancy, and social isolation. Long term, they are at risk for poor health and mental health episodes. However, many depressed adolescents do not receive treatment.[119]

Second, integrated care works. Primary care physicians are often the first point of contact for these patients and, if properly trained, have the opportunity to identify and guide treatment of depression. Unfortunately, the traditional fragmented approach tends to squander this opportunity; however, the collaborative care model has been proven to generate "significant improvements in depressive symptoms and functional impairment."[120] One study showed that approximately 40% of parents of children with mental health conditions who reported a need for care coordination also reported that their need was unmet.[121]

Third, the return on investment through the ACO's employment of the collaborative model is positive. Put another way, inadequate care through lack of use of this best practice treatment model contributes to poor physical health outcomes and high costs.[122]

The ACO model aligns the financial and professional incentives and motivators to allow integration of mental and physical pediatric care. As the National Alliance on Mental Illness bluntly states in its family guide, *Integration of Mental Health and Pediatric Primary Care*, "As individuals, we are not fragmented, we are whole people."[123] This initiative fits the ACO targeting model for selecting the biggest bang for the buck. However, even with these major financing obstacles removed by the shared savings model, optimum integrated pediatric care still faces significant barriers.

Despite the existence of guidelines, primary care and child psychiatrists often lack awareness and understanding of the possibilities. This is out of the traditional practice comfort zone for many, and there are limited shared traditions. With this manual and those like it in the hands of physician champions, these remaining barriers can be overcome. This is a prime example of why physician leadership is so vital to ACO success.

**I Get It—We Need to Integrate, but How?**
Incorporating behavioral and physical care for adults and children in the ACO model is relatively new, as of the date of this Manual. However, CIN/ACOs can build on established principles of collaborative care and early ACO initiatives to fashion the structure most appropriate to your patient population, payer contract, access to skilled providers in your region, and cultural readiness

- **Awareness**—It is essential to share information about child psychiatrists and other experts with primary care, other providers, and patients. At present, exposure to child and adolescent mental health training in medical schools varies.[124] *JAMA* reports, "Pediatric [primary care clinicians] often cite concerns about inadequate training and time to comprehensively address adolescent mental health needs."[125]

Various approaches are being undertaken to close this gap in knowledge. In New York, five academic child and adolescent psychiatry divisions are collaborating to provide education and consultation to primary care physicians around the state via telephone, face-to-face, and telepsychiatry modalities. They are also partnering to provide a formal "mini-fellowship" over a three-day period.

Often an ACO's options for pushing pediatric mental healthcare knowledge must be simpler and more pragmatic. The following approaches are recommended for consideration:

- Incorporating child psychiatrists in all pediatric care planning.
- Creating written ACO protocols and guidelines on collaborative childcare.
- Scheduling periodic multidisciplinary "lunch-and-learn" or service-line meetings to cross-pollinate approaches and foster new shared traditions.

For additional ideas for pushing knowledge to primary care, see the American Academy of Child and Adolescent Psychiatry's *Facts for Families*, educational handouts, website resources, *Guide to Building Collaborative Mental Health Care Partnerships in Pediatric Primary Care*, guidelines on *When to Seek Referral of Consultation with Child and Adolescent Psychiatrists*, and *Strategies for System Change in Mental Health: A Chapter Action Kit*.

- **Integration Models**
  - **Lessons from the IMPACT Model**—One Child Psychiatrist Accountable Care Workgroup member stated that, "We can be leaders in primary care by supporting the institution of the IMPACT Model of collaborative care of mental disorders in primary care offices. I participate in such a program and can attest to its effectiveness in three ways: (1) medication management is more successful in this model than in usual care; (2) we are getting more people into psychotherapy; and (3) we are identifying patients with serious mental disorders who require referral to specialty care. Almost all my work is non-billable, but the ACO that employs me sees me as an important part of overall quality improvement and cost control."

    The IMPACT Model essentially is comprised of collaborative care among primary care, psychiatry, and a case manager; outcomes measurement, such as PHQ-9 for depression; and stepped care—that is, care regularly adjusted based on clinical outcomes and an evidence-based algorithm. Consistent with our Workgroup member's experience, studies have shown the IMPACT Model to improve care and lower costs, especially in patients with co-morbidities.[126]

  - **Lessons from ACOs**—The *Health Affairs* survey of behavioral and physical health integration (undifferentiated between adults and children) in ACOs revealed several common models, congruent with the IMPACT Model and similar collaborative care models. Most used what they called the "primary care expansion model" and a few used the "reverse integration model." All were viewed as viable and appropriate to the circumstances of each ACO.

1. **Primary Care Expansion Model**—The goal is to empower the Patent-Centered Medical Home primary care physicians to expand their care capabilities and to know when to refer the more complex behavioral health services. They fall into one of three categories:

   a. **Consulting Model**—A consulting service is developed for the primary care physician with local psychiatrists, usually off premises. For example, the pediatric ACO University Hospitals Rainbow Care Connection in Cleveland, Ohio, integrates behavioral health services with primary care using social workers and telepsychiatry modalities.

   b. **Co-Location Model**—Primary care and psychiatry share a physical space. Degrees of connectivity can vary from consultations to "warm handoffs."

   c. **Embedded Mode**—The psychiatrist works directly with the primary care team.

   *Strategic Note:* The ACO's incentive to lower overall patient population costs makes it financially feasible to extend the reach of the consultation model through standing protocols, phone calls, texts, and telepsychiatry. These were not compensated in the fee-for-service system but may well present a positive return on investment, particularly in underserved areas. One surveyed ACO leader stated that they, like our Workgroup member's experience related in the IMPACT Model section, paid the psychiatrist his or her fee-for-service hourly rate equivalent *not* to schedule patients so as to be accessible for consultation.

2. **Reverse Integration Model**—Primary care providers are integrated into existing behavioral health programs. The relatively few ACOs using this model had Medicaid contracts, and also had large disadvantaged populations or a high burden of severe mental illness.

   **Now let's apply this to child care in an ACO.** In its family guide on integrating pediatric care, the National Alliance of Mental Illness states that of the various models, "There is no single right way to integrate services and supports." But it does make the general recommendation that, "for most youth, the pediatric primary care setting is the most practical location for the integrated care because most families and youth access care in primary care offices, while youth with serious mental health issues should be referred."[127] A corollary for Medicaid children for locating at the first point of contact might be the health department in some settings.

B.  **Co-Management of Complex Patients**—Complicated mental health issues should be recognized early through the integration models outlined above, and then referred to the child psychiatrist through an organized process. After the referral, the psychiatrist helps the primary care team identify the child's clinical needs and advises on interim management issues, such as medication and crisis management. A care coordinator should be involved and should share updates with primary care on such things as current psychotropic medications and psychotherapeutic interventions. The child psychiatrist should lead discharge planning and decisions on intervention with various agencies and providers. Throughout, the primary care practice maintains a critical role in ongoing communication on the child's condition to ensure complex care coordination and family liaison.

*Strategic Note:* Co-management agreements are important to ensure partnerships between consultants, primary care, child psychiatrists, and other specialists in any ACO arrangement. Clear plans for co-management align the approach to care and provide a framework for quality and cost-effective care. Particularly in pediatrics, specialists and specialized care teams for children with chronic and complex illnesses are often in centralized locations such as children's hospitals, geographically separated from the community where patients live. Centralization of specialty resources evolved because of the small number of children in treatment and the limited numbers of pediatric specialists.

It is important to ensure patients attributed to the ACO get coordinated care through their medical home or are organized through the pediatric specialist, with communication links to the primary care physician, specialists, and family. Inclusion of the family, patient, primary care physician, and specialists in these decisions developing the best care structure for the patient is critical in preventing supplication of services, utilization of higher-cost services (*e.g.*, emergency departments at children's hospitals for illnesses treatable in the community), and access to care. For example, a child with diabetes may have the management of diabetes on a day-to-day basis from a nurse or other individual at the pediatric endocrinologist's office, but routine care for well child visits and acute illnesses are managed in the primary care medical home.

Careful development of co-management agreements, formal or informal, between the specialists and primary care physicians, and including the family in the planning, will allow access to care at the most appropriate site tailored to the individual child and medical needs.

C.  **Best Practices**—Clinically valid practices work. One member of the companion Pediatrics Accountable Care Workgroup noted that "Even in the high-cost areas, we need to use what evidence we have. Don't just throw the kitchen sink at it." Another stated simply that "Many things can be protocolized. That translates into lower costs."

One example of evidence-based best practices may be found in the Choosing Wisely® initiative:

- **Don't routinely prescribe an antipsychotic medication to treat behavioral and emotional symptoms of childhood mental disorders in the absence of approved or evidence-supported indications.** There are both on- and off-label clinical indications for antipsychotic use in children and adolescents. FDA-approved and/or evidence-supported indications for antipsychotic medications in children and adolescents include psychotic disorders, bipolar disorder, tic disorders, and severe irritability in children with autism spectrum disorders. There is increasing evidence that antipsychotic medication may be useful for some disruptive behavior disorders.

  Children and adolescents should be prescribed antipsychotic medications only after having had a careful diagnostic assessment with attention to comorbid medical conditions and a review of the patient's prior treatments. Efforts should be made to combine both evidence-based pharmacological and psychosocial interventions and support.

  Limited availability of evidence-based psychosocial interventions may make it difficult for every child to receive this ideal combination. Discussion of potential risks and benefits of medication treatment with the child and their guardian is critical. A short- and long-term treatment and monitoring plan to assess outcome, side effects, metabolic status and discontinuation, if appropriate, is also critical. The evidence base for use of atypical antipsychotics in preschool and younger children is limited and therefore further caution is warranted in prescribing in this population.

- **Don't prescribe antipsychotic medications to patients for any indication without appropriate initial evaluation and appropriate ongoing monitoring.** Metabolic, neuromuscular, and cardiovascular side effects are common in patients receiving antipsychotic medications for any indication, so thorough initial evaluation to ensure that their use is clinically warranted, and ongoing monitoring to ensure that side effects are identified, are essential.

  "Appropriate initial evaluation" includes the following: (a) thorough assessment of possible underlying causes of target symptoms including general medical, psychiatric, environmental, or psychosocial problems; (b) consideration of general medical conditions; and (c) assessment of family history of general medical conditions, especially of metabolic and cardiovascular disorders. "Appropriate ongoing monitoring" includes re-evaluation and documentation of dose, efficacy, and adverse effects; and targeted assessment, including assessment of movement disorder or neurological symptoms; weight, waist circumference, and/or BMI; blood pressure; heart rate; blood glucose level; and lipid profile at periodic intervals.

- **Don't routinely prescribe two or more antipsychotic medications concurrently.** Research shows that use of two or more antipsychotic medications occurs in 4% to 35% of outpatients and 30% to 50% of inpatients. However, evidence for the efficacy and safety of using multiple antipsychotic medications is limited, and risk for drug interactions, noncompliance, and medication errors is increased. Generally, the use of two or more antipsychotic medications concurrently should be avoided except in cases of three failed trials of monotherapy, which included one failed trial of Clozapine where possible, or where a second antipsychotic medication is added with a plan to cross-taper to monotherapy.

    D. **Other**—For more detail on the above-prioritized initiatives and information on others, please refer to the *Accountable Care Manual for Child Psychologists* at www.ncmedsoc.org/physician-resources/accountable-care/aco-toolkits.

    E. **PCSP Standards**—The NCQA Patient-Centered Specialty Practice standards regarding care team and patient coordination are recommended generally for all specialists, including child psychiatrists.

II. **Metrics**

    A. **Overview**—After determining the initiatives involving this specialty that are most appropriate for your CIN/ACO, to incentivize the desired behavior and outcomes, it is recommended that clinically valid metrics track adherence to the chosen activities and accomplishment of the desired results. Starting with the MACRA measures (see Table 7-4), use the available array of measures from various sources as a "menu" from which to start, and then tailor, prioritize, and weight them to fit your incentivization goals.

**TABLE 7-4.** MACRA's Quality Payment Program MIPS Measures Relevant to Child Psychiatry

| MEASURE NAME | MEASURE DESCRIPTION |
| --- | --- |
| ADHD: Follow-Up Care for Children Prescribed Attention-Deficit/ Hyperactivity Disorder (ADHD) Medication | Percentage of children aged 6-12 and newly dispensed a medication for attention-deficit/hyperactivity disorder (ADHD) who had appropriate follow-up care. Two rates are reported. 1. Percentage of children who had one follow-up visit with a practitioner with prescribing authority during the 30-Day Initiation Phase. 2. Percentage of children who remained on ADHD medication for at least 210 days and who, in addition to the visit in the Initiation Phase, had at least two additional follow-up visits with a practitioner within 270 days (9 months) after the Initiation Phase ended. |
| Anti-Depressant Medication Management | Percentage of patients aged 18 years and older who were treated with anti-depressant medication, had a diagnosis of major depression, and who remained on an anti-depressant medication treatment. Two rates are reported. 1. Percentage of patients who remained on an anti-depressant medication for at least 84 days (12 weeks). 2. Percentage of patients who remained on an anti-depressant medication for at least 180 days (6 months). |

*Continued on next page*

**TABLE 7-4.** MACRA's Quality Payment Program MIPS
Measures Relevant to Child Psychiatry (continued)

| MEASURE NAME | MEASURE DESCRIPTION |
|---|---|
| Care Plan | Percentage of patients aged 65 years and older who have an advance care plan or surrogate decision maker documented in the medical record or documentation in the medical record that an advance care plan was discussed but the patient did not wish or was not able to name a surrogate decision maker or provide an advance care plan. |
| Child and Adolescent Major Depressive Disorder (MDD): Suicide Risk Assessment | Percentage of patient visits for those patients aged 6- 17 years with a diagnosis of major depressive disorder with an assessment for suicide risk. |
| Tobacco Use and Help with Quitting Among Adolescents | The percentage of adolescents aged 12-20 years with a primary care visit during the measurement year for whom tobacco use status was documented and received help with quitting if identified as a tobacco user. |
| Weight Assessment and Counseling for Nutrition and Physical Activity for Children and Adolescents | Percentage of patients aged 3-17 years who had an outpatient visit with a primary care physician (PCP) or Obstetrician/Gynecologist (OB/GYN) and who had evidence of the following during the measurement period. Three rates are reported. 1. Percentage of patients with height, weight, and body mass index (BMI) percentile documentation. 2. Percentage of patients with counseling for nutrition. 3. Percentage of patients with counseling for physical activity. |

# DERMATOLOGISTS

I. **Why and How You May Want to Utilize Dermatologists in Your CIN/ACO**

A. **Primary Care/Dermatologist Coordination**—Perhaps the most practical utilization of dermatologists in value-based care is implementation of the following proven approaches involving coordination between the ACO patient's primary care physician and the dermatologist:

1. Early detection of systemic diseases. Many diseases are identifiable by dermatologic diagnosis. If the dermatologist knows to alert the attributed patient's treating physician and uses the ACO's digital access to their medical record to better evaluate the diagnosis, then a material number of early diagnoses can help to optimize treatment.

2. Dermatologists support treating primary care physicians, especially regarding skin cancer. While the incidence of skin cancer is increasing, so is the shortage of dermatologists. Primary care physicians can be better informed on indicators of skin cancer and other diseases, follow basic criteria for when to refer or when not to, and co-manage with the dermatologist.[128] Value-based care has unleashed technological aids to this coordination, from standing protocols and telephone accessibility to teledermatology. Teledermatology is one of the fastest-growing areas of telemedicine today—both store-and-forward and full-motion interactive video modalities.[129]

B. **Site-of-Service Optimization, Especially Mohs Surgery**—Moving procedures to lower-cost sites when consistent with best practice is the proverbial "low-hanging fruit" for all providers in value care, including dermatologists. One particularly viable initiative is the single visit in-office pathology, surgery, and reconstruction for appropriate Mohs surgery.

C. **Use of Best Practices**—A core set of evidence-based guidelines for dermatologists is recommended in ACOs. This practice will improve quality, which lowers costs. The Choosing Wisely® guidelines of the American Academy of Dermatology, and Improving Wisely guidelines of the American College of Mohs Surgery are recommended for consideration.

1. Don't prescribe oral antifungal therapy for suspected nail fungus without confirmation of fungal infection.

2. Don't perform sentinel lymph node biopsy or other diagnostic tests for the evaluation of early, thin melanoma because they do not improve survival.

3. Don't treat uncomplicated, nonmelanoma skin cancer less than 1 centimeter in size on the trunk and extremities with Mohs micrographic surgery.

4. Don't use oral antibiotics for treatment of atopic dermatitis unless there is clinical evidence of infection.

5. Don't routinely use topical antibiotics on a surgical wound.

6. Don't use systemic (oral or injected) corticosteroids as a long-term treatment for dermatitis.

7. Don't use the skin prick tests such as the radioallergosorbent test (RAST) for the routine evaluation of eczema.

8. Don't routinely use microbiologic testing in the evaluation and management of acne.

9. Don't routinely use antibiotics to treat bilateral swelling and redness of the lower leg unless there is clear evidence of infection.

10. Don't routinely prescribe antibiotics for inflamed epidermal cysts.[130]

**D. Other**—For more detail on the above-prioritized initiatives and information on others, please refer to the *Accountable Care Manual for Dermatologists* at: www.ncmedsoc.org/physician-resources/accountable-care/aco-toolkits/

**II. Metrics**

**A. Overview**—After determining the initiatives involving this specialty that are most appropriate for your CIN/ACO, to incentivize the desired behavior and outcomes, it is recommended that clinically valid metrics track adherence to the chosen activities and accomplishment of the desired results. Use the available array of measures from various sources as a "menu" from which to start, and then tailor, prioritize, and weight them to fit your incentivization goals. The measures in Table 7-5 may be one such body of measures to consider.

**TABLE 7-5.** MACRA's Quality Payment Program MIPS Measures Relevant to Dermatology

| MEASURE NAME | MEASURE DESCRIPTION |
|---|---|
| Biopsy Follow-Up | Percentage of new patients whose biopsy results have been reviewed and communicated to the primary care/referring physician and patient by the performing physician. |
| Closing the Referral Loop: Receipt of Specialist Report | Percentage of patients with referrals, regardless of age, for which the referring provider receives a report from the provider to whom the patient was referred. |
| Documentation of Current Medications in the Medical Record | Percentage of visits for patients aged 18 years and older for which the eligible professional attests to documenting a list of current medications using all immediate resources available on the date of the encounter. This list must include ALL known prescriptions, over-the-counters, herbals, and vitamin/mineral/dietary (nutritional) supplements AND must contain the medications' name, dosage, frequency, and route of administration. |
| Melanoma: Continuity of Care - Recall System | Percentage of patients, regardless of age, with a current diagnosis of melanoma or a history of melanoma whose information was entered, at least once within a 12-month period, into a recall system that includes: a target date for the next complete physical skin exam, AND a process to follow up with patients who either did not make an appointment within the specified timeframe or who missed a scheduled appointment. |

**TABLE 7-5.** MACRA's Quality Payment Program MIPS
Measures Relevant to Dermatology (continued)

| MEASURE NAME | MEASURE DESCRIPTION |
|---|---|
| Melanoma: Coordination of Care | Percentage of patient visits, regardless of age, with a new occurrence of melanoma who have a treatment plan documented in the chart that was communicated to the physician(s) providing continuing care within one month of diagnosis. |
| Melanoma: Overutilization of Imaging Studies in Melanoma | Percentage of patients, regardless of age, with a current diagnosis of Stage 0 through IIC melanoma or a history of melanoma of any stage, without signs or symptoms suggesting systemic spread, seen for an office visit during the one-year measurement period, for whom no diagnostic imaging studies were ordered. |
| Preventive Care and Screening: Screening for High Blood Pressure and Follow-Up Documented | Percentage of patients aged 18 years and older seen during the reporting period who were screened for high blood pressure AND a recommended follow-up plan is documented based on the current blood pressure (BP) reading as indicated. |
| Preventive Care and Screening: Tobacco Use: Screening and Cessation Intervention | Percentage of patients aged 18 years and older who were screened for tobacco use one or more times within 24 months AND who received cessation counseling intervention if identified as a tobacco user. |
| Psoriasis: Clinical Response to Oral Systemic or Biologic Medications | Percentage of psoriasis patients receiving oral systemic or biologic therapy who meet minimal physician- or patient-reported disease activity levels. It is implied that establishment and maintenance of an established minimum level of disease control as measured by physician- and/or patient-reported outcomes will increase patient satisfaction with and adherence to treatment. |
| Tobacco Use and Help with Quitting Among Adolescents | The percentage of adolescents aged 12-20 years with a primary care visit during the measurement year for whom tobacco use status was documented and who received help with quitting if identified as a tobacco user. |
| Tuberculosis (TB) Prevention for Psoriasis, Psoriatic Arthritis and Rheumatoid Arthritis Patients on a Biological Immune Response Modifier | Percentage of patients whose providers are ensuring active tuberculosis prevention through yearly negative standard tuberculosis screening tests or are reviewing the patient's history to determine if they have had appropriate management for a recent or prior positive test. |

# EMERGENCY PHYSICIANS

I. **Why and How You May Want to Utilize Emergency Physicians in Your CIN/ACO**

The Emergency Medicine Workgroup found that there were significant ACO opportunities that are concrete, high-impact, and not available in the fee-for-service setting. The fundamental differences opening the door for this change are:

- Linking with the ACO's primary care members, emergency medicine physicians are no longer as isolated in trying to coordinate for patients entering and departing their emergency department, but now stand at the center of a full continuum of care. The newly available opportunities create a compelling reason any ACO should seek out and reward emergency physicians.

- Switching to value-based reimbursement provides strong financial support for primary care to provide access and coordination both before and after ED admission. **This is particularly important now that significantly more newly covered patients under the Affordable Care Act are expected to seek non-emergency care through their local ED unless alternative access to primary care is made available.**

These themes are reflected in the recommended initiatives that follow. For ease of understanding, the recommended initiatives follow the care continuum. Note, however, that the Emergency Medicine ACO Workgroup believes that the "biggest bang for the buck" for emergency physicians will be in controlling the transition of patients back to the ACO upon discharge.

A. **Pre-Emergency Department Referral**

1. **Staff Alternative Urgent Care Sites and Triage Hotlines**—Who better than emergency physicians to see patients with urgent but less acute conditions? Emergency physician practices should contemplate setting up and/or staffing urgent care clinics and handling after-hours referrals from the ACO member practices. One North Carolina ACO saw a direct correlation in decreased ED use with the opening of their after-hours clinic.

    Similarly, trained nurse coordinators can staff an ED triage hotline, with access to an emergency physician. One study showed this practice leading to a 24% reduction in Levels 3, 4, and 5 acuity ED visits.[131]

    The American College of Emergency Physicians notes, "Ultimately, in order to improve [ACO] care coordination, emergency medicine may need to diversify the options available for the management of inpatients. Observation units are an expanding area of growth as are ED-run follow-up clinics and call centers. . . ."[132]

2. **Leadership on ACO ED Utilization Clinical Subcommittee**—Several of the greatest opportunities to optimize ED utilization must be driven by primary care providers in the community. Heretofore, the emergency

physician could have little impact on misreferrals or default self-referrals due to lack of alternative access. The ACO setting changes all of that. If emergency physicians simply plug into an ACO's clinical team working on ED utilization, they can lead creation of the valuable continuum of care bridge missing for all these years. You are on a team now, not in a silo.

Basically, the ACO's patients must have access to care other than having to default to the ED. Under shared savings, ACO physicians are not highly financially incentivized to see these patients. They also are incentivized to provide after-hours care and make available urgent care alternative sites, perhaps run by emergency physicians. Topics emergency physicians can help refine include:

- Urgent care clinic access to emergency physician diagnostic support.
- Integration of dataflow so referred patient is accompanied by relevant information and designation of a contact person.
- Redirection.
- Transportation issues stifling access to alternative sites.
- Education of primary care physicians on appropriate referrals.
- Referral management protocols.
- Alternative access to emergency physician diagnostic and treatment decision support (such as telephone, email, video conference, telemedicine). "Patients with certain medical conditions (*e.g.*, COPD, CHF, and cellulitis) tend to have recurrent exacerbations of their condition that lead to frequent ED utilization. By working with ACOs to determine goals of ED care including alternatives to admission, such as observation admissions or next-day community follow-up plans, EDs may be able to provide just as good, if not potentially better, care at a much lower cost."[133]
- Patient education materials regarding tools available and site-of-care alternatives.

3. **Increase Access by Primary Care for Complex Urgent Issues Diagnosis and Treatment Support**—A recent RAND study found that office-based physicians increasingly rely on EDs to evaluate complex patients.[134] Obviously, in many cases, this evaluation function could be performed without referral of the patient to the ED and its associated costs. The primary care physician in an ACO should have better access to multiple specialties, including the emergency physician. Alternative means of accessing your knowledge, as previously discussed, such as following your standard protocols on proper referral, email, telephone, using taped talks to educate other physicians or patients, etc., seem to present efficiency and time-saving opportunities.

4. **Skilled Nursing Facility Referral Management**—Often a skilled nursing facility (SNF) will not fully understand when a patient truly should be admitted to a hospital or rushed to the ED. On the other hand, the ED may not know the care capabilities of the SNF and err on the side of caution in accepting non-acute referrals. The patient is often not articulate, and the transfer often lacks background information or contact person information. Prior to ED referrals from an SNF, emergency physicians can develop protocols and exercise due diligence on SNF capabilities to better manage patient referrals and treatment.

B. **Intra-ED Initiatives**

Emergency physicians can show value in the new healthcare by streamlining the care process once the patient has been referred to the ED and connecting them to the ACO care continuum. For example, at Aurora Sinai Medical Center in Milwaukee, all patients are triaged by a physician, nurse practitioner, or physician assistant. Non-emergent patients are educated about appropriate ED use to reduce unnecessary future visits and actually are scheduled for a follow-up appointment with a primary care physician. This accounted for a 23% reduction in annual ED visits.[135] Suggested intra-ED ACO initiatives include:
- Patient education and engagement.
- Nurse navigator in the ED.
- Low acuity fast track.
- Expedited triage.
- Check-in kiosks.
- Split-flow management.
- Containment of inappropriate hospital admissions using evidence-based best practices.
- Connection upon discharge to ACO's primary care network.

C. **ED Discharge Management**

Of all the significant ACO opportunities available to emergency physicians, the ones presenting themselves at the moment of discharge are the most potent. Previously physicians often had a very frayed safety net or care network to which to connect their patients. Patients then sadly, and expensively, became "frequent fliers" due to the lack of access. Because of the change incentives, with an ACO network that has incorporated as many community health resources as feasible (this is required by the MSSP), you should for the first time have a place to hand off your patient, their health information, and their care plan.

1. **Discharge Handoff to ACO Medical Home**—Often, under fee-for-service, physicians would not accept new Medicare patients or the wait times (Boston[136]) effectively precluded realistic follow-up care. For ACO patients, it should be a goal for every one of them to walk out of the ED

with a primary care appointment in hand. The ACO data system should pass along relevant medical information and your suggested chronic care plan.

This sounds naïve until we remember that the cost difference between a primary care and ED visit is on the order of 10:1 and up to 40:1. Avoided hospital and intensive care admissions through meaningful follow-up only increase those savings. With primary care participating in this considerable portion of those savings, under ACOs, they have a huge incentive to take these patient handoffs. The American College of Emergency Physicians even suggests that emergency physicians consider providing home health services to improve transitions of care.[137]

2. **Management of Drug-Related "Frequent Fliers"**—A number of effective strategies are available in an ACO setting to address the "frequent flier" problems related to drug usage. Because these frequent fliers often use several EDs, EDs should track patient usage. Prescription monitoring programs help differentiate the dependent or entrepreneurial patient from the one truly experiencing severe pain for which an opiate is appropriate. The ED can involve the patient in dependency counseling, connecting the patient to pain clinics, psychiatric help, or analgesic services.

D. **Awareness/Leadership/Urgency: Emergency Medicine's Role in Guiding Change**

Emergency medicine physicians need to know what an ACO is, how to recognize one with a likelihood of success, and the professional opportunities and risks involved. Leaders need to get up to speed and be catalysts for this transformative change. These champions need to act with confidence, but also with a sense of urgency. This is mentioned as a strategy in and of itself because the biggest risk of failure of the accountable care movement and either collapse of Medicare and Medicaid or default to Draconian alternatives is lack of informed physician leadership. If you do not become involved, there is a good chance that the roles of emergency medicine will be missed and, like some early ACOs, you will not be involved at all in the shared savings pool distribution. Every successful ACO starts with a few champions. Why not have one be an emergency physician? As Bert Coffer, MD, said: "If you don't have a seat at the table, you are on the menu."

E. **Avoidance of Expensive Drugs and Procedures with Marginal Value**

Opportunities for improved care and cost also exist in pharmacy and procedure selection. Again, staying with the evidence base, think about the most cost-effective medications. This value-based thinking will benefit the patients clinically and financially and benefit the shared savings. Choosing Wisely®, an initiative of the American Board of Internal Medicine (ABIM) Foundation, is a resource "to help physicians and patients engage in conversations to reduce overuse of tests and procedures and support physician efforts to help patients make smart and effective care choices" (See, http://wwwabimfoundation.org/initiatives/choosing-wisely.aspx). The recommendations of the American College of Emergency Physicians to the Choosing Wisely® initiative can be accessed at: http://www.choosingwisely.org/doctor-patient-lists/american-college-of-emergency-physicians.

II. **Metrics**

    A. **Overview**—After determining which initiatives involving this specialty are most appropriate for your CIN/ACO, to incentivize the desired behavior and outcomes, it is recommended that clinically valid metrics track adherence to the chosen activities and accomplishment of the desired results. Perhaps use the following array of measures from various sources as a "menu" from which to start, and then tailor, prioritize, and weight them to fit your incentivization goals.

    B. **MACRA Quality Payment Program MIPS Measures Relevant to Emergency Medicine**

        1. **Quality—50% of total score:** Select 6 measures including one **Outcome** measure (or high priority measure if an outcome measure is not applicable) and report each on at least 60% of eligible Medicare and non-Medicare patient/visits for the entire year. Suggestions for your specialty include but are not limited to the following:

- #1 Diabetes: Hemoglobin A1c Poor Control—High Priority
- #65 Appropriate Treatment for Children with Upper Respiratory Infection (URI)—High Priority
- #66 Appropriate Testing for Children with Pharyngitis*—High Priority
- #76 Prevention of catheter-related bloodstream infections (CRBSI)—central venous catheter insertion protocol—High Priority
- #91 Acute Otitis Externa (AOE): Topical Therapy*—High Priority
- #93 Acute Otitis Externa (AOE): Systemic Antimicrobial Therapy—Avoidance of Inappropriate Use*—High Priority
- #116 Avoidance of Antibiotic Treatment in Adults with Acute Bronchitis*—High Priority
- #130 Documentation and Verification of Current Medications in the Medical Record—High Priority
- #187 Stroke and Stroke Rehabilitation: Thrombolytic Therapy*
- #254 Ultrasound Determination of Pregnancy Location for Pregnant Patients with Abdominal Pain*
- #255 Rh Immunoglobulin (Rhogam) for Rh-Negative Pregnant Women at Risk of Fetal Blood Exposure Pain*
- #317 Preventive Care and Screening: Screening for High Blood Pressure and Follow-Up Documented*

- #326 Atrial Fibrillation and Atrial Flutter: Chronic Anticoagulation Therapy
- #331: Adult Sinusitis: Antibiotic Prescribed for Acute Sinusitis (Appropriate Use)*—High Priority
- #332: Adult Sinusitis: Appropriate Choice of Antibiotic: Amoxicillin Prescribed for Patients with Acute Bacterial Sinusitis (Appropriate Use)*—High Priority
- #333: Adult Sinusitis: Computerized Tomography (CT) for Acute Sinusitis (Overuse)*—High Priority
- #415 Emergency Medicine: Emergency Department Utilization of CT for Minor Blunt Head Trauma for Patients Aged 18 Years and Older*—High Priority
- #416 Emergency Medicine: Emergency Department Utilization of CT for Minor Blunt Head Trauma for Patients Aged 2 through 17 Years*—High Priority
- #419 Overuse of Neuroimaging for Patients with Primary Headache and A Normal Neurological Examination—High Priority

*These 13 measures (plus EHR-only measure 107) make up the Emergency Medicine Specialty Measures Set.

2. **PI: Promoting Interoperability** *(formerly ACI)*—**25% of total score:** Replaces the Medicare EHR Incentive Program also known as Meaningful Use. A minimum of the following base measures is required if reporting this category. *Note that EHRs certified to a 2014 edition report a different set of measures.*
   - Conduct security risk analysis
   - ePrescribe
   - Provide patient electronic access
   - Send a summary of care
   - Receive/accept a summary of care

3. **IA: Improvement Activities—15% of total score:** Attest that you completed up to 2 high-weighted activities or 4 medium-weighted activities for a minimum of 90 days. Groups with 15 or fewer participants or if you are in a rural or health professional shortage area, attest that you completed 1 high-weighted or 2 medium-weighted activities for a minimum of 90 days. *There are over 90 possible measures to choose from. The following are suggestions only:*
   - Collection and use of patient experience and satisfaction data on access (**medium-weighted**).
   - Annual registration in the Prescription Drug Monitoring Program (**medium-weighted**).
   - Engagement of new Medicaid patients and follow-up (**high-weighted**).

- Engage patients and families to guide improvement in the system of care (**medium-weighted**).
- Implementation of documentation improvements for practice/process improvements (**medium-weighted**).
- Implementation of improvements that contribute to more timely communication of test results (**medium-weighted**).

4. **Other Resources from CMS**—*MIPS Measures Guide for Emergency Medicine Clinicians* offers a non-exhaustive sample of measures and activities for the Quality, Improvement Activities, and Advancing Care Information performance categories that may apply in 2017 to these specialists.

# GYNECOLOGISTS

I.   **Why and How You May Want to Utilize Gynecologists in Your CIN/ACO**
     *NOTE: As the contributors in value-based care are distinctly different for physicians practicing obstetrics, a separate treatment for obstetricians is found on page 161.*

A.   **As Primary Care First Point of Contact for Many Women**—Many women view their OB/GYN as their only physician or as their primary care physician. This may be by choice, but it may be by necessity, particularly in rural areas. In the *Medical Economics* article entitled "Young Minority Women Bypass Primary Care for OB/GYN," survey results reported the following:

   • More than half the women aged 18 to 40 years say their OB/GYN is the only physician they see on an annual basis.
   • 68% of women 41 and over also saw primary care physicians.
   • Roughly 40% of the women surveyed reported having chronic conditions such as diabetes, obesity, or hypertension.[138]

   One Gynecology Accountable Care Workgroup member commented that gynecologists are often the "first contact for women." In a rural area without primary care access, they will remain the primary care physician by default, but in an ACO setting with access to a primary care-led Patient-Centered Medical Home (PCMH), primary care treatment will often be commenced, then an appropriate referral made to the PCMH. Another Workgroup member stated that, "If they are unassigned, we try to keep them in the ACO" by facilitating a physician/patient relationship within the ACO. The savings alone in avoided emergency department visits would justify this initiative. "ACOG [The American Congress of Obstetricians and Gynecologists] has long said ob-gyns have a tradition of providing preventive care to women and that the specialty knows how to provide women a point of entry to the healthcare system."[139] Jeffrey Cain, MD, a former Chairman of the American Academy of Family Physicians, has stated that he expects gynecologists to start working more closely with primary care physicians as we move toward team-based care.[140]

   One physician noted, "If the gynecologist is the primary care physician, he/she must provide COMPREHENSIVE primary care (*i.e.*, wellness and prevention, GYN services) AND care for simple chronic management (*i.e.*, htn, obesity, diabetics, screening, complete immunizations, etc.)." A proactive coordinated relationship with a primary care physician is recommended. This avoids a default to multiple specialist referrals, further fragmenting the patient's care.

   ***Strategic Note:*** Use Co-Management Plan Agreements—When the gynecologist is assuming primary care duties, co-management plan agreements are important to ensure partnerships between gynecologists, primary care physicians, and other specialists. Clear plans align the approach to care and a framework for efficient coordination of care. It creates pathways for communication, feedback, and transition management. The patient should be included in the planning of these protocols. The gynecologist's presumed first option should now be coordination with the primary care practice, but with channels to the appropriate specialists on the team.

This practice will lead to a double whammy of ACO value-add contributions: First, the contact, diagnosis, and referral stand to generate better care and substantial savings. Second, even "default" primary care triage and treatment by the gynecologist can access all of the mentioned high-value ACO opportunities of prevention and wellness, chronic care management, reduced hospitalizations, care transitions, and multispecialty coordination of complex patients.

B. **As Specialists Coordinating with the CIN/ACO Care Team**—Your colleagues are often confronted and confounded by medical concerns requiring clinical expertise only within the gynecological sphere. The accountable care model opens up heretofore unavailable new possibilities to provide that expertise at the point of care and even to the patient. One Gynecology Accountable Care Workgroup member noted that simply by the ACO's gynecologists being on the same Electronic Medical Record System with the other specialties, he estimated that they opined on at least one or two questions per day, resulting in "huge cost savings." Another commended the practice of periodic lunch-and-learn sessions with referring physicians. A more targeted approach that has proven effective is to contact the top referrers exhibiting poor practices relative to evidence-based best practices. The gynecologists send them the clinically valid guidelines and monitor adherence.

Per the American Congress of Obstetrics and Gynecology, "Nearly one-third of rural women live in counties with no OB/GYN at all. Location is a serious disadvantage for these women."[141] They have higher rates of cervical cancer; receive fewer mammograms, pap smears and colorectal screenings; and are less likely to receive family planning services.[142] Given the obvious improvement in quality of care and reduced expenditures through improved health status, if gynecological "knowledge" is pushed into a rural or other area without ready access, value-based payment such as in an ACO now unleashes new opportunities. Care will improve if the gynecologist is linked to the point-of-care provider through the ACO's health information exchange. Likewise, telemedicine and established telephone or email access protocols through the ACO can help close this gap. One Workgroup member commented that, "In an ACO, you've got to be the director of female health care."

If a gynecologist sees a persistent but avoidable problem, they might proactively reach out and share the guidelines within the ACO. One example provided by the Workgroup was the decision to share guidelines with primary care physicians regarding when to refer a woman who is bleeding too much. "When it gets this bad, it's time to send them." This simple ACO knowledge-sharing produced real results.

An ACO model mitigates the problem that current insurance may limit coverage of women's health services. Because such care will result in better quality and more savings, the ACO could compensate those services via a monthly fee.

A woman with a gynecological issue often will have other medical concerns, such as anxiety relative to an unplanned pregnancy. Many ACOs prioritize on multidisciplinary care of the high-risk, high-cost heretofore unmanaged patient—the 10% driving the 50% of total costs. Our fragmented, "siloed" fee-for-service system has repeatedly let these patients fall between the cracks. The ACO's data analysis might reveal a woman with gynecological issues who is also morbidly obese, diabetic, depressed, and exhibiting cardiac issues. Shared protocols, access via technology, "lunch and learns," and other interventional collaboration efforts often result in an ACO's greatest care and financial improvements.

One study of women suffering from depression who received collaborative care displayed 50% fewer symptoms after one year. Multidisciplinary teams reviewed multiple health concerns on a weekly basis.

C. **Follow Evidence-Based Practices**—One source of best practices is the Safety Certification in Outpatient Practice Excellence for Women's Health Program (SCOPE) developed by the American Congress of Obstetricians and Gynecologists (ACOG). This program details elements comparable to the National Committee for Quality Assurance metrics. The SCOPE program is a voluntary program used for assessing the patient safety concepts and techniques in the gynecology office.

Because the women's healthcare profession has demonstrated experience with clinical best practices, providers in this area can lead the incorporation and development of similar initiatives for ACOs. Gynecologist guidelines and metrics can frame providing patient assessment and evaluations, prescribing and monitoring medication, serving as a liaison to medical issues, being a member of the Patient-Centered Medical Home, consulting to the public healthcare system, and acting as an advocate for the patient.

The multidisciplinary Choosing Wisely® initiative is a good beginning source of guidelines:

- **Don't perform routine annual cervical cytology screening (Pap tests) in women 30-65 years of age.** In average risk women, annual cervical cytology screening has been shown to offer no advantage over screening performed at three-year intervals. However, a well-woman visit should occur annually for patients with their healthcare practitioner to discuss concerns and problems and have appropriate screening with consideration of a pelvic examination.

- **Don't treat patients who have mild dysplasia of less than two years in duration.** Mild dysplasia (Cervical Intraepithelial Neoplasia [CIN 1]) is associated with the presence of the human papillomavirus (HPV) which does not require treatment in average risk women. Most women with CIN 1 on biopsy have a transient HPV infection that will usually clear in less than 12 months and, therefore, does not require treatment.

- **Don't screen for ovarian cancer in asymptomatic women at average risk.** In population studies, there is only fair evidence that screening of asymptomatic women with serum CA-125 level and/or transvaginal ultrasound can detect ovarian cancer at an earlier stage than it can be detected in the absence of screening. Because of the low prevalence of ovarian cancer and the invasive nature of the interventions required after a positive screening test, the potential harms of screening outweigh the potential benefits.

D. **Site of Service**—Site-of-service differentials can make a big difference in costs, without a difference in care. One Workgroup member related that sharing the site-of-service financial implications was "astounding." The top identified areas to focus on were surgery, imaging, and nutrition consulting. A five-to-one price differential between hospital and clinic was used as an example for the latter. Posting site-of-service statistics naming gynecologists provided effective "social pressure."

E. **Other**—Please see *The Accountable Care Manual for Gynecologists*, which may be downloaded at www.ncmedsoc.org/physician-resources/accountable-care/aco-toolkits.

F. **PCSP Standards**—The NCQA Patient-Centered Specialty Practice standards regarding care team and patient coordination are recommended generally for all specialists, including gynecologists.

II. **Metrics**

A. **Overview**—After determining which initiatives involving this specialty are most appropriate for your CIN/ACO, to incentivize the desired behavior and outcomes, it is recommended that clinically valid metrics track adherence to the chosen activities and accomplishment of the desired results. Perhaps use the following array of measures from various sources as a "menu" from which to start, and then tailor, prioritize, and weight them to fit your incentivization goals (see Table 7-6).

**TABLE 7-6.** MACRA Quality Payment Program MIPS Measures
Relevant to Gynecology and Obstetrics

| MEASURE NAME | MEASURE DESCRIPTION |
| --- | --- |
| Appropriate Workup Prior to Endometrial Ablation | Percentage of women, aged 18 years and older, who underwent endometrial sampling or hysteroscopy with biopsy before undergoing an endometrial ablation. |
| Biopsy Follow-Up | Percentage of new patients whose biopsy results have been reviewed and communicated to the primary care/referring physician and patient by the performing physician. |
| Breast Cancer Screening | Percentage of women aged 50-74 years who had a mammogram to screen for breast cancer. |
| Care Plan | Percentage of patients aged 65 years and older who have an advance care plan or surrogate decision maker documented in the medical record or documentation in the medical record that an advance care plan was discussed but the patient did not wish or was not able to name a surrogate decision maker or provide an advance care plan. |
| Cervical Cancer Screening | Percentage of women aged 21-64 years who were screened for cervical cancer using either of the following criteria: * Women aged 21-64 who had cervical cytology performed every 3 years; * Women aged 30-64 who had cervical cytology/human papillomavirus (HPV) co-testing performed every 5 years. |
| Chlamydia Screening and Follow Up | The percentage of female adolescents 16 years of age who had a chlamydia screening test with proper follow-up during the measurement period. |
| Chlamydia Screening for Women | Percentage of women aged 16-24 years who were identified as sexually active and who had at least one test for chlamydia during the measurement period. |
| Closing the Referral Loop: Receipt of Specialist Report | Percentage of patients with referrals, regardless of age, for which the referring provider received a report from the provider to whom the patient was referred. |
| Controlling High Blood Pressure | Percentage of patients aged 18-85 years who had a diagnosis of hypertension and whose blood pressure was adequately controlled (<140/90mmHg) during the measurement period. |
| Documentation of Current Medications in the Medical Record | Percentage of visits for patients aged 18 years and older for which the eligible professional attested to documenting a list of current medications using all immediate resources available on the date of the encounter. This list must include ALL known prescriptions, over-the-counters, herbals, and vitamin/mineral/dietary (nutritional) supplements AND must contain the medications' name, dosage, frequency and route of administration. |
| Non-Recommended Cervical Cancer Screening in Adolescent Females | The percentage of adolescent females aged 16-20 years who were screened unnecessarily for cervical cancer. |
| Osteoporosis Management in Women Who Had a Fracture | The percentage of women aged 50-85 who suffered a fracture and who either had a bone mineral density test or received a prescription for a drug to treat osteoporosis in the six months after the fracture. |

*Continued on next page*

TABLE 7-6. MACRA Quality Payment Program MIPS Measures
Relevant to Gynecology and Obstetrics (continued)

| MEASURE NAME | MEASURE DESCRIPTION |
|---|---|
| Performing Cystoscopy at the Time of Hysterectomy for Pelvic Organ Prolapse to Detect Lower Urinary Tract Injury | Percentage of patients who underwent cystoscopy to evaluate for lower urinary tract injury at the time of hysterectomy for pelvic organ prolapse. |
| Preventive Care and Screening: Body Mass Index (BMI) Screening and Follow-Up Plan | Percentage of patients aged 18 years and older with a BMI documented during the current encounter or during the previous six months AND with a BMI outside of normal parameters, for whom a follow-up plan was documented during the encounter or during the previous six months of the current encounter. Normal Parameters: Age 18 years and older BMI ≥ 18.5 and < 25 kg/m$^2$ |
| Preventive Care and Screening: Influenza Immunization | Percentage of patients aged 6 months and older seen for a visit between October 1 and March 31 who received an influenza immunization OR who reported previous receipt of an influenza immunization. |
| Preventive Care and Screening: Screening for High Blood Pressure and Follow-Up Documented | Percentage of patients aged 18 years and older seen during the reporting period who were screened for high blood pressure AND a recommended follow-up plan is documented based on the current blood pressure (BP) reading as indicated. |
| Preventive Care and Screening: Tobacco Use: Screening and Cessation Intervention | Percentage of patients aged 18 years and older who were screened for tobacco use one or more times within 24 months AND who received cessation counseling intervention if identified as a tobacco user. |
| Preventive Care and Screening: Unhealthy Alcohol Use: Screening and Brief Counseling | Percentage of patients aged 18 years and older who were screened for unhealthy alcohol use using a systematic screening method at least once within the last 24 months AND who received brief counseling if identified as an unhealthy alcohol user. |
| Proportion of Patients Sustaining a Bladder Injury at the Time of Any Pelvic Organ Prolapse Repair | Percentage of patients undergoing any surgery to repair pelvic organ prolapse who sustained an injury to the bladder recognized either during or within 1 month after surgery. |
| Proportion of Patients Sustaining a Bowel Injury at the Time of Any Pelvic Organ Prolapse Repair | Percentage of patients undergoing surgical repair of pelvic organ prolapse that was complicated by a bowel injury at the time of index surgery that was recognized intraoperatively or within 1 month after surgery. |
| Proportion of Patients Sustaining a Ureter Injury at the Time of Any Pelvic Organ Prolapse Repair | Percentage of patients undergoing pelvic organ prolapse repairs who sustained an injury to the ureter recognized either during or within 1 month after surgery. |
| Tobacco Use and Help with Quitting Among Adolescents | The percentage of adolescents aged 12- 20 years with a primary care visit during the measurement year for whom tobacco use status was documented and who received help with quitting if identified as a tobacco user. |

**TABLE 7-6.** MACRA Quality Payment Program MIPS Measures
Relevant to Gynecology and Obstetrics (continued)

| MEASURE NAME | MEASURE DESCRIPTION |
|---|---|
| Urinary Incontinence: Assessment of Presence or Absence of Urinary Incontinence in Women Aged 65 Years and Older | Percentage of female patients aged 65 years and older who were assessed for the presence or absence of urinary incontinence within 12 months. |
| Urinary Incontinence: Plan of Care for Urinary Incontinence in Women Aged 65 Years and Older | Percentage of female patients aged 65 years and older with a diagnosis of urinary incontinence with a documented plan of care for urinary incontinence at least once within 12 months. |

B.  **Blue Cross Measures Relevant to Gynecologists and Obstetrics**—The Blue Cross Blue Shield of North Carolina Tiered Network utilizes administrative claims data in an effort to identify high-quality, low-cost providers and to help consumers make more informed choices for their medical care. They note: "Transparent methodology provides physicians with access to information on how their performance compares to their peers on nationally accepted quality measures as well as local cost efficiency benchmarks." The quality measures chosen for the obstetrics/gynecology specialty include:

- Percentage of women 40-69 years of age who had a mammogram to screen for breast cancer.
- Percentage of women 21-64 years of age who received one or more Pap tests to screen for cervical cancer.
- Percentage of women 16-20 years of age who were identified as sexually active and who had at least one test for chlamydia during the measurement year.
- Percentage of women 21-24 years of age who were identified as sexually active and who had at least one test for chlamydia during the measurement year.
- Percentage of hysterectomy with potentially avoidable complications.
- Percentage of deliveries with a potentially avoidable complication.[143]

# HOSPITALISTS

I.  **Why and How You May Want to Utilize Hospitalists in Your CIN/ACO**

The incorporation of hospitalists into an ACO allows for attainment of efficiencies because of hospitalists' continuous provision of patient care, rather than the periodic rounds performed by internists and other specialists.[144] "Hospitalists position themselves to manage through the entire spectrum and episodes of illness," explains R. Jeffrey Taylor, President and COO of IPC The Hospitalist Company. "That skill set and continuity of care will be crucial for ACOs."[145]

A.  **Hospitalist as Co-Manager**

Hospitalists are tasked with the management and coordination of care throughout the inpatient experience and facilitate communication among care providers, both inside and outside the hospital. The positive impact of these skillsets is particularly significant with complex patient populations.

A study was performed at the University of the Rochester School of Medicine on the effect of co-management by a geriatric hospitalist and orthopedic surgeons. The intervention was performed on older patients suffering from multiple co-morbidities who are treated for a hip fracture at The Geriatric Fracture Center (GFC). In this intervention, co-management included "a strong emphasis on co-ownership, mutual respect, and communication."[146]

The study included 314 patients; 193 patients were considered more complex, as they suffered from more co-morbid conditions and dementia. The other 121 patients, who comprised the control group received usual care. Despite being a more acute population, the intervention group experienced more favorable results throughout the entire episode of their care, such as:[147]

- Shorter times to surgery (24.1 vs. 37.4 hours)
- Fewer post-operative infections (2.3% vs. 19.8%)
- Fewer overall complications (30.6% vs. 46.3%)
- Shorter length of stay (4.6 vs. 8.3 days)
- Lower use of physical restraint (0% vs. 14.1%)

*Strategic Note:* A clearly defined co-management structure should be established in order to prevent "dumping," where specialists and primary care physicians transfer responsibility of an admitted patient to hospitalists. Dumping forces hospitalists to shoulder all responsibility for patients during their inpatient stay, often providing care that exceeds their capabilities. This is especially important because hospitalists are put at an increased legal risk.[148] Co-management agreements should reflect an understanding of:

- Shared goals, reflecting the mission of the ACO.
- Patients' needs.
- Value proposition of hospitalists and other providers.
- Scope of hospitalists' abilities.

- Workload capacity of hospitalists.
- Resources necessary to perform assigned tasks.
- Co-management agreements should evolve with time.[149]

One suggested method is to develop metrics related to how co-management is handled in the organization. Metrics are generally an effective way to ensure that trends such as dumping are not developing in the hospital setting. Data should be collected at baseline, as well as continuously over time. Any identified problems should be addressed immediately in order to ensure that bad habits do not become established.

## B. Hospitalist Involvement in Post-Discharge Care

In an effort to rethink their role in the clinical setting, successful hospitalists have expanded their scope beyond traditional inpatient care, in both clinical and non-clinical capacities.

### 1. Clinical Role in Patient Discharge

Additional clinical roles include both pre- and post-hospitalization care, such as admission and rehabilitation. A National Taiwan University Hospital experiencing a 22% readmission rate after discharge from the hospitalist ward implemented a Post-Discharge Transitional Care (PDTC) program, operated by nurses and hospitalists.[150] The program consisted of the following activities for 30 days post-discharge:

- Disease-specific care plan established at discharge.
- Disease-specific indicators monitored through:
  - Patient hotline
  - Scheduled follow-up calls (days 1, 3, 7, 14 and 30).
- Hospitalist-run outpatient clinic.

If a disease worsened, it was reported to the patient's hospitalist and further management was discussed, including counseling, referral to the hospitalist-run clinic, or referral to the ED. Within 30 days of discharge, the intervention group had significantly lower rates of readmission (14% vs. 22%) and death (1% vs. 3%).

There have previously been mixed responses to hospitalist-run clinics in the United States; under a fee-for-service model, many hospitals have ultimately had to subsidize these clinics. However, under the ACO model, there is much more financial incentive to provide care through this type of model.

### 2. Non-Clinical Role in Patient Discharge

Hospitalists have the opportunity to play a key role in the handoff of patients after discharge, such as back to their primary care physicians. In the ACO setting, hospitals are suddenly finding themselves invested in the patient's successful transition out of the hospital, due to the fact that they are now financially penalized for readmissions within 30 days.

There are six principles that hospitalists should follow to ensure a successful patient handoff.

1. **Communicate in an Effective, Convenient Manner**—Hospitalists should find a method of communication that is most convenient for the majority of the primary care physicians with whom they have relationships; when necessary, customization of method may be necessary. Only convey information that is essential for primary care physicians to know.

2. **Utilize the Knowledge of Primary Care Physicians**—The opinions of primary care physicians should be incorporated into complex medical decisions and design of care. There are multiple benefits to incorporating a primary care physician's expertise regarding a specific patient. First, patients will be comforted knowing that their primary care physician's opinion has been included. Second, it is essential that one clear message regarding post-discharge instructions be communicated to the patient in order to avoid confusion. Lastly, there is a much higher chance that a primary care physician will enforce post-discharge instructions if they agree on the course of action.

3. **Timeliness of Communication is Essential**—Hospitalists should connect with primary care physicians in a timely manner at the following points: admission, before major medical decisions (especially those that might be irreversible), and at discharge.

4. **Include the Patient**—The patient should be an active part of the medical decision-making process, and the primary care physician can advise how to best facilitate patient participation.

5. **Be on the Patient's Side**—Hospitalists run the risk of being viewed as a "gatekeeper" of the hospital system. To overcome this impression, hospitalists need to make it clear that they are the patient's advocate.

6. **Always Interact in a Polite and Gracious Manner**—Even if the hospitalist's initial interactions with the primary care physician are awkward or unsuccessful, the hospitalist should still continue to be gracious and polite. All relationships have the potential to improve.[151]

   *Strategic Note:* The Society of Hospital Medicine (SHM) has recently introduced the Post-Acute Care Toolbox, targeting patients transitions from short-term hospital stays to skilled nursing facilities. The recommendations presented in the toolbox comes from both 1) evidence-based medicine, and 2) the opinions of industry experts. For more information, please visit http://www.hospitalmedicine.org/Web/Quality___Innovation/Implementation_Toolkit/pact/Overview_PACT.aspx.

C. **Hospitalist Involvement in Quality Improvement Initiatives**
   "One of the most important material changes we have seen is that hospital medicine has developed its own research and educational agenda and platform,"

explained Dr. Arora, co-chair of the Society of Hospital Medicine's Physicians in Training Committee, "The field's expanding non-clinical opportunities are emerging as another drawing card. Hospitalists are increasingly becoming involved in informatics, quality improvement, and medical education, and partnering with administration in a variety of areas."[152]

For example, the University of California at San Francisco launched a high-value care initiative in the Department of Hospital Medicine in March 2012, co-led by a hospitalist and the administrator of the Division of Hospital Medicine. The initiative had three main goals:

1. Identify areas of waste in the hospital (defined as areas of high cost with no associated improvement in health outcomes) using financial and clinic data.
2. Utilize evidence-based interventions that promote value and quality of care.
3. Drive cultural change though evidence-based cost awareness education.

Dr. Christopher Moriates, co-chair of the committee responsible for the initiative, explained, "We're not just creating these pilot programs and asking people to do more. We're really thinking through these interventions as complete packages. We're really baking it into our culture. As we address what people actually do and change the systems around . . . it becomes standard practices and thus more likely to be sustainable."[153]

During the first year, six projects were undertaken, including: reduce unnecessary nebulizer use, curb overuse and inappropriate use of gastric stress ulcer prophylaxis, encourage better blood utilization stewardship, improve the use of telemetry, scale back on inappropriate/repeat inpatient echocardiograms, and reduce the number of ionized calcium labs. Early results have shown that the plan is working. In particularly, unnecessary nebulizer usage has decreased by more than 50% on a high-acuity medical ward.

Dr. Shaun Frost, president of the Society of Hospital Medicine, predicted the future demand for hospitalists involved with quality improvement initiatives, explaining, "Young physicians interested in hospital medicine must embrace the fact that an important part of the job today is working on systems aspects of care, to improve care processes. Hospital medicine has always seen itself as a specialty whose role is to help hospitals deliver better care. But with healthcare reform evolving, hospitalists will have an even larger role in organizing care delivery."[154]

***Strategic Note:*** The Society for Hospital Medicine (SHM) has joined Choosing Wisely®, an initiative through the American Board of Internal Medicine (ABIM) foundation to promote conversations between physicians and patients concerning the careful selection about medical tests and procedures. The goal of the campaign is to for patients to choose care that is evidence-based, not duplicative, free from harm and absolutely necessary.[155] Five topics have been selected in the area of Adult Hospital Medicine:

1. "Don't place, or leave in place, urinary catheters for incontinence or convenience or monitoring of output for non-critically ill patients (acceptable indications: critical illness, obstruction, hospice, perioperatively for <2 days for urologic procedures; use weights instead to monitor diuresis)."
2. "Don't prescribe medications for stress ulcer prophylaxis to medical inpatients unless at high risk for GI complications."
3. "Avoid transfusions of red blood cells for arbitrary hemoglobin or hematocrit thresholds and in the absence of symptoms of active coronary disease, heart failure or stroke."
4. "Don't order continuous telemetry monitoring outside of the ICU without using a protocol that governs continuation."
5. "Don't perform repetitive CBC and chemistry testing in the face of clinical and lab stability."

To learn more about the SHM Choosing Wisely® Adult and Pediatric recommendations, as well as the Choosing Wisely® Case Study Competition, please visit http://www.hospitalmedicine.org/choosingwisely.

***Strategic Note:*** Hospitalists should pay attention to Physician Fee Schedules, which are constantly being updated to include new Current Procedural Terminology (CPT) codes that they can utilize in their expanded roles. In particular, there has been a trend of CMS focusing on developing new CPT codes in the areas of transitional care, coordination and counseling. For example, codes 99495 and 99496 were introduced in the 2013 Physician Fee Schedule, both of which must include:

- Communication (direct contact, telephone or electronic) with the patient and/or caregiver within 2 business days of discharge;
- Medical decision making of moderate complexity during the service period; and
- A face-to-face visit (within 14 days of discharge for 99495 and within 7 days of discharge for 99496). [156]

While solely focusing on areas incentivized by fee schedules is not encouraged, aligning initiatives according to new developments in fee schedules can be an effective method for ensuring a smooth transition from volume- to value-based care.

D. **Expanded Scope of Clinical Activities for Hospitalists**

There are several additional clinical functions that can be performed by hospitalists that are strongly aligned with the principles of the ACO model. Some examples are listed below.

1. **Emergency Department Triage**[157]

Emergency departments (EDs) across the country face a bottleneck of patients that are waiting to be admitted to the hospital, resulting in long wait times, low patient satisfaction, and poor outcomes. One root cause of this problem is that EDs rely on input of physicians from varying departments concerning the admission of a patient. According to a pre- and post-intervention study performed at Johns Hopkins Bayview Medical Center, the use of hospitalists as triage consultants to the ED has proven to decrease admission time from approximately 2.5 hours to 20 minutes, with no significant differences in mortality rates.

### 2. Emergency Department Surgery[158]

There is a nationwide shortage of surgeons available to perform acute care procedures, caused by such factors as increased specialization of surgeons, declining reimbursement, increasing malpractice liability risks, aging surgeon population, unwillingness to prioritize ambulatory surgery over elective surgery, and more. The Institute of Medicine published a report entitled "Hospital-Based Emergency Care: At the Breaking Point" that cited the closing of several EDs across the country due to an insufficient surgical treatment capacity, thus limiting access of care to communities. A trial at the University of California—San Francisco revealed positive outcomes from the use of hospitalists as both surgeons and triages to specialty surgeons when necessary.

*Strategic Note:* Many hospital systems regard the use of hospitalists as a strategy to decrease the cost of providing care, which is strongly aligned with the goals of an ACO. One study regarding the use of hospitalists in 12 randomly selected communities detected a correlation between the varied use of hospitalists and the predominant type of reimbursement present in the market. A higher presence of hospitalists was observed in markets where payers reimbursed providers under various methods of fixed payments, such as capitation, per diem, and DRG case rates. On the contrary, a lower utilization of hospitalists was noted in markets where the primary method of reimbursement was more varied, including fee-for-service components.[159]

### 3. Skilled Nursing Facility

Another strategy utilized by hospitals to decrease the costs of providing care to inpatients is to transition patients who are not yet ready to go into an intermediary skilled nursing facility (SNF). This tactic is especially effective for the 5% of patients who account for approximately 50% of hospital costs. Industry experts believe that hospitalists are key to the success of SNFs, particularly as more complex patients are transferred to these settings to decrease the total cost of care.[160]

### E. Hospitalists as Public Health Managers

The Institute of Medicine has identified the three core functions of public health as assessment, assurance, and policy development. Assessment is defined as the gathering and analysis of data related to population health. Assurance is ensuring the availability of high-quality, necessary health services to communities. Lastly, policy is developed as a way to ensure that the goals of assessment and assurance are met.

ACOs, by definition, are responsible for managing the healthcare of a specific patient population. Therefore, activities related to improving the overall health status of this population are highly aligned with the fundamental principles of value-based care. While hospitalists traditionally only focus on a small subset of the population—inpatients—they are well-equipped to tackle a whole host of public health and population health management-related activities. Table 7-7 details specific initiatives within the three core functions of public health—assessment, assurance, and policy—that hospitalists have successfully engaged in.[161]

***Strategic Note:*** The involvement of hospitalists in public health and population health management may be viewed as inefficient from the hospital's perspective. By historically focusing on individual patient care, hospitalists have developed a reputation as being able to achieve improved outcomes and cost savings in the acute care setting. Therefore, the hospital might view the shift from individual to population management as uneconomical, especially because there is currently minimal reimbursement for these efforts. However, it is important to note that improved populations health will ultimately lead to cost savings under the ACO model, and therefore may be considered cost-effective in the long run.[162]

F.  **Hospitalist Involvement in Palliative Care**

Recent trends have increased the amount of time that patients spend in the inpatient setting in their last six months of life, with 67% of Americans dying in the hospital setting.[163] The integration of hospitalists into palliative care provides several opportunities for improving the quality of care at the end of life. Clinic-based physicians are, by nature, unable to maintain a constant presence at a patient's bedside. Hospitalists, on the other hand, have a constant presence that has several potential benefits.

First, hospitalists may be able to more provide care in a more objective manner because they have not developed a long-term relationship with the patient; this can also enable hospitalists to more easily evaluate a patient's physiological impairments. Second, hospitalists' abilities to communicate with other providers within the hospital setting will allow them to better coordinate interdisciplinary care. Lastly, hospitalists can use this opportunity to develop expertise in caring for terminally ill patients, including treatment for pain, discussion of treatment options, and clarifying goals of care with patients and families. Furthermore, hospitalists can educate other providers on the proper techniques for palliative care.[164]

One medical center in Wisconsin uses tools from the Society for Hospital Medicine's Project BOOST (Better Outcomes for Older Adults through Safe

Transitions) in order to improve palliative care. All patients under hospitalist care are assessed for a series of risk factors when admitted; the medical center developed protocols based on Project BOOST tools in response to certain identified risk factors. For example, the use of a Palliative Care Quality Indicators Checklist can prompt hospitalists to order palliative consult. Since the introduction of these new policies, the medical center has seen reduced readmissions, increased patient satisfaction, and increased usage of palliative consults for the target patient population. Dr. Andrew McDonagh, head of the medical center's hospitalist service, explained that "doing our job well as hospitalists will be more than just addressing medical needs but tailoring our care to the individual patient. Palliative care helps us better define appropriate care for these patients."[165]

G. **Other**—Please see *The Accountable Care Manual for Hospitalists*, which may be downloaded at www.ncmedsoc.org/physician-resources/accountable-care/aco-toolkits.

H. **PCSP Standards**—The NCQA Patient-Centered Specialty Practice standards regarding care team and patient coordination are recommended generally for all specialists, including hospitalists.

II. **Metrics**

   A. **Examples of Measures that Measure Hospitalist Performance**

   1. **Medicare**—Any provider organization participating in a Medicare Shared Savings Program ACO contract holds the provider accountable for meeting 33 different quality measures. According to experts, "A conservative view of the hospitalist's role in an ACO suggests the hospitalist can influence at least half of these quality measures, ranging from preventive health to care coordination to the treatment of at-risk patients."[166] Although hospitalists do have the potential to impact the majority of these factors, they only *should* work to impact fewer factors. Other factors should be the responsibility of nurses or primary care physicians.

   Table 7-7 depicts these 33 different quality measures:

**TABLE 7-7.** Quality Measures Providers Are Accountable for

| # | CATEGORY | QUALITY MEASURE |
|---|----------|-----------------|
| 1 | Patient/ Caregiver Experience | Getting Timely Care, Appointments, and Information |
| 2 | | How Well Your Doctors Communicate |
| 3 | | Patients' Rating of Doctor |
| 4 | | Access to Specialists |
| 5 | | Health Promotion and Education |
| 6 | | Shared Decision Making |
| 7 | | Health Status/Functional Status |

*Continued on next page*

**TABLE 7-7.** Quality Measures Providers Are Accountable for (continued)

| # | CATEGORY | QUALITY MEASURE |
|---|----------|-----------------|
| 8 | Care Coordination/ Patient Safety | Risk Standardized, All Condition Readmissions |
| 9 | | ASC Admissions: COPD or Asthma in Older Adults |
| 10 | | ASC Admission: Heart Failure |
| 11 | | Percent of PCPs Who Qualified for EHR Incentive Payment |
| 12 | | Medication Reconciliation |
| 13 | | Falls: Screening for Fall Risk |
| 14 | Preventive Health | Influenza Immunization |
| 15 | | Pneumococcal Vaccination |
| 16 | | Adult Weight Screening and Follow-up |
| 17 | | Tobacco Use Assessment and Cessation Intervention |
| 18 | | Depression Screening |
| 19 | | Colorectal Cancer Screening |
| 20 | | Mammography Screening |
| 21 | | Proportion of Adults Who Had Blood Pressure Screened in Past 2 Years |
| 22 | At-Risk Population Diabetes | Hemoglobin A1c Control (HbA1c) (<8%) |
| 23 | | Low-Density Lipoprotein (LDL) (<100 mg/dL) |
| 24 | | Blood Pressure (BP) < 140/90 |
| 25 | | Tobacco Non-Use |
| 26 | | Aspirin Use |
| 27 | | Percent of Beneficiaries with Diabetes Whose Hba1c in Poor Control (>9%) |
| 28 | At-Risk Population Hypertension | Percent of Beneficiaries with Hypertension Whose BP <140/90 |
| 29 | At-Risk Population IVD | Percent of Beneficiaries with IVD with Complete Lipid Profile and LDL Control < 100mg/dl |
| 30 | | Percent of Beneficiaries with IVD Who Use Aspirin or Other Antithrombotic |
| 31 | At-Risk Population HF | Beta-Blocker Therapy for LVSD |
| 32 | At-Risk Population CAD | Drug Therapy for Lowering LDL Cholesterol |
| 33 | | ACE Inhibitor or ARB Therapy for Patients with CAD and Diabetes and/or LVSD |

2. **Patient Quality Reporting System (PQRS)**—The Medicare Shared Savings Program regulations state that any physician participating in an ACO will be treated as also participating in the PQRS program and will quality for PQRS incentive payments. This is highly beneficial because the hospital will provide substantial support for the reporting requirements for the PQRS program.

Table 7-8, provided by the Society for Hospital Medicine, depicts which of the PQRS measures can be impacted by hospitalists.

**TABLE 7-8.** 2014 PQRS Measures for Hospitalists

## 2014 PQRS Measures for Hospitalists*

| PQRS NUMBER AND MEASURE TITLE | NQS DOMAIN | REPORTING METHODOLOGY |
|---|---|---|
| 1: Diabetes: Hemoglobin A1c Poor Control | Effective Clinical Care | 1, 2, 3, 4, 5, 6 |
| 2: Diabetes: LDL-C Control | Effective Clinical Care | 1, 2, 3, 6 |
| 5: Heart Failure: ACE/ARB for LVSD | Effective Clinical Care | 2, 3, 6 |
| 8: Heart Failure: Beta-Blocker for LVSD | Effective Clinical Care | 2, 3, 4, 5, 6 |
| 24: Osteoporosis: Communication Post-Fracture | Communication and Care Coordination | 1, 2 |
| 31: Stroke: VTE Prophylaxis | Effective Clinical Care | 1, 2 |
| 32: Stroke: DC on Antithrombotic Therapy | Effective Clinical Care | 1, 2 |
| 33: Stroke: Anticoagulation for AFib | Effective Clinical Care | 2 |
| 35: Stroke: Screening for Dysphagia | Effective Clinical Care | 1, 2 |
| 36: Stroke: Rehabilitation Services | Effective Clinical Care | 1, 2 |
| 40: Osteoporosis: Management Post-Fracture | Effective Clinical Care | 1, 2 |
| 47: Advance Care Plan | Communication and Care Coordination | 1, 2 |
| 56: CAP: Vital Signs | Effective Clinical Care | 1, 2 |
| 59: CAP: Empiric Antibiotics | Effective Clinical Care | 1, 2 |
| 76: Prevention of CRBSI: CVC Insertion Protocol | Patient Safety | 1, 2 |
| 117: Diabetes: Eye Exam | Effective Clinical Care | 1, 2, 3, 6 |
| 119: Diabetes: Medical Attention for Nephropathy | Effective Clinical Care | 1, 2, 3, 6 |
| 130: Documentation of Current Medications | Patient Safety | 1, 2, 3, 6 |
| 163: Diabetes: Foot Exam | Effective Clinical Care | 1, 2, 3, 6 |
| 187: Stroke: Thrombolytic Therapy | Effective Clinical Care | 2 |
| 228: Heart Failure: LVF Testing | Effective Clinical Care | 2 |

Reporting Methodology
1. Claims   2. Registry   3. EHR   4. Group Practice Reporting Option (GPRO)   5. ACO (only for ACO Participants)   6. Measures Groups

* SHM has identified these measures to be reportable by hospitalists as applicable to their practice. For more information, contact the CMS Helpdesk at 866-288-8912 or qnetsupport@hcqis.org.

shm
Society of Hospital Medicine

# NEPHROLOGISTS

I.    **Why and How You May Want to Utilize Nephrologists in Your CIN/ACO**

    A.  **Quarterbacks of the ESRD Team**—End-stage renal disease (ESRD) is the highest-cost patient population in the entire Medicare program. With so many dollars at stake per patient, if there are effective initiatives to mitigate avoidable costs while improving the quality of care, these patients should be targeted as high-value populations for CINs and ACOs. There are effective treatments, and nephrologists are key to their success.

    B.  **Early Identification of and Intervention for At-Risk Patients**—Delaying dialysis, through (1) earlier identification of at-risk patients, and (2) use of interventions that slow further degeneration of kidney function, is the biggest "bang for the buck" a nephrologist can make in the quality and cost of care for individual patients. Treatment of a patient for as little as six months to a year prior to dialysis dramatically decreases mortality and cost.[167] One of the physicians on the TAC Physician Advisory Committee opined that because of the "absolute evidence that early referral to nephrology is associated with marked improvement in outcomes," it is "one of the best examples we have for clinical outcomes impact from a specialty."[168]

        The success of an ACO venture relies upon its ability to identify and refer such at-risk patients prior to a crisis-event. As one of the physician members of the Workgroup noted "earlier referral is key." One member of the Workgroup drew an analogy between patients with kidney damage and antenatal care: in both instances we (1) can identify a definite approaching medical event, and (2) know that the outcome of that medical event is frequently determined by the advance care received. Nephrologists have the capacity to slow, stop, or even reverse the progression of kidney disease, provided they have the opportunity to intervene in advance.[169]

        Whereas, under the siloed fee-for-service model, nephrologists were very careful to avoid any impression of "poaching" patients from referring physicians; within an ACO, incentives are aligned for greater coordination between specialists and the primary care physician. The first, fundamental, step is for primary care providers to be educated and have access to simplified guidelines to direct when a referral should be made.[170]

        The systemic use of urinalysis screening to identify and refer such patients is one way to accomplish this. Nephrologists also have an important role in educating primary care physicians on best practices to avoid further kidney damage, most specifically through the avoidance of non-steroid anti-inflammatory drugs.[171] Your savings are higher for the health problems you avoid—in other words, for the patients you do not see—than for the problems you personally treat.

**Examples:**
- Consolidate clinical guidelines for dissemination to and referral by primary care physicians to nephrologists during routine checkups.
- Lunch-and-Learn segments focusing on early chronic kidney disease recognition and intervention.[172]
- Regular "Case Study" emails to primary care physicians, outlining examples of cases of when to make a referral and what information to include in that referral.

C. **Nephrologist-Led Primary Care Teams for Complex Patients**—The level of coordination and transition management of complex high-risk patients is both one of the greatest failings of the fee-for-service system and one of the greatest opportunities under accountable care.[173] These patients commonly comprise around 10%-20% of the patient population, yet consume 50%-70% of the total costs. Because this management yields significant overall contributions to the Triple Aim, they are considered "low-hanging fruit" by ACOs. The ACO model provides the opportunity to formalize and reward nephrologists' existing leadership in treating complex patients and coordinating care across multiple specialties.[174] Nephrologists are ideally suited to serve leadership roles in such efforts:

> *The nephrologist—a central provider for patients with chronic kidney disease, end-stage renal disease, or kidney transplants—assumes a critical position in addressing the primary care needs of these patients, who tend to require frequency of contact. A care coordination role has emerged for the nephrology healthcare team due to the extensive co-morbidities of these patients as well as to the interdisciplinary models in dialysis and transplantation involved in their care.[175]*

A patient's care team needs to coordinate, know their roles, practice to the top of their licenses, and be supervised by a nephrologist. "Supervision" is a carefully chosen role, and one with which nephrologists have ample experience.

Assembling the team for systematized care of a complex patient population presents structural and logistical difficulties; however, CIN/ACOs can rely on nephrologists' existing expertise in coordination of complex care, and build on established principles of collaborative care and early ACO initiatives to fashion the structure most appropriate to your patient population, payer contract, access to skilled providers in your region, and cultural readiness.

- **Engage in Palliative Dialysis**—The field of nephrology is shifting from an exclusive focus on increasing survival to one that provides greater attention to quality of life. There is an opportunity to integrate the advances of palliative medicine into the comprehensive treatment of those patients.[176]

A discussion on the site and nature of service is particularly important when considered in the context of patient-centered care for palliative dialysis. As Dr. Lewis Cohen, Director of the Renal Palliative Care Initiative, noted, "The tradition in nephrology—as in medicine in general—has been to view death as an enemy to be overcome by any means. A generational shift has taken place, with some balance now being provided by interest in quality of life."[177] This increasing appreciation for quality of life and the importance of advance planning by an informed patient supplied with the necessary support system to implement those decisions has engendered support for the development of clinical guidelines for palliative dialysis.[178]

There are many patients who simply need some dialysis to avoid uremic symptoms and avoid fluid overload and heart failure. And, as one of our Workgroup members noted, this objective—when considered in the context of the patient's choice—should be kept in mind. Currently, dialysis treatment plans, reflecting the structure and expectations of the Quality Incentive Program, are typically treated in an "all or nothing" approach. The protocol is to "chase phosphorus, albumin, and adequacy in patients" where such ideal numbers will not improve life expectancy or quality to any appreciable degree.[179] Instead, nephrologists could further refine existing protocols for this subset of patients, offering an easier, more comfortable treatment, shorter times, less rigorous dietary restrictions, and even fewer than the standard three treatments a week.

Barriers, however, continue to exist to the institution of such a more *tailored* approach. The most notable obstacle is the current metrics under which dialysis facilities are graded and compensated. These metrics "punish" facilities for the withdrawal or reduction of dialysis, despite evidence that such a one-dimensional assessment may not accurately reflect clinical best practices or the best interests of patients.[180] The question of how to quantify the quality of care for ESRD continues to be a difficult one; however, the realignment and restructuring introduced with an ACO presents an important opportunity as it equips—as advocates for their patients—with new resources and alliances to address this problem.

D. **Other**—For more detail on the above-prioritized initiatives and information on others, please refer to the *Accountable Care Manual for Nephrologists* at www.ncmedsoc.org/physician-resources/accountable-care/aco-toolkits.

E. **PCSP Standards**—The NCQA Patient-Centered Specialty Practice standards regarding care team and patient coordination are recommended generally for all specialists, including nephrologists.

II. **Metrics**

A. **Overview**—After determining the initiatives involving this specialty that are most appropriate for your CIN/ACO, to incentivize the desired behavior and outcomes, it is recommended that clinically valid metrics track adherence to the chosen activities and accomplishment of the desired results. Starting with the MACRA Quality Payment Program measures, use the available array of measures from various sources as a "menu" from which to start, and then tailor, prioritize, and weight them to fit your incentivization goals (see Table 7-10).

**TABLE 7-10.** MACRA's Quality Payment Program MIPS Measures Relevant to Nephrology

| MEASURE NAME | MEASURE DESCRIPTION |
|---|---|
| Adult Kidney Disease: Blood Pressure Management | Percentage of patient visits for those patients aged 18 years and older with a diagnosis of chronic kidney disease (CKD) stage 3, 4, or 5, not receiving Renal Replacement Therapy [RRT] with a blood pressure < 140/90 mmHg OR ≥ 140/90 mmHg with a documented plan of care. |
| Adult Kidney Disease: Catheter Use at Initiation of Hemodialysis | Percentage of patients aged 18 years and older with a diagnosis of End-Stage Renal Disease (ESRD) who initiate maintenance hemodialysis during the measurement period, whose mode of vascular access is a catheter at the time maintenance hemodialysis is initiated. |
| Adult Kidney Disease: Catheter Use for Greater Than or Equal to 90 Days | Percentage of patients aged 18 years and older with a diagnosis of ESRD receiving maintenance hemodialysis for greater than or equal to 90 days whose mode of vascular access is a catheter. |
| Adult Kidney Disease: Referral to Hospice | Percentage of patients aged 18 years and older with a diagnosis of ESRD who withdraw from hemodialysis or peritoneal dialysis who are referred to hospice care. |
| Age-Appropriate Screening Colonoscopy | The percentage of patients greater than 85 years of age who received a screening colonoscopy from January 1 to December 31. |
| Appropriate Follow-up Imaging for Incidental Abdominal Lesions | Percentage of final reports for abdominal imaging studies for asymptomatic patients aged 18 years and older with one or more of the following noted incidentally with follow-up imaging recommended: Liver lesion ≤ 0.5 cm, Cystic kidney lesion < 1.0 cm, Adrenal lesion ≤ 1.0 cm. |
| Diabetes: Hemoglobin A1c (HbA1c) Poor Control (>9%) | Percentage of patients aged 18-75 years with diabetes who had hemoglobin A1c > 9.0% during the measurement period. |
| Documentation of Current Medications in the Medical Record | Percentage of visits for patients aged 18 years and older for which the eligible professional attests to documenting a list of current medications using all immediate resources available on the date of the encounter. This list must include ALL known prescriptions, over-the-counters, herbals, and vitamin/mineral/dietary (nutritional) supplements AND must contain the medications' name, dosage, frequency and route of administration. |
| Pain Assessment and Follow-Up | Percentage of visits for patients aged 18 years and older with documentation of a pain assessment using a standardized tool(s) on each visit AND documentation of a follow-up plan when pain is present. |
| Pain Brought Under Control Within 48 Hours | Patients aged 18 and older who report being uncomfortable because of pain at the initial assessment (after admission to palliative care services) that report pain was brought to a comfortable level within 48 hours. |

# NEUROLOGISTS

I. **Why and How You May Want to Utilize Neurologists in Your CIN/ACO**

A. **Coaching to Improve Primary Care and EMT Diagnosis, Referral, and Co-Management**—Our analysis has shown that movement in the accountable care era from fragmented care to coordinated care for patients with neurological issues presents significant opportunity to increase the quality of care and reduce the costs of care and suffering of these patients. As one neurologist stated, "With the intent of ACOs in improving 'health care' as opposed to 'sick care,' there should be an intense focus on working with primary care providers." Neurologists are natural educators and consultants. They are key resources to primary care physicians on their support team for patients with neurological issues.

Opportunities across disease states were found to exist in areas of coaching to improve primary care diagnosis and referral, teleconferencing, integration of treatment protocols with primary care, including urgent care centers, and increased availability to patients. Extending knowledge further "upstream," the neurologist, as educator, will be particularly helpful to patients through such things as group teleconferences, webinars, and web-based videos. Neurologists will add value through more engagement along the more active end of the continuum when patients are hospitalized, with active participation on the hospital's medical staff.

These multidisciplinary teams can be virtual, but also concrete in the form of Stroke Clinics, Headache Clinics, or the Geisinger Clinic's Neurosciences Institute.

Another manifestation of this extension of knowledge by neurologists is the strategic opportunity represented by allied provider care navigators and coordinators. These may be employees of the Patient-Centered Medical Home of the ACO, but work at the direction of neurologists, at such things as supporting access to non-physician/institute resources for patients with dementia; epilepsy compliance to reduce ED visits or hospitalizations; and patient self-management and management of stroke-inducing hypertension and diabetes.

In summary, the neurologists' skill sets of teaching and consulting when used across the care continuum and aided by technology seem to present proverbial "low-hanging fruit" opportunities for neurologists in the accountable care era. Occurring in every strategic initiative, this represents the singular most promising accountable care theme for neurologists. Important singularly, this recurring core strategy is even more potent cumulatively.

B. **Sharing of Stroke Primary and Secondary Prevention Best Practices**

**Prevention—Two Stages**

**1. Primary Prevention**

Education and Training: An important component in a neurology strategy within your ACO is education and training of primary care providers, care coordinators, and ACO patients with one or more major risk factors for stroke. Such education and training can help prevent the occurrence of a first stroke and could be coordinated through a stroke prevention and treatment clinic. The neurology group could provide training materials as well as a neurologist/teacher to lead the training. This training would have a double focus—both upstream—on primary care providers/care coordinators and on at-risk patients.

Training materials and sessions would aim (1) to sensitize primary care providers to recognize leading indicators or risk factors for potential stroke as well as to appropriate proactive follow-up measures once these indicators are identified and (2) to make the dangers of stroke concrete for at-risk patients as well as to equip them to take charge of their own care. Additionally, the neurology group would coordinate with the patient care coordinators at the ACO to help develop protocols for the early identification of risk factors and combinations of risk factors, assessment of the level of risk, and appropriate, proactive follow up measures. Consultation could be available on an ongoing basis.[181] These efforts are complimentary to the ACO's initiatives regarding diabetes, hypertension, mental health, and obesity management. The relevant metrics here would be relatively straightforward, measuring the improvement in occurrences of primary stroke and in major stroke risk factors, say, over six-month intervals following above interventions.

**2. Secondary Prevention/Ongoing Treatment**

The single best predictor of stroke is a previous stroke. An estimated 30% of survivors of an initial ischemic stroke (which accounts for 87% of all strokes) will have a subsequent stroke within five years. Eighteen percent of these strokes will be fatal. Stroke also carries with it a serious risk of (1) cardiac involvement, with 5% of stroke survivors suffering a heart attack within a year, and (2) depression, with an estimated 40% of stroke patients experiencing depression with the year following the stroke.

Secondary stroke prevention is well-suited to a model of care that aims at preventing long-term morbidity and mortality because (1) patients who suffer an initial stroke are easily identified and (2) risk modification strategies can significantly decrease the likelihood of recurrence. With a stroke prevention and treatment team or clinic overseen by a neurologist, stroke patients would have a ready source for follow-up care, reducing both recurrence and hospital readmission. In conjunction with primary care providers, such a team or clinic could also provide services for other high-risk patients and/or offer guidance and consultation services to the primary care providers for these patients.

For patients who have already suffered stroke, the follow-up would be more intensive and broad-ranging, encompassing aggressive follow-up for high blood pressure (*e.g.,* with diuretics or ACE inhibitors), high cholesterol (*e.g.,* with statins), and other risks factors; and counseling on lifestyles changes such as diet, exercise, cessation of tobacco smoking, and moderation of alcohol consumption. For patients for whom more intensive care is deemed necessary, the team or clinic would employ nurses to reach out to patients to engage them in their own recovery and to ensure prompt and regular follow-ups.

Neurologists would provide patient educational services and content, leveraging technology. Neurologists would play a leading role in the emerging demand for preventive stroke services by making risk factor modification a part of the neurological examination and by providing long-term follow-up and appropriate care in a stroke prevention clinic.[182] In addition to the measures outlined for the prevention of primary stroke, patients who have already suffered from stroke would be enrolled in a specialized program for stroke prevention lead by physicians and nurses.

Again, the relevant metrics here would be relatively straightforward, measuring the improvement in occurrences of secondary stroke and in major stroke risk factors, say, over six-month intervals following above specialized interventions.

C. **Sharing of Standards for Diagnosis, Treatment, and Referral Regarding Epilepsy**—Epileptic seizures can be caused by almost anything that affects the brain, but is characteristically due to a spectrum of seizure syndromes and disorders that range in their severity and treatment outcomes. In March 2012, the Institute of Medicine released its landmark study, *Epilepsy Across the Spectrum: Promoting Health and Understanding*, the first authoritative independent appraisal of epilepsy in the United States. The study makes it clear that there are significant gaps in provision of high-quality healthcare for many Americans burdened with epilepsy and its associated health problems. Optimal treatment is complex and must be tailored for each patient.

Epilepsy is the fourth most common neurological disorder in the United States — after migraine, stroke, and Alzheimer disease. An estimated 2.2 million Americans have epilepsy, with 150,000 new U.S. cases diagnosed every year; about one in 26 people will develop epilepsy at some time in their lives. The estimated U.S. annual direct medical care cost of epilepsy is $9.6 billion, according to the report.[183]

Virtual or concrete "Epilepsy Centers" improve care, lower costs, and are ideal for accountable care. Each center would be well integrated into the health system and locality that it is a part of as well as into the network of centers. Strong ties and partnerships with state health departments and other healthcare providers, particularly those focused on other neurological disorders, could expand the reach of coverage to people with epilepsy who are in rural and underserved areas through use of telemedicine, outreach clinics, and other relevant mechanisms. People with epilepsy and their families, as well as researchers and healthcare providers, could also benefit from the compilation and analysis of quality, outcomes, and health services data provided by all centers in the network.[184]

Even without the existence of a fully functioning epilepsy center, ACO opportunities exist for neurologist leadership in (1) patient education to dispel the stigma blocking people from coming forward; (2) educating primary and emergency care providers on the "mimickers of epilepsy" and standards of diagnosis, treatment, and referral, optimizing care in emergency departments and reducing stays in hospitals; (3) streamlining diagnosis to reduce hospitalization; (4) training epilepsy nurses and EEG technologists; (5) teleneurology; and (6) expedition of mental health involvement to rein in avoidable hospitalization and diagnostic costs of pseudo-seizures.

Ideally, the expertise of ACOs' multidisciplinary teams involved in managing complex epilepsy should include psychiatry, psychology, counseling, social work, occupational therapy, neuroradiology, clinical nurse specialists, neurophysiology, neurology, neurosurgery, and neuroanaesthesia. Through technology, could this be made available to ACOs statewide from a central leveraging center?

Teams should have MRI and video telemetry facilities available to them. The neurosurgeon in the multidisciplinary team should have specialist experience of and/or training in epilepsy surgery and have access to invasive electroencephalography recording facilities. Information should be provided to children, young people, and adults and families and/or care givers as appropriate about the reasons for considering surgery. Metrics for this disease state could include measuring improvements in diagnosis and reduction in hospital stays for epileptic patients.

D. **Other**—For more detail on the above-prioritized initiatives and information on others, please refer to the *Accountable Care Manual for Neurologists* at www.ncmedsoc.org/physician-resources/accountable-care/aco-toolkits.

E. **PCSP Standards**—The NCQA Patient-Centered Specialty Practice standards regarding care team and patient coordination are recommended generally for all specialists, including nephrologists.

## II. Metrics

**A. Overview**—After determining the initiatives involving this specialty that are most appropriate for your CIN/ACO, to incentivize the desired behavior and outcomes, it is recommended that clinically valid metrics track adherence to the chosen activities and accomplishment of the desired results. Starting with the MACRA Quality Payment Program measures (see Table 7-11), use the available array of measures from various sources as a "menu" from which to start, and then tailor, prioritize, and weight them to fit your incentivization goals.

**TABLE 7-11.** MACRA's Quality Payment Program MIPS Measures Relevant to Neurology

| MEASURE NAME | MEASURE DESCRIPTION |
| --- | --- |
| Amyotrophic Lateral Sclerosis (ALS) Patient Care Preferences | Percentage of patients diagnosed with Amyotrophic Lateral Sclerosis (ALS) who were helped in planning for end-of-life issues (e.g., advance directives, invasive ventilation, hospice) at least once annually. |
| Care Plan | Percentage of patients aged 65 years and older who have an advance care plan or surrogate decision maker documented in the medical record or documentation in the medical record that an advance care plan was discussed but the patient did not wish or was not able to name a surrogate decision maker or provide an advance care plan. |
| Closing the Referral Loop: Receipt of Specialist Report | Percentage of patients with referrals, regardless of age, for which the referring provider receives a report from the provider to whom the patient was referred. |
| Dementia: Caregiver Education and Support | Percentage of patients, regardless of age, with a diagnosis of dementia whose caregiver(s) were provided with education on dementia disease management and health behavior changes AND referred to additional resources for support within a 12-month period. |
| Dementia: Cognitive Assessment | Percentage of patients, regardless of age, with a diagnosis of dementia for whom an assessment of cognition is performed and the results reviewed at least once within a 12-month period. |
| Dementia: Counseling Regarding Safety Concerns | Percentage of patients, regardless of age, with a diagnosis of dementia or their caregiver(s) who were counseled or referred for counseling regarding safety concerns within a 12-month period. |
| Dementia: Functional Status Assessment | Percentage of patients, regardless of age, with a diagnosis of dementia for whom an assessment of functional status is performed and the results reviewed at least once within a 12-month period. |
| Dementia: Management of Neuropsychiatric Symptoms | Percentage of patients, regardless of age, with a diagnosis of dementia who have one or more neuropsychiatric symptoms who received or were recommended to receive an intervention for neuropsychiatric symptoms within a 12-month period. |
| Dementia: Neuropsychiatric Symptom Assessment | Percentage of patients, regardless of age, with a diagnosis of dementia and for whom an assessment of neuropsychiatric symptoms is performed, and results reviewed at least once in a 12-month period. |

**TABLE 7-11.** MACRA's Quality Payment Program MIPS
Measures Relevant to Neurology (continued)

| MEASURE NAME | MEASURE DESCRIPTION |
|---|---|
| Documentation of Current Medications in the Medical Record | Percentage of visits for patients aged 18 years and older for which the eligible professional attests to documenting a list of current medications using all immediate resources available on the date of the encounter. This list must include ALL known prescriptions, over-the-counters, herbals, and vitamin/mineral/dietary (nutritional) supplements AND must contain the medications' name, dosage, frequency and route of administration. |
| Documentation of Signed Opioid Treatment Agreement | All patients 18 and older prescribed opiates for longer than six weeks duration who signed an opioid treatment agreement at least once during opioid therapy documented in the medical record. |
| Epilepsy: Counseling for Women of Childbearing Potential with Epilepsy | All female patients of childbearing potential (aged 12-44 years) diagnosed with epilepsy who were counseled or referred for counseling for how epilepsy and its treatment may affect contraception or pregnancy at least once a year |
| Evaluation or Interview for Risk of Opioid Misuse | All patients aged 18 and older prescribed opiates for longer than six weeks duration evaluated for risk of opioid misuse using a brief validated instrument (e.g., Opioid Risk Tool, SOAPP-R) or patient interview documented at least once during opioid therapy in the medical record. |
| Opioid Therapy Follow-up Evaluation | All patients aged 18 and older prescribed opiates for longer than six weeks duration who had a follow-up evaluation conducted at least every three months during opioid therapy documented in the medical record. |
| Overuse of Neuroimaging for Patients with Primary Headache and A Normal Neurological Examination | Percentage of patients with a diagnosis of primary headache disorder for whom advanced brain imaging was not ordered. |
| Parkinson's Disease: Cognitive Impairment or Dysfunction Assessment | All patients with a diagnosis of Parkinson's disease who were assessed for cognitive impairment or dysfunction in the past 12 months. |
| Parkinson's Disease: Medical and Surgical Treatment Options Reviewed | All patients with a diagnosis of Parkinson's disease (or caregiver(s), as appropriate) who had the Parkinson's disease treatment options (e.g., non-pharmacological treatment, pharmacological treatment, or surgical treatment) reviewed at least annually. |
| Parkinson's Disease: Psychiatric Symptoms Assessment | All patients with a diagnosis of Parkinson's disease who were assessed for psychiatric symptoms (e.g., psychosis, depression, anxiety disorder, apathy, or impulse control disorder) in the past 12 months. |
| Parkinson's Disease: Rehabilitative Therapy Options | All patients with a diagnosis of Parkinson's disease (or caregiver(s), as appropriate) who had rehabilitative therapy options (e.g., physical, occupational, or speech therapy) discussed in the past 12 months. |

*Continued on next page*

**TABLE 7-11.** MACRA's Quality Payment Program MIPS
Measures Relevant to Neurology (continued)

| MEASURE NAME | MEASURE DESCRIPTION |
|---|---|
| Preventive Care and Screening: Body Mass Index (BMI) Screening and Follow-Up Plan | Percentage of patients aged 18 years and older with a BMI documented during the current encounter or during the previous six months AND with a BMI outside of normal parameters, a follow-up plan is documented during the encounter or during the previous six months of the current encounter. Normal Parameters: Age 18 years and older BMI ≥ 18.5 and < 25 kg/m$^2$ |
| Preventive Care and Screening: Screening for High Blood Pressure and Follow-Up Documented | Percentage of patients aged 18 years and older seen during the reporting period who were screened for high blood pressure AND for whom a recommended follow-up plan is documented based on the current blood pressure (BP) reading as indicated. |
| Preventive Care and Screening: Tobacco Use: Screening and Cessation Intervention | Percentage of patients aged 18 years and older who were screened for tobacco use one or more times within 24 months AND who received cessation counseling intervention if identified as a tobacco user. |
| Preventive Care and Screening: Unhealthy Alcohol Use: Screening and Brief Counseling | Percentage of patients aged 18 years and older who were screened for unhealthy alcohol use using a systematic screening method at least once within the past 24 months AND who received brief counseling if identified as an unhealthy alcohol user. |
| Quality of Life Assessment for Patients with Primary Headache Disorders | Percentage of patients with a diagnosis of primary headache disorder whose health-related quality of life (HRQoL) was assessed with a tool(s) during at least two visits during the 12-month measurement period AND whose health-related quality of life score stayed the same or improved. |
| Stroke and Stroke Rehabilitation: Discharged on Antithrombotic Therapy | Percentage of patients aged 18 years and older with a diagnosis of ischemic stroke or transient ischemic attack (TIA) who were prescribed antithrombotic therapy at discharge. |
| Tobacco Use and Help with Quitting Among Adolescents | The percentage of adolescents aged 12-20 years with a primary care visit during the measurement year for whom tobacco use status was documented and received help with quitting if identified as a tobacco user. |

# OBSTETRICIANS

I.    **Why and How You May Want to Utilize Obstetricians in Your CIN/ACO**

A.    **Care Management for High-Risk Patients**—High-risk patients most often become high-cost patients. As such, they require special attention. Obstetricians are in a unique position to minimize the incidence of complex high-cost newborns through prenatal care and focused attention on high-risk pregnancies, and also to mitigate the impact of high-risk births through coordination of care. With some training and appropriate data collection, staff could learn to identify high-risk patients and pay special attention to their needs. Rather than simply following up with these patients, staff should coordinate their overall care.

For example, if a patient's obstetrician recommends a neurology consult, then staff should help set up the appointment and follow up with the patient. As the patient's *de facto* primary care physician, the obstetrician is specially equipped to oversee this important care coordination. Further, because pregnant mothers represent more than one patient, OBs have a special responsibility to oversee their care coordination. In an ACO setting, data analytics information identifying high-risk patients can be obtained early enough to avoid or mitigate catastrophic costs and acute care needs.

Such coordination will be especially important for premature babies, low birth weight births, and high-risk pregnancies. Premature babies often have many medical conditions and complications that need attention, and obstetricians in your ACO should coordinate their care to achieve optimal results. Further, mothers of premature babies sometimes need coordinated care as well.

In North Carolina, the Pregnancy Medical Home Program provides pregnancy care management programs to manage high-risk patients. Obstetricians conduct a prenatal risk assessment, identify high-risk pregnancies, provide comprehensive care management, and conduct post-partum assessments, including screen for depression and connecting mothers to primary care. One physician working within the Pregnancy Medical Home Program stated that he had at his fingertips pathways, best practices, and feedback on C-sections and post-natal visits. Most importantly, "We know outliers—we have the data," he said.

B.    **Embracing the Duality of the OB/GYN as Primary Care Physician and Specialist**—ACOs are founded on coordination and integration, and primary care physicians (PCPs) are specially positioned to direct and oversee these processes. PCPs are already primed to manage patients with multiple medical conditions, and such care management is essential to the ACO model. As hospitals and physician groups create ACOs, they will look to the experience and leadership of PCPs. This process is especially relevant to OB/GYNs, who are both specialists and PCPs.

*Note:* The particular value-care roles of gynecologists as PCPs and specialists are addressed in the gynecology section of this manual.

Many OB/GYNs consider themselves PCPs, and many women view their OB/GYN as their PCP. For large numbers of women, the only doctor they see on a regular basis is their OB/GYN. This phenomenon has been furthered by developments in family medicine. In fact, family medicine training no longer is required to cover contraceptives, IUD insertion, or pregnancy counseling, and this will only increase the number of women looking to their OB/GYNs for primary care. In turn, OB/GYNs act as a gateway to other specialized care. This type of patient management is critical to the functioning of your ACO.

It must be noted that the PCP/specialist duality is a complicated matter. For example, few OB/GYNs will have a patient referred to them as a PCP; they will be referred as specialists. However, therein lies a distinct advantage for OB/GYNs and their ACOs: Women will seek their guidance in their PCP capacity regarding specialist referrals, while they also will receive specialist referrals from other PCPs. So, the PCP/specialist duality, though complicated, actually may serve as an important asset to your ACO.

It is important for ACOs to realize the benefits of giving leadership roles to PCPs, including OB/GYNs. It is just as important for OB/GYNs to take those leadership roles. We learned several lessons from the 1990s, but one of the most critical was the danger of top-down health protocols. To stand by is to let hospitals and payers dictate the future to physicians. As noted, fuller development of strategies for the physician practicing gynecology is included in the section that focuses on gynecological care.

The OB/GYN Accountable Care Workgroup and the Pediatric Accountable Care Workgroup independently determined that closer coordination was truly a "low-hanging fruit" opportunity for population management and value-based payment. For example, one OB/GYN Accountable Care Workgroup member reported that his practice refers to the family's pediatrician at 36 weeks of pregnancy whenever the mother is on methadone. "The baby might need them." Another example offered by the Pediatricians Accountable Care Workgroup was to refer certain families to the OB/GYN for family planning and prenatal care.

C. **Patient and Physician Engagement**—In a value-based health system, the overall health of the patient is critical, but it is not a one-way effort from physician to patient. The patient must be actively involved in her own care. Obstetricians should strive to increase engagement in care on both sides of the relationship. Patient engagement adds great value to medical care, but it has been underutilized in the fee-for-service model.

In an environment where patient engagement is low, a patient could miss an appointment due to forgetfulness or a scheduling conflict. Her doctor, operating in a volume-based system, might not follow up with any urgency. The patient could then experience a medical emergency and be transported to the emergency department for care. She might give birth prematurely.

An ACO could add considerable value to the care of a patient by preventing the missed appointment or by following up with the patient quickly to reschedule. It has been repeatedly shown that following up with patients after a visit helps patients stay engaged in their medical care, leading to better results. For pregnant women, patient engagement can lead to fewer costly birth complications and a reduction in any number of health issues for mother and child.

To increase patient engagement, your ACO might provide more staff—or rearrange current staff duties—to better understand their life circumstances and barriers to healthcare, and to communicate with patients before and after visits. Communication should be through various means, including phone calls, emails, and standard mail. Staff should ensure that patients are following the advice given during their visit and answer questions that patients may have. You should also consider "e-visits," where you can offer limited consultation to patients who find travel difficult and who may not need any sort of physical examination. E-visits might be especially beneficial to pregnant women who are experiencing unusual pain and discomfort.

***Strategic Note:*** Hiring and/or training staff and nurses to implement the above strategies seems daunting. This manual does not advocate immediate changes, however, in this section or in others suggesting change. Small changes in the right direction can help your ACO add value to its practice, and administrative changes can be achieved in small steps.

D. **Follow National Guidelines**—Reducing hospitalizations is a key strategy for ACOs, as hospitalization is quite costly. Two ways to reduce hospitalizations are care coordination and patient engagement, as discussed above. Still another way to reduce hospitalizations is to follow national guidelines regarding obstetrical care. Recent years have seen revisions in recommendations for hysterectomies, C-sections, elective deliveries, nulliparous issues, breastfeeding, antenatal steroids, and procedures for reducing newborn bloodstream infections.

There are several nationally recognized bodies of guidelines to review for illustration purposes. The following two sets of guidelines are part of the multidisciplinary Choosing Wisely® initiative:

**1. The American College of Obstetricians and Gynecologists**
   • **Don't schedule elective, non-medically indicated inductions of labor or cesarean deliveries before 39 weeks 0 days gestational age.** Delivery prior to 39 weeks 0 days has been shown to be associated with an increased risk of learning disabilities and a potential increase in morbidity

and mortality. There are clear medical indications for delivery prior to 39 weeks 0 days based on maternal and/or fetal conditions. A mature fetal lung test, in the absence of appropriate clinical criteria, is not an indication for delivery.

- **Don't schedule elective, non-medically indicated inductions of labor between 39 weeks 0 days and 41 weeks 0 days unless the cervix is deemed favorable.** Ideally, labor should start on its own initiative whenever possible. Higher Cesarean delivery rates result from inductions of labor when the cervix is unfavorable. Healthcare practitioners should discuss the risks and benefits with their patients before considering inductions of labor without medical indications.

2. **Society for Maternal-Fetal Medicine**
   - **Don't do an inherited thrombophilia evaluation for women with histories of pregnancy loss, intrauterine growth restriction (IUGR), preeclampsia, and abruption.** Scientific data supporting a causal association between either methylenetetrahydrofolate reductase (MTHFR) polymorphisms or other common inherited thrombophilia and adverse pregnancy outcomes, such as recurrent pregnancy loss, severe preeclampsia, and IUGR, are lacking. Specific testing for antiphospholipid antibodies, when clinically indicated, should be limited to lupus anticoagulant, anticardiolipin antibodies, and beta 2 glycoprotein antibodies.
   - **Don't place a cerclage in women with short cervix who are pregnant with twins.** Women with a short cervical length who are pregnant with twins are at very high risk for delivering preterm, but the scientific data, including a meta-analysis of data published on this issue, shows that cerclage in this clinical situation not only is not beneficial, but may in fact be harmful, i.e., associated with an increase in preterm births.
   - **Don't offer noninvasive prenatal testing (NIPT) to low-risk patients or make irreversible decisions based on the results of this screening test.** NIPT has only been adequately evaluated in singleton pregnancies at high risk for chromosomal abnormalities (material age 35; positive screening; sonographic findings suggestive of aneuploidy; translocation carrier at increased risk for trisomy 13, 18 or 21; or prior pregnancy with a trisomy 13, 18, or 21). Its utility in low-risk pregnancies remains unclear. False positive and false negative results occur with NIPT, particularly for trisomy 13 and 18. Any positive NIPT result should be confirmed with invasive diagnostic testing prior to a termination of pregnancy. If NIPT is performed, adequate pretest counseling must be provided to explain the benefits and limitations.
   - **Don't screen for intrauterine growth restriction (IUGR) with Doppler blood flow studies.** Studies that have attempted to screen pregnancies for

the subsequent occurrence of IUGR have produced inconsistent results. Furthermore, no standards have been established for the optimal definition of an abnormal test, best gestational age for the performance of the test, or the technique for its performance. However, once the diagnosis of IUGR is suspected, the use of antenatal fetal surveillance, including umbilical artery Doppler flow studies, is beneficial.

- **Don't use progestogens for preterm birth prevention in uncomplicated multifetal gestations.** The use of progestogens has not been shown to reduce the incidence of preterm birth in women with uncomplicated multifetal gestations.

The OB/GYN Accountable Care Workgroup offered the following common-sense recommendations from the national literature:

- The immediate availability of contraception to help increase the interval between pregnancies and to prevent unwanted pregnancies particularly in high-risk patients with multiple co-morbidities.
- Ensuring that high-risk obstetrical patients deliver in an appropriate level facility (perinatal regionalization).
- Minimizing labor elective induction in nulliparous patients to reduce the Cesarean section rate.

E. **Other**—For more detail on the above-prioritized initiatives and information on others, please refer to the *Accountable Care Manual for Obstetricians* at www.ncmedsoc.org/physician-resources/accountable-care/aco-toolkits

F. **PCSP Standards**—The NCQA Patient-Centered Specialty Practice standards regarding care team and patient coordination are recommended generally for all specialists, including obstetricians.

II. **Metrics**

A. **Overview**—After determining the initiatives involving this specialty that are most appropriate for your CIN/ACO, to incentivize the desired behavior and outcomes, it is recommended that clinically valid metrics track adherence to the chosen activities and accomplishment of the desired results. Perhaps use the following array of measures from various sources as a "menu" from which to start, and then tailor, prioritize, and weight them to fit your incentivization goals.

B. **Examples of Metrics to Measure Obstetrical Performance:**

- Cesarean section rates.
- Elective induction for patient or obstetrician convenience.[185]
- ICU and NICU usage and costs.
- Preterm births.
- Nulliparous term singleton vertex.
- Low birth weight rates.
- Anesthesia complication rates.

- Prenatal substance exposure rates.
- Infant and mother mortality rates.
- AHRQ's birth trauma rate.
- Laboratory costs.
- Imaging costs.
- Pharmaceutical costs.
- Hospitalization rates.
- Post-partum health.
- Hospital readmission reduction.
- Electronic information exchange.
- Prophylactic antibiotics for Cesarean delivery.[186]
- 17-P utilization.
- Post-partum:
  - Post-partum depression assessment.
  - Family planning.
  - Coordination with PCPs for mother and child.
- Entry of patients into prenatal care prior to 14 weeks.
- Use of antenatal corticosteroids.
- Use of long-acting reversible contraception on selected patient populations.

"[W]ell-designed quality measures in surgery, cardiology, and infertility have catalyzed changed, improved care, and reduced gaps in quality. We argue that the same can be done in obstetrics"[187] (see Table 7-12).

**TABLE 7-12.** MACRA's Quality Payment Program MIPS
Measures Relevant To Obstetrics and Gynecology

| MEASURE NAME | MEASURE DESCRIPTION |
|---|---|
| Appropriate Workup Prior to Endometrial Ablation | Percentage of women, aged 18 years and older, who undergo endometrial sampling or hysteroscopy with biopsy before undergoing an endometrial ablation |
| Biopsy Follow-Up | Percentage of new patients whose biopsy results have been reviewed and communicated to the primary care/referring physician and patient by the performing physician |
| Breast Cancer Screening | Percentage of women 50-74 years of age who had a mammogram to screen for breast cancer. |
| Care Plan | Percentage of patients aged 65 years and older who have an advance care plan or surrogate decision maker documented in the medical record or documentation in the medical record that an advance care plan was discussed but the patient did not wish or was not able to name a surrogate decision maker or provide an advance care plan |
| Cervical Cancer Screening | Percentage of women 21-64 years of age who were screened for cervical cancer using either of the following criteria: * Women age 21-64 who had cervical cytology performed every 3 years * Women age 30-64 who had cervical cytology/ human papillomavirus (HPV) co-testing performed every 5 years |

**TABLE 7-12.** MACRA's Quality Payment Program MIPS Measures
Relevant To Obstetrics and Gynecology (continued)

| MEASURE NAME | MEASURE DESCRIPTION |
|---|---|
| Chlamydia Screening and Follow Up | The percentage of female adolescents 16 years of age who had a chlamydia screening test with proper follow-up during the measurement period |
| Chlamydia Screening for Women | Percentage of women 16-24 years of age who were identified as sexually active and who had at least one test for chlamydia during the measurement period |
| Closing the Referral Loop: Receipt of Specialist Report | Percentage of patients with referrals, regardless of age, for which the referring provider receives a report from the provider to whom the patient was referred |
| Controlling High Blood Pressure | Percentage of patients 18-85 years of age who had a diagnosis of hypertension and whose blood pressure was adequately controlled (<140/90mmHg) during the measurement period |
| Documentation of Current Medications in the Medical Record | Percentage of visits for patients aged 18 years and older for which the eligible professional attests to documenting a list of current medications using all immediate resources available on the date of the encounter. This list must include ALL known prescriptions, over-the-counters, herbals, and vitamin/mineral/dietary (nutritional) supplements AND must contain the medications' name, dosage, frequency and route of administration. |
| Non-Recommended Cervical Cancer Screening in Adolescent Females | The percentage of adolescent females 16-20 years of age who were screened unnecessarily for cervical cancer |
| Osteoporosis Management in Women Who Had a Fracture | The percentage of women age 50-85 who suffered a fracture and who either had a bone mineral density test or received a prescription for a drug to treat osteoporosis in the six months after the fracture |
| Performing Cystoscopy at the Time of Hysterectomy for Pelvic Organ Prolapse to Detect Lower Urinary Tract Injury | Percentage of patients who undergo cystoscopy to evaluate for lower urinary tract injury at the time of hysterectomy for pelvic organ prolapse |
| Preventive Care and Screening: Body Mass Index (BMI) Screening and Follow-Up Plan | Percentage of patients aged 18 years and older with a BMI documented during the current encounter or during the previous six months AND with a BMI outside of normal parameters, a follow-up plan is documented during the encounter or during the previous six months of the current encounter Normal Parameters: Age 18 years and older BMI ≥ 18.5 and < 25 kg/m² |
| Preventive Care and Screening: Influenza Immunization | Percentage of patients aged 6 months and older seen for a visit between October 1 and March 31 who received an influenza immunization OR who reported previous receipt of an influenza immunization |
| Preventive Care and Screening: Screening for High Blood Pressure and Follow-Up Documented | Percentage of patients aged 18 years and older seen during the reporting period who were screened for high blood pressure AND a recommended follow-up plan is documented based on the current blood pressure (BP) reading as indicated |

*Continued on next page*

**TABLE 7-12.** MACRA's Quality Payment Program MIPS Measures
Relevant To Obstetrics and Gynecology (continued)

| MEASURE NAME | MEASURE DESCRIPTION |
|---|---|
| Preventive Care and Screening: Tobacco Use: Screening and Cessation Intervention | Percentage of patients aged 18 years and older who were screened for tobacco use one or more times within 24 months AND who received cessation counseling intervention if identified as a tobacco user |
| Preventive Care and Screening: Unhealthy Alcohol Use: Screening & Brief Counseling | Percentage of patients aged 18 years and older who were screened for unhealthy alcohol use using a systematic screening method at least once within the last 24 months AND who received brief counseling if identified as an unhealthy alcohol user |
| Proportion of Patients Sustaining a Bladder Injury at the Time of any Pelvic Organ Prolapse Repair | Percentage of patients undergoing any surgery to repair pelvic organ prolapse who sustains an injury to the bladder recognized either during or within 1 month after surgery |
| Proportion of Patients Sustaining a Bowel Injury at the time of any Pelvic Organ Prolapse Repair | Percentage of patients undergoing surgical repair of pelvic organ prolapse that is complicated by a bowel injury at the time of index surgery that is recognized intraoperatively or within 1 month after surgery |
| Proportion of Patients Sustaining a Ureter Injury at the Time of any Pelvic Organ Prolapse Repair | Percentage of patients undergoing pelvic organ prolapse repairs who sustain an injury to the ureter recognized either during or within 1 month after surgery |
| Tobacco Use and Help with Quitting Among Adolescents | The percentage of adolescents 12 to 20 years of age with a primary care visit during the measurement year for whom tobacco use status was documented and received help with quitting if identified as a tobacco user |
| Urinary Incontinence: Assessment of Presence or Absence of Urinary Incontinence in Women Aged 65 Years and Older | Percentage of female patients aged 65 years and older who were assessed for the presence or absence of urinary incontinence within 12 months |
| Urinary Incontinence: Plan of Care for Urinary Incontinence in Women Aged 65 Years and Older | Percentage of female patients aged 65 years and older with a diagnosis of urinary incontinence with a documented plan of care for urinary incontinence at least once within 12 months |

# ONCOLOGISTS

I.  **Why and How You May Want to Utilize Oncologists in Your CIN/ACO**

A.  **Avoidable Costs Signal Opportunity**—A combination of high costs and a high degree of ability to avoid those costs presents significant opportunity for oncologists in accountable care. A February 2012 report by United Healthcare revealed substantial unjustified variation in oncology care delivery, including a 10:1 variation in imaging for metastatic patients, wide differences in end-of-life advanced care planning, a 2:1 cost variation in treatment of Stage 1 ER-neg EHR-2-unexpressed breast cancer, and wide variance on symptom management and access that led to differences in ED and hospitalization costs.[188]

Recent data supports the significant value-add upside available for involving oncologists in ACOs: WellPoint reports that 26% of oncology admissions are related to symptoms of treatment-related toxicity, led by dehydration, neutropenia or fever, pain, anemia, infection, and DVT. They found widespread variation in use of CSF with chemotherapy, and that imaging was often repeated unnecessarily with 90% of use not consistent with national guidelines. They reported a 20-fold variation in cost for equally effective treatments.[189]

Predictive models indicate a total potential ACO cancer care savings of 6.7%-13.5% derived from the following areas:

- Chemotherapy pathway adherence          1.0%-3.0%
- Avoidable emergency department utilization   0.6%-1.1%
- Avoidable hospital admissions              4.0%-7.0%
- Diagnostics (imaging, lab)                 0.2%-0.5%
- End-of-life diagnostic planning            0.9%-1.9%

With the average cancer cost of $1.3 million/1,000 Medicare lives, a Medicare ACO with 17,000 lives and a 12% savings rate would yield $2.5 million in savings related to better cancer care, as illustrated in Table 7-13.[190]

**TABLE 7-13.** Calculation of ACO Cancer Cost-Savings Potential

| VARIABLE | PER 1,000 POPULATION |
|---|---|
| Cancer incidence rates (age >65) | 21 |
| Average cancer cost per patient | $80,000 |
| Average cancer cost per population | $1,680,000 |
| Potential cancer cost-savings rate | 10% |
| Potential cancer cost savings | $168,000 |
| "Average size" ACO annual savings (per 15,000 Medicare lives) = $2,520,000 ||

### B. Initiatives

#### 1. Multidisciplinary Team Care Models

While this model may fairly be viewed as a means to an end for initiatives discussed below and not an end in itself, it leverages oncologist influence to address the looming manpower shortage and drives key initiatives, so is best highlighted separately.

One oncologist, who is a member of a multispecialty ACO, described their team as comprised of an oncologist medical director, a psychologist, an oncological pharmacist, a nutritionist, a chaplain, an embedded internist, and a social worker. The psychologist developed an excellent questionnaire tool to see what people's needs actually are. (Cancer patients chronically under-report needs.) The use of the tool prompts good responses and assists the team in anticipating and addressing needs early. For example, the social worker may help with insurance or home incompatibility issues, the dietician may recommend Ensure, and the chaplain may assist with end-of-life advance care planning.

Comprehensive care improves quality and lowers costs. Workflow is improved, further enhancing savings. In this transition phase from fee-for-service to value-based payment, it was noted that this approach "pays for itself" because the oncologist actually can see more patients while also guiding more comprehensive best practice care.

Another oncologist, who specializes in breast cancer treatment, formed a multidisciplinary and multispecialty clinic around women's health.

Within the Team Care Model, all noted the advantage of having a well-trained nurse practitioner or oncological pharmacist host live teaching sessions for patients with similar diagnoses or who are taking the same drug. For example, the latter realizes savings because it allows use of less-expensive drugs that have higher chances of nausea or complications if not properly taken by the patient.

#### 2. Patient Engagement

Because of the complexity and intensity of cancer treatment with its associated increased chances for error on one hand and opportunities for informed patient self-management on the other, deep patient engagement is especially critical. "Under accountable care, engaging patients and families as partners in care will be an essential strategy for achieving the best possible patient outcomes while also reducing costs to the health system."[191]

##### a. Assessment for Oral Therapy

While patient orientation is applicable to all patients and families, patients who are prescribed oral therapies face additional risks and therefore require a more concerted approach to education and engagement. Managing an oral regimen requires patients to take on significant responsibilities, including acquiring the drug, following often complex dosing schedules, and reporting symptoms and side effects to their care team in a timely way. Studies have found that patients' failure to take their prescriptions appropriately leads to unnecessary side effects and complications, suboptimal patient outcomes, and higher overall healthcare costs. Oncologists need to make a careful initial assessment regarding whether a patient is a good candidate for oral therapies to help avoid these potential complications and additional costs (see Table 7-14).[192]

**TABLE 7-14.** Distinguishing Patients Who Are Able to Take on Responsibility for Oral Therapies

| IDEAL CANDIDATES | POOR CANDIDATES |
|---|---|
| Understand importance of specific therapy to their disease | Lack a support system at home |
| Are able to make the commitment to comply with treatment regimen | Are already taking multiple non-cancer drug therapies |
| Can swallow pills or liquids | Have emotional or psychological conditions, especially depression |
| Are able to manage drug costs | Have cognitive, memory, or visual impairment |
| Have good communication skills or committed caregiver who can communicate on their behalf | Have a history of missed appointments |
| | Have a poor relationship with provider |
| | Have a poor understanding of therapy |
| | Have daily routines that would be disrupted by regimen |

## b. Meaningful Patient Involvement and Continuous Education

Given the complexity of oncology care, cancer programs should seek to engage patients as partners at their first interaction and to reinforce key messages throughout the care continuum.

As a starting point, many providers have found that it is helpful to provide explicit instructions to patients about their role and responsibilities relative to their cancer treatment. The Mayo Clinic's cancer center, for instance, offers a new patient orientation via an orientation booklet and DVD. The 12-minute DVD introduces the cancer center, as well as its philosophy of care, physical layout, and resources.[193] The video also encourages patients to take an active role in their care.

The Mayo Clinic has found that this introduction leads to better patient use of available resources, lower patient anxiety, and greater patient involvement. While other, more time-intensive methods (such as classes and drop-in sessions) were tried, they were ultimately unsuccessful because of high drop-off rates.[194]

### c. Medication Management: Prescribing and Educating

Drugs administered in an infusion center are routinely subject to multiple checks by the pharmacy and nursing staff. Despite the fact that oral drugs carry many of the same, if not more, risks as infused drugs, the prescribing process usually works very differently. According to a survey of National Cancer Institute-designated cancer centers, 24% require physicians to indicate the patient's diagnosis on the script and 21% of cancer centers perform double checks on oral drug orders, leaving patients at risk of dangerous errors. Instituting multiple checks as well as a patient education session on the prescribed medications can reduce errors and improve patient outcomes and satisfaction.

### d. Medication Management: Technological Aids

Providing detailed, personalized counseling is an essential step for ensuring patients have the information they need to manage their oral therapies safely, but patients also need ongoing support to remember to take their drugs as prescribed. Fortunately, there are many easy-to-use, low-cost tools designed to help patients adhere to their medication schedules.

For example, "my Community Pillbox" is a smart phone application designed to help patients remember to take their medication. Patients upload their medication schedules to their phones. As they take their medications, they check off each one. If a patient forgets to take a scheduled dose, the screen displays an exclamation mark, indicating a missed medication. If questions arise, the application links to information about each drug and also includes contact information for the patient's providers. Currently the application is available to patients at no cost.

Another example, Vitality Glow Cap is a programmable cap that can be attached to any standard pill bottle. When it is time for a patient to take a scheduled dose, the cap begins to glow. If a dose is missed, the cap alerts the patient by beeping. If the bottle remains unopened for a specified period of time, the cap can email or phone the patient or a family member. Each cap costs $5 and can be used repeatedly.

### 3. Triage Nursing: Reducing Hospitalizations and Emergency Department Utilization

According to the Oncology Roundtable of The Advisory Board Company, addressing avoidable emergency department visits is one of the greatest "opportunities for driving value in cancer care."[195] Cancer and its treatments produce numerous and often debilitating symptoms, side effects, and complications. Although these issues reduce patients' quality of life and, if left unchecked, can ultimately result in poorer patient outcomes, patients often do not report them to their care team.

One analysis conducted by researchers at the Cleveland Clinic found that during a typical clinic visit, cancer patients voluntarily report one symptom to their care team. However, when the researchers conducted a systematic assessment, the median number of symptoms experienced by patients was 10. Notably, these symptoms were often significant or even debilitating.

These data are concerning both because they suggest that patients are suffering unnecessarily and because uncontrolled symptoms can develop into more serious complications leading to emergency department (ED) visits and hospitalizations. The ED is a suboptimal site of care for cancer patients for multiple reasons. First, ED clinicians often feel ill-equipped to manage cancer patients. Second, cancer patients often have compromised immune systems, and they may be more likely to be exposed to pathogens in the ED. Third, the ED is more expensive than other treatment settings; the UNC researchers estimate that treating cancer patients' uncontrolled symptoms in the clinic setting would reduce costs by 50%.

The Team Care concept can be used to educate the patient to ED alternatives, raise awareness of access to the team through the triage nurse hotline, and address non-cancer issues. It would enhance continuity of care and keep the feedback loop intact.

To address this issue, Consultants in Medical Oncology & Hematology (CMOH), a private practice in Drexel Hill, Pennsylvania, developed a comprehensive nurse-led phone triage system. Patients can call with questions about test results, symptoms, and other care needs. The phone is answered by a clinic nurse who addresses patients' concerns by following a set of algorithms based on Oncology Nursing Society guidelines. The phone triage line, which received approximately 3,500 calls in 2010, operates from 7:00 a.m. to 6:00 p.m. on weekdays. After 6:00 p.m., calls are redirected to an answering service, which can connect patients to on-call physicians. The physicians have remote access to the practice's EMR, allowing them to access patient records and follow the same symptom management algorithms used by the nurses.

At CMOH, 75% of patient concerns can be managed with instructions for at home self-care. Another 10% of patients are scheduled to come in for an office visit within 24 hours, and just 7% are referred to the ED.

The success of the phone triage system depends not only on the clinic's management of phone calls but also on patient participation. To that end, CMOH's patients are instructed from the start of their cancer treatment that they need to play an active role in their care, ask questions, express concerns, and immediately report all symptoms to the care team. This message is reinforced with patients by the physicians and staff at regular intervals.

The data suggest that CMOH's phone triage system has enabled the practice to identify and address patients' symptoms before they become crises. Between 2005 and 2010, CMOH experienced steady declines in their number of ED visits per patient per year. In 2010, they had an average of just one ED visit per patient. Similarly, inpatient admissions also declined dramatically. Notably, both of these gains were achieved despite overall growth in CMOH's patient volumes.

4. **Advanced Planning for Survivorship and End-of-Life Care**

Under the fee-for-service system, cancer survivors are often lost in transition and disregard oncologists' recommendations. Off-loading follow-up from oncologists to oncology nurse practitioners and primary care providers creates savings while stemming the oncologist shortage. Survivorship strategies fit well into the aforementioned Team Care approach.

Studies have shown that when patients' end-of-life care preferences are known and followed, patients live longer and die happier. Such patient-centered care also reduces costs by avoiding aggressive—and expensive—treatment for patients who do not wish such treatment.

Currently, our medical system is focused on performing aggressive interventions at any cost—if hospitals have the resources, they will use them. This aggressive treatment is the default for patients who do not make their end-of-life preferences known. Currently, only one out of three adults Americans have advance directives that detail these preferences. Oncologists can play a central role in encouraging patients and their families to discuss and make end-of-life plans in advance. Medical Orders for Scope of Treatment (MOST) and Physician Orders for Life Sustaining Treatment (POLST) can be useful documents for seriously ill patients possibly nearing death.

5. **Unleash the Power of Data**

Rapid advances of healthcare technology will provide powerful business intelligence analytics to identify and treat otherwise high-risk/higher-cost patients, have decision support at the point of care, and communicate real-time across the cancer care team, among other attributes. Public reporting of oncologists' quality of care will become common.

With oncologists in front of this trend, it can be used to lower overall costs without defaulting to lower oncologist incomes. As Atul Gawande, MD stated, "In cystic fibrosis, a decision was made to make outcomes data public. There was a risk that sites would drop out of the program, but that didn't happen. Instead, providers started to devour the data. The poorly performing sites made visits to the high performers. They began to unlock the secrets. This is what happens when data is made public."[196]

6. **Reduce Unjustified Variation in Care**

The Oncology Accountable Care Workgroup suspected that there is widespread unjustified variation in care, thus suggesting that the development of evidence-based best practices and monitoring of adherence will reap quality and cost improvements.

**Examples: Choosing Wisely® Guidelines**—The American Society of Clinical Oncology (ASCO) is one of nine specialty societies participating in the Choosing Wisely® campaign directed to curb use of common tests and treatments not supported by clinical evidence. ASCO was specific that its participation was driven by the goal of ensuring that all cancer care is "high-value" care. The list of guidelines includes:

- Computed tomography (CT) scans should be limited in asymptomatic patients following curative-intent treatment for aggressive lymphoma.
- Inferior vena cava filters should not be routinely used in patients with acute venous thromboembolism.
- Do not transfuse more than the minimum number of red blood cell units necessary to relieve symptoms of anemia or to return a patient to safe hemoglobin range (7-8 g/dL in stable non-cardiac inpatients).
- Do not test for thrombophilia in adults with venous thromboembolism occurring in the setting of major transient risk factors such as surgery, trauma, or prolonged immobility.
- Do not administer plasma or prothrombin complex concentrates for non-emergent reversal of vitamin K antagonists (i.e., outside the setting of major bleeding, intracranial hemorrhage, or anticipated emergent surgery).
- Avoid unnecessary anticancer therapy, including chemotherapy, in patients with advanced solid-tumor cancers who are unlikely to benefit, and instead, focus on symptom relief and palliative care.
- For early-stage breast cancer and prostate cancer that are at low risk of spreading, do not use advanced-imaging technologies (positron emission tomography [PET], CT, and radionuclide bone scans) for determining the cancer's spread.
- For individuals who have completed curative treatment for breast cancer, and who have no symptoms of recurrence, advanced-imaging tests (PET, CT, and radionuclide bone scans) and routine blood tests for certain biomarkers (CEA, CA 15-3, CA 27-29) should not be used to screen for cancer recurrences.
- Avoid administering white blood cell stimulating factors to patients who have a very low risk for febrile neutropenia (less than 20%).

7. **Use Technology to Extend *Tecum* Care Reach**

Whether across the hall, across town, or across the county, technology can aid the operation and workflow of seamless cancer care teams. Referral protocols, telephone, email, teleconference access to primary care and allied providers, and web-driven instruction videos and portals can all allow you to provide value-adding knowledge at the point of care. This not only promotes better quality through more timely access to critical diagnostic or treatment clinical input, but can generate savings from avoiding unnecessary referrals and admissions.

Use of technology in such a manner was penalized by the fee-for-service system but will be handsomely rewarded under value-based care. Rural patients will not be deprived of the benefits of collaborative care.

8. **Examples of Application of These Initiatives**

The Oncology ACO in Florida, comprised of Baptist Health of South Florida and the Advanced Medical Specialties practice, identified 226 patients, with a baseline annual cost of $23,054,596.00, or $102,295.00 per patient. The medical oncologists were the primary care physicians for the cancer patients. They targeted patients with the most common cancers (breast, digestive system, leukemia and lymphoma, female and male reproductive, and respiratory) with three or more E&M services the prior year. They used the CMS and Quality Oncology Practice Initiative (QOPI) metrics. The targeted initiatives were (1) patient education and the patient experience (understanding one's illness, appropriate setting of goals, focusing on symptomatic control, allying with key healthcare surrogates); (2) chemotherapy spend control through strict adherence to pathways, and chemotherapy education; (3) better utilization of hospice and palliative care services; (4) ED use management through education, access, palliative care, and transition management; and (5) process improvement through hospital embedded care navigators and flow design for surgery, anesthesia, imaging, and radiation therapy.

The "lessons learned" they reported were to pick committed partners; that data is important but complex; that signing the contract is the beginning, not the end; and that the oncologist practice becomes the *de facto* medical home for the patients. They intend to connect across the care continuum with the rest of the Clinically Integrated Network at the health system.[197]

WellPoint is promoting an Oncology Medical Home with three key components: (1) adherence to pathways, with emphasis on chemotherapy and supportive care and on using USON Level 1 pathways where appropriate; (2) coordination of care and disease management, with coordination with other specialists, proactive telephone support by nurse coordinators, and evaluation of acute events in the office and not emergency department; and (3) end-of-life care, with coordination with hospice.

Their lessons learned over three years are that standardization and development of appropriate metrics takes time. They noted the tension with the oncology FFS business model being tied to the delivery of chemotherapy.[198]

**C. Other**—Please see *The Accountable Care Manual for Oncologists*, which may be downloaded at www.ncmedsoc.org/physician-resources/accountable-care/aco-toolkits.

**D. PCSP Standards**—The NCQA Patient-Centered Specialty Practice standards regarding care team and patient coordination are recommended generally for all specialists, including oncologists.

**II.  Metrics**

**A. Overview**—After determining the initiatives involving this specialty that are most appropriate for your CIN/ACO, to incentivize the desired behavior and outcomes, it is recommended that clinically valid metrics track adherence to the chosen activities and accomplishment of the desired results. Perhaps use the array of measures from various sources as a "menu" from which to start, and then tailor, prioritize, and weight them to fit your incentivization goals (see Table 7-15).

**TABLE 7-15.** MACRA's Quality Payment Program MIPS Measures Relevant to Oncology

| MEASURE NAME | MEASURE DESCRIPTION |
|---|---|
| Care Plan | Percentage of patients aged 65 years and older who have an advance care plan or surrogate decision maker documented in the medical record or documentation in the medical record that an advance care plan was discussed but the patient did not wish or was not able to name a surrogate decision maker or provide an advance care plan. |
| Closing the Referral Loop: Receipt of Specialist Report | Percentage of patients with referrals, regardless of age, for which the referring provider receives a report from the provider to whom the patient was referred. |
| Documentation of Current Medications in the Medical Record | Percentage of visits for patients aged 18 years and older for which the eligible professional attests to documenting a list of current medications using all immediate resources available on the date of the encounter. This list must include ALL known prescriptions, over-the-counters, herbals, and vitamin/mineral/dietary (nutritional) supplements AND must contain the medications' name, dosage, frequency and route of administration. |
| HER2 Negative or Undocumented Breast Cancer Patients Spared Treatment with HER2-Targeted Therapies | Proportion of female patients (aged 18 years and older) with breast cancer who are human epidermal growth factor receptor 2 (HER2)/neu negative who are not administered HER2-targeted therapies. |

*Continued on next page*

**TABLE 7-15.** MACRA's Quality Payment Program MIPS
Measures Relevant to Oncology (continued)

| MEASURE NAME | MEASURE DESCRIPTION |
|---|---|
| KRAS Gene Mutation Testing Performed for Patients with Metastatic Colorectal Cancer Who Receive Anti-epidermal Growth Factor Receptor (EGFR) Monoclonal Antibody Therapy | Percentage of adult patients (aged 18 or over) with metastatic colorectal cancer who receive anti-epidermal growth factor receptor monoclonal antibody therapy for whom KRAS gene mutation testing was performed. |
| Oncology: Medical and Radiation - Pain Intensity Quantified | Percentage of patient visits, regardless of patient age, with a diagnosis of cancer currently receiving chemotherapy or radiation therapy in which pain intensity is quantified. |
| Oncology: Medical and Radiation - Plan of Care for Pain | Percentage of visits for patients, regardless of age, with a diagnosis of cancer currently receiving chemotherapy or radiation therapy who report having pain with a documented plan of care to address pain. |
| Oncology: Radiation Dose Limits to Normal Tissues | Percentage of patients, regardless of age, with a diagnosis of breast, rectal, pancreatic, or lung cancer receiving 3D conformal radiation therapy who had documentation in medical record that radiation dose limits to normal tissues were established prior to the initiation of a course of 3D conformal radiation for a minimum of two tissues. |
| Patients with Metastatic Colorectal Cancer and KRAS Gene Mutation Spared Treatment with Anti-epidermal Growth Factor Receptor (EGFR) Monoclonal Antibodies | Percentage of adult patients (aged 18 or over) with metastatic colorectal cancer and KRAS gene mutation spared treatment with anti-EGFR monoclonal antibodies. |
| Preventive Care and Screening: Screening for High Blood Pressure and Follow-Up Documented | Percentage of patients aged 18 years and older seen during the reporting period who were screened for high blood pressure AND a recommended follow-up plan is documented based on the current blood pressure (BP) reading as indicated. |
| Preventive Care and Screening: Tobacco Use: Screening and Cessation Intervention | Percentage of patients aged 18 years and older who were screened for tobacco use one or more times within 24 months AND who received cessation counseling intervention if identified as a tobacco user. |
| Preventive Care and Screening: Unhealthy Alcohol Use: Screening and Brief Counseling | Percentage of patients aged 18 years and older who were screened for unhealthy alcohol use using a systematic screening method at least once within the last 24 months AND who received brief counseling if identified as an unhealthy alcohol user. |
| Proportion Admitted to Hospice for Fewer Than 3 Days | Proportion of cancer patients who died, who were admitted to hospice and spent fewer than 3 days there. |
| Proportion Admitted to the Intensive Care Unit (ICU) in the Last 30 Days of Life | Proportion of patients who died from cancer admitted to the ICU in the last 30 days of life. |
| Proportion Not Admitted to Hospice | Proportion of patients who died from cancer who were not admitted to hospice. |

**TABLE 7-15.** MACRA's Quality Payment Program MIPS
Measures Relevant to Oncology (continued)

| MEASURE NAME | MEASURE DESCRIPTION |
|---|---|
| Proportion of Patients Who Died from Cancer with More Than One Emergency Department Visit in the Last 30 Days of Life | Proportion of patients who died from cancer with more than one emergency department visit in the last 30 days of life. |
| Proportion Receiving Chemotherapy in the Last 14 Days of Life | Proportion of patients who died from cancer who received chemotherapy in the last 14 days of life. |
| Prostate Cancer: Avoidance of Overuse of Bone Scan for Staging Low-Risk Prostate Cancer Patients | Percentage of patients, regardless of age, with a diagnosis of prostate cancer at low (or very low) risk of recurrence receiving interstitial prostate brachytherapy, OR external beam radiotherapy to the prostate, OR radical prostatectomy, OR cryotherapy who did not have a bone scan performed at any time since diagnosis of prostate cancer. |
| Radical Prostatectomy Pathology Reporting | Percentage of radical prostatectomy pathology reports that include the pT category, the pN category, the Gleason score and a statement about margin status. |
| Tobacco Use and Help with Quitting Among Adolescents | The percentage of adolescents aged 12-20 years with a primary care visit during the measurement year for whom tobacco use status was documented and received help with quitting if identified as a tobacco user. |
| Trastuzumab Received by Patients with AJCC Stage I (T1c) - III and HER2 Positive Breast Cancer Receiving Adjuvant Chemotherapy | Proportion of female patients (aged 18 years and older) with AJCC stage I (T1c) - III, human epidermal growth factor receptor 2 (HER2) positive breast cancer receiving adjuvant chemotherapy who are also receiving trastuzumab. |

# OPHTHALMOLOGISTS

I. **Why and How You May Want to Utilize Ophthalmologists in Your CIN/ACO**
The pupils provide the body's best window to blood vessels and nerves, and many diseases exhibit manifestations in and around the eyes. The ability to detect and access to an ACO's electronic data registry places ophthalmologists in position to be an ACO's early warning system and care coordinators, especially for diabetic patients.

"Like plastic surgeons and dermatologists, a great many ophthalmologists have experience with retail medicine through noninsurance-covered services like Lasik, cosmetic blepharoplasty, and eyeglasses. This extra experience in the importance of driving down costs and improving patient satisfaction in a true healthcare market may be useful in demonstrating how to improve outcomes for others in an ACO less adept at this way of thinking about healthcare. Additionally, the need to coordinate screening for diabetic retinopathy with primary care through better information exchange is an enormous opportunity for ophthalmologists."[199]

A. **Disease Management and Connecting with the Primary Care Team**—This includes diabetes management and making appropriate referrals for patients who may have chronic diseases but may not currently work with a primary care provider. The ophthalmologist can serve as a touchpoint in the patient's care and ensure through proper follow-up that the patient ultimately is also connected with their primary care team. Examples of conditions ophthalmologists can identify for appropriate referral and follow-up are hypertension, diabetes, brain tumors, sleep apnea, thyroid disease, and cancers.

B. **Use of Best Practices**—A useful source of core best practices may be found in the recommendations of the American Academy of Ophthalmology to the Choosing Wisely® program sponsored by the ABIM Foundation:

1. "Don't perform preoperative medical tests for eye surgery unless there are specific medical indications.
2. Don't routinely order imaging tests for patients without symptoms or signs of significant eye disease.
3. Don't order antibiotics for adenoviral conjunctivitis.
4. Don't routinely provide antibiotics before or after intravitreal injections.
5. Don't place punctal plugs for mild dry eye before trying other medical treatments."[200]

    Additionally, the American Academy of Ophthalmology's Preferred Practice Patterns identify useful best practices for ophthalmologists.[201]

C. **Optimize Site-of-Service**—Providers are encouraged to move procedures to lower-cost facilities or outpatient sites when consistent with best practices. Particular opportunity exists for providing alternatives to the emergency department, which has a pronounced patient engagement aspect, discussed below.

For example, when a patient presents at an emergency department with double vision, the patient will likely need to undergo a series of expensive tests to rule out a variety of causes. However, if seen in the ophthalmologists' office, the specialized expertise of the clinician can rule out certain conditions and thereby reduce the number of tests that may need to be completed.

One way this can be accomplished is by offering after-hours access for patients to avoid potentially unnecessary emergency department use. Additionally, ophthalmologists should focus on avoiding expensive in-hospital procedures when the same procedure can be done in a less-expensive setting with the same or better-quality outcomes, such as a physician's office or ambulatory surgical center.

D. **Drug Management**—An ophthalmologist's use of best practices in determining the best drug for treatment may lead to cost reductions. For example, when treating macular degeneration, comparative effectiveness research[202] has shown that treatment of age-related macular degeneration (AMD) in cases of severe, or "wet," as of 2016, AMD, with both Lucentis and Avastin produce similar outcomes on visual acuity. However, the costs of these drugs vary greatly, with Lucentis costing approximately $2,000.00 per dose while Avastin costs $50.00 per dose.

E. **Use of Telehealth**—With the onset of a multitude of telehealth technology options entering the market, many ophthalmologists are well-equipped to increase access to care and improve the patient experience by its use. For example, some ophthalmologists are now studying the accuracy and reliability of using telehealth for diagnosing and screening diabetic retinopathy and macular edema with some success.[203] Particularly when a patient has co-morbidities such as diabetes and hypertension, the effectiveness of telehealth in these cases may produce cost savings as well as a better patient experience and increased patient engagement and adherence.[204]

F. **Other**—Please see *The Accountable Care Manual for Ophthalmologists*, which may be downloaded at www.ncmedsoc.org/physician-resources/accountable-care/aco-toolkits.

G. **PCSP Standards**—The NCQA Patient-Centered Specialty Practice standards regarding care team and patient coordination are recommended generally for all specialists, including ophthalmologists.

II. **Metrics**

A. **Overview**—After determining the initiatives involving this specialty that are most appropriate for your CIN/ACO, to incentivize the desired behavior and outcomes, it is recommended that clinically valid metrics track adherence to the chosen activities and accomplishment of the desired results. Use the available array of measures from various sources as a "menu" from which to start, and then tailor, prioritize, and weight them to fit your incentivization goals.

**B. Examples of Possible Ophthalmology Performance Measures**—Ophthalmologists can consult the 19 IRISES® Clinical Quality Registry measures approved by the Centers for Medicare & Medicaid Services (CMS).[205] See Table 7-16.

**TABLE 7-16.** MACRA's Quality Payment Program MIPS Measures Relevant to Ophthalmology

| MEASURE NAME | MEASURE DESCRIPTION |
|---|---|
| Adult Primary Rhegmatogenous Retinal Detachment Surgery: No Return to the Operating Room Within 90 Days of Surgery | Patients aged 18 years and older who had surgery for primary rhegmatogenous retinal detachment who did not require a return to the operating room within 90 days of surgery. |
| Adult Primary Rhegmatogenous Retinal Detachment Surgery: Visual Acuity Improvement Within 90 Days of Surgery | Patients aged 18 years and older who had surgery for primary rhegmatogenous retinal detachment and achieved an improvement in their visual acuity, from their preoperative level, within 90 days of surgery in the operative eye. |
| Age-Related Macular Degeneration (AMD): Counseling on Antioxidant Supplement | Percentage of patients aged 50 years and older with a diagnosis of age-related macular degeneration (AMD) or their caregiver(s) who were counseled within 12 months on the benefits and/or risks of the Age-Related Eye Disease Study (AREDS) formulation for preventing progression of AMD. |
| Age-Related Macular Degeneration (AMD): Dilated Macular Examination | Percentage of patients aged 50 years and older with a diagnosis of age-related macular degeneration (AMD) who had a dilated macular examination performed which included documentation of the presence or absence of macular thickening or hemorrhage AND the level of macular degeneration severity during one or more office visits within 12 months. |
| Care Plan | Percentage of patients aged 65 years and older who have an advance care plan or surrogate decision maker documented in the medical record or documentation in the medical record that an advance care plan was discussed but the patient did not wish or was not able to name a surrogate decision maker or provide an advance care plan. |
| Cataract Surgery with Intraoperative Complications (Unplanned Rupture of Posterior Capsule Requiring Unplanned Vitrectomy) | Percentage of patients aged 18 years and older who had cataract surgery performed and had an unplanned rupture of the posterior capsule requiring vitrectomy. |
| Cataract Surgery: Difference Between Planned and Final Refraction | Percentage of patients aged 18 years and older who had cataract surgery performed and who achieved a final refraction within +/- 1.0 diopters of their planned (target) refraction. |
| Cataracts: 20/40 or Better Visual Acuity within 90 Days Following Cataract Surgery | Percentage of patients aged 18 years and older with a diagnosis of uncomplicated cataract who had cataract surgery and no significant ocular conditions impacting the visual outcome of surgery and had best-corrected visual acuity of 20/40 or better (distance or near) achieved within 90 days following the cataract surgery. |

**TABLE 7-16.** MACRA's Quality Payment Program MIPS
Measures Relevant to Ophthalmology (continued)

| MEASURE NAME | MEASURE DESCRIPTION |
|---|---|
| Cataracts: Complications within 30 Days Following Cataract Surgery Requiring Additional Surgical Procedures | Percentage of patients aged 18 years and older with a diagnosis of uncomplicated cataract who had cataract surgery and had any of a specified list of surgical procedures in the 30 days following cataract surgery which would indicate the occurrence of any of the following major complications: retained nuclear fragments, endophthalmitis, dislocated or wrong power IOL, retinal detachment, or wound dehiscence. |
| Cataracts: Improvement in Patient's Visual Function within 90 Days Following Cataract Surgery | Percentage of patients aged 18 years and older who had cataract surgery and had improvement in visual function achieved within 90 days following the cataract surgery, based on completing a preoperative and post-operative visual function survey. |
| Cataracts: Patient Satisfaction within 90 Days Following Cataract Surgery | Percentage of patients aged 18 years and older who had cataract surgery and were satisfied with their care within 90 days following the cataract surgery, based on completion of the Consumer Assessment of Healthcare Providers and Systems Surgical Care Survey. |
| Closing the Referral Loop: Receipt of Specialist Report | Percentage of patients with referrals, regardless of age, for which the referring provider receives a report from the provider to whom the patient was referred. |
| Diabetes: Eye Exam | Percentage of patients aged 18-75 years with diabetes who had a retinal or dilated eye exam by an eye care professional during the measurement period or a negative retinal exam (no evidence of retinopathy) in the 12 months prior to the measurement period. |
| Diabetic Retinopathy: Communication with the Physician Managing Ongoing Diabetes Care | Percentage of patients aged 18 years and older with a diagnosis of diabetic retinopathy who had a dilated macular or fundus exam performed with documented communication to the physician who manages the ongoing care of the patient with diabetes mellitus regarding the findings of the macular or fundus exam at least once within 12 months. |
| Diabetic Retinopathy: Documentation of Presence or Absence of Macular Edema and Level of Severity of Retinopathy | Percentage of patients aged 18 years and older with a diagnosis of diabetic retinopathy who had a dilated macular or fundus exam performed which included documentation of the level of severity of retinopathy and the presence or absence of macular edema during one or more office visits within 12 months. |
| Documentation of Current Medications in the Medical Record | Percentage of visits for patients aged 18 years and older for which the eligible professional attests to documenting a list of current medications using all immediate resources available on the date of the encounter. This list must include ALL known prescriptions, over-the-counters, herbals, and vitamin/mineral/dietary (nutritional) supplements AND must contain the medications' name, dosage, frequency and route of administration. |

*Continued on next page*

**TABLE 7-16.** MACRA's Quality Payment Program MIPS
Measures Relevant to Ophthalmology (continued)

| MEASURE NAME | MEASURE DESCRIPTION |
|---|---|
| Preventive Care and Screening: Screening for High Blood Pressure and Follow-Up Documented | Percentage of patients aged 18 years and older seen during the reporting period who were screened for high blood pressure AND a recommended follow-up plan is documented based on the current blood pressure (BP) reading as indicated. |
| Preventive Care and Screening: Tobacco Use: Screening and Cessation Intervention | Percentage of patients aged 18 years and older who were screened for tobacco use one or more times within 24 months AND who received cessation counseling intervention if identified as a tobacco user. |
| Primary Open-Angle Glaucoma (POAG): Optic Nerve Evaluation | Percentage of patients aged 18 years and older with a diagnosis of primary open-angle glaucoma (POAG) who have an optic nerve head evaluation during one or more office visits within 12 months. |
| Primary Open-Angle Glaucoma (POAG): Reduction of Intraocular Pressure (IOP) by 15% OR Documentation of a Plan of Care | Percentage of patients aged 18 years and older with a diagnosis of primary open-angle glaucoma (POAG) whose glaucoma treatment has not failed (the most recent IOP was reduced by at least 15% from the pre-intervention level) OR if the most recent IOP was not reduced by at least 15% from the pre-intervention level, a plan of care was documented within 12 months. |
| Tobacco Use and Help with Quitting Among Adolescents | The percentage of adolescents aged 12-20 years with a primary care visit during the measurement year for whom tobacco use status was documented and received help with quitting if identified as a tobacco user |

# ORTHOPEDISTS

I.  **Why and How You May Want to Utilize Orthopedists in Your CIN/ACO**
    Orthopedics is one of the few clinical areas projected to grow in revenue over
    the next 10-15 years. It is also ideally suited to episode payment initiatives due
    to the relatively bounded nature of key procedures. Thus, orthopedics has been
    at the epicenter of the bundled payment movement. The predicted "ACO 2.0"
    evolution includes multiple bundled payment initiatives intertwined in the ACO's
    full continuum of care strategy.[206]

    A.  **Device and Supplies Cost Reductions**—Standardization of implants, devices,
        and supplies tends to lead to cost reductions through volume discounting and
        manpower efficiencies.

    B.  **Compress Unjustified Variability Contrary to Evidence-Based Best
        Practice**—Starting with the orthopedist subcommittee of the ACO Clinical
        Committee, determine among peers the clinically valid, severity-adjusted
        best practices you agree to follow. Monitor the variability of ACO physicians
        against those standards and report to the group, with individual identifiers,
        on a regular basis. It is common that accomplished peers are surprised at the
        degree of variability and the associated avoidable costs and complications.
        The selection of best practices must be determined by peers to achieve buy-in.

        A useful source of core best practices may be found in the recommendations
        of the American Academy of Orthopedic Surgeons to the Choosing Wisely®
        program sponsored by the ABIM Foundation:

        1.  **"Avoid performing routine post-operative deep vein thrombosis ultra-
            sonography screening in patients who undergo elective hip or knee
            arthroplasty.** Since ultrasound is not effective at diagnosing unsuspected
            deep vein thrombosis (DVT) and appropriate alternative screening tests
            do not exist, if there is no change in the patient's clinical status, routine
            post-operative screening for DVT after hip or knee arthroplasty does not
            change outcomes or clinical management.

        2.  **Don't use needle lavage to treat patients with symptomatic osteoarthri-
            tis of the knee for long-term relief.** The use of needle lavage in patients
            with symptomatic osteoarthritis of the knee does not lead to measurable
            improvements in pain, function, 50-foot walking time, stiffness, tender-
            ness, or swelling.

        3.  **Don't use glucosamine and chondroitin to treat patients with symp-
            tomatic osteoarthritis of the knee.** Both glucosamine and chondroitin
            sulfate do not provide relief for patients with symptomatic osteoarthritis
            of the knee.

        4.  **Don't use lateral wedge insoles to treat patients with symptomatic medial
            compartment osteoarthritis of the knee.** In patients with symptomatic

osteoarthritis of the knee, the use of lateral wedge or neutral insoles does not improve pain or functional outcomes. Comparisons between lateral and neutral heel wedges were investigated, as were comparisons between lateral wedged insoles and lateral wedged insoles with subtalar strapping. The systematic review concludes that there is only limited evidence for the effectiveness of lateral heel wedges and related orthoses. In addition, the possibility exists that those who do not use them may experience fewer symptoms from osteoarthritis of the knee.

5. **Don't use post-operative splinting of the wrist after carpal tunnel release for long-term relief.** Routine post-operative splinting of the wrist after the carpal tunnel release procedure showed no benefit in grip or lateral pinch strength or bowstringing. In addition, the research showed no effect in complication rates, subjective outcomes, or patient satisfaction. Clinicians may wish to provide protection for the wrist in a working environment or for temporary protection. However, objective criteria for their appropriate use do not exist. Clinicians should be aware of the detrimental effects including adhesion formation, stiffness, and prevention of nerve and tendon movement."[207]

*Strategic Note:* The current fragmented fee-for-service model makes it difficult to coordinate across specialties for such problems as chronic back pain. Primary care physicians, anesthesiologist pain specialists, and orthopedists in an ACO, however, are incentivized to collaborate and develop a uniform, evidence-based approach.

Paul Levin, M.D., Vice Chairman of the Department of Orthopedic Surgery at Montefiore Medical Center in New York City, stated, "If you look at the management of acute low back pain care in the U.S., it's widely recognized that it's over treated with no benefit to the patient and associated with that is an excessive use of expensive medical services. We've already embarked on this mission over the past year, even before we were officially an ACO program. The primary focus is on the education of primary care physicians and ensuring rapid access to a spine specialist when the primary care provider believes it is warranted. Lectures are delivered at the primary care sites reviewing evidence-based guidelines, red flags, and the basics of performing an appropriate history and physical examination of the patient with acute low back pain. If you talk to the PCPs, they are most excited about gaining a comfort level in caring for these patients and streamlining the process for orthopedic evaluation."[208]

C. **Optimize Site-of-Service**—Seek to move procedures to lower-cost facilities or outpatient sites when consistent with best practices. Particular opportunity exists for providing alternatives to the emergency department, which has a pronounced patient engagement aspect, discussed below. The Orthopaedists

Accountable Care Workgroup emphasized that active optimization of site-of-service was truly "low-hanging fruit." They emphasize this as a straightforward way of achieving early savings.

D. **Workflow Management**—This is sometimes called "care redesign." Freed from the fragmentation of the fee-for-service system, work to optimize patient flow and provider coordination across the continuum of care. Better scheduling and pre-op readiness will generate savings.

E. **Patient Engagement**—Patient education is essential for success. Patients need to know when it is appropriate to present to an emergency department. A detailed patient handbook and journal are recommended. Better physician-patient communications are the best way to engage a patient. The hospitalist can coordinate better with the primary care providers. A transition health coach or "Patient Navigator" can actively follow up, including home visits.

Tom Hunt, Executive Administrator of MidAmerica Orthopedics in Chicago, suggests that, "Orthopedic surgeons can specifically focus on realizing the greatest savings within ACOs by decreasing hospital length of stays, readmissions, and use of the emergency room. If the surgeon and his or her team can be sure they have preoperative, intraoperative, and discharge planning organized before their patient arrives at the hospital, length of stay will be controlled, and discharge will be timely."[209]

F. **Post-Acute Care Management**—Patient engagement, discharge planning, active follow up and communication, managing complex high-risk, high-cost care with post-acute care providers, have been shown to present significant opportunities for care improvement, reduced complications and readmissions, and cost savings.

G. **"Push" Knowledge Upstream to Medical Home**—Barbara Bergin, MD, an orthopedic surgeon with Texas Orthopedics, Sports and Rehabilitation Associates in Austin, commented that, "Orthopedics is almost a primary care field of practice. We don't just do surgery. Believe it or not, the majority of our practices are actually centered on the conservative treatment of musculoskeletal disorders and not doing surgery. . . . **We're one of the specialties an ACO . . . is going to seek out for maximum efficiency and control of the patient's medical care.**"[210]

II. **Metrics**

A. **Overview**—After determining the initiatives involving this specialty that are most appropriate for your CIN/ACO, to incentivize the desired behavior and outcomes, it is recommended that clinically valid metrics track adherence to the chosen activities and accomplishment of the desired results. Start with available measure sets from various sources as a "menu" and then tailor, prioritize, and weight them to fit your incentivization goals.

B. **Examples of Possible Orthopedic Performance Measures**

- Avoidance of expensive in-hospital procedures when the same treatment can be done in a less-expensive setting, such as a physician's office.
- Preventive services measures including early detection and screening for conditions such as lower back pain and musculoskeletal injuries.
- Implementation of ACO integrated care protocols.
- Open line of communication between primary care and orthopedic care team.
- Establishment of baseline care plans for total joint replacement and assessment of patient performance against the plans.
- Effective, efficient, evidence-based supply chain management.
- Creating informed decisions for patients and families re: pain management, home health, rehab, and other recovery-related services.

See Table 7-17 for quality payment measures.

**TABLE 7-17. MACRA's Quality Payment Program MIPS Measures Relevant to Orthopedists**

| MEASURE NAME | MEASURE DESCRIPTION |
|---|---|
| Care Plan | Percentage of patients aged 65 years and older who have an advance care plan or surrogate decision maker documented in the medical record or documentation in the medical record that an advance care plan was discussed but the patient did not wish or was not able to name a surrogate decision maker or provide an advance care plan. |
| Closing the Referral Loop: Receipt of Specialist Report | Percentage of patients with referrals, regardless of age, for which the referring provider receives a report from the provider to whom the patient was referred. |
| Documentation of Current Medications in the Medical Record | Percentage of visits for patients aged 18 years and older for which the eligible professional attests to documenting a list of current medications using all immediate resources available on the date of the encounter. This list must include ALL known prescriptions, over-the-counters, herbals, and vitamin/mineral/dietary (nutritional) supplements AND must contain the medications' name, dosage, frequency and route of administration. |
| Functional Status Assessment for Total Hip Replacement | Percentage of patients 18 years of age and older with primary total hip arthroplasty (THA) who completed baseline and follow-up patient-reported functional status assessments. |
| Functional Status Assessment for Total Knee Replacement | Percentage of patients 18 years of age and older with primary total knee arthroplasty (TKA) who completed baseline and follow-up patient-reported functional status assessments. |
| Osteoarthritis (OA): Function and Pain Assessment | Percentage of patient visits for patients aged 21 years and older with a diagnosis of OA with assessment for function and pain. |
| Patient-Centered Surgical Risk Assessment and Communication | Percentage of patients who underwent a non-emergency surgery who had their personalized risks of post-operative complications assessed by their surgical team prior to surgery using a clinical data-based, patient-specific risk calculator and who received personal discussion of those risks with the surgeon. |

**TABLE 7-17.** MACRA's Quality Payment Program MIPS
Measures Relevant to Orthopedists (continued)

| MEASURE NAME | MEASURE DESCRIPTION |
|---|---|
| Perioperative Care: Selection of Prophylactic Antibiotic - First- or Second-Generation Cephalosporin | Percentage of surgical patients aged 18 years and older undergoing procedures with the indications for a first- or second-generation cephalosporin prophylactic antibiotic who had an order for a first- or second-generation cephalosporin for antimicrobial prophylaxis. |
| Perioperative Care: Venous Thromboembolism (VTE) Prophylaxis (When Indicated in ALL Patients) | Percentage of surgical patients aged 18 years and older undergoing procedures for which venous thromboembolism (VTE) prophylaxis is indicated in all patients, who had an order for Low Molecular Weight Heparin (LMWH), Low- Dose Unfractionated Heparin (LDUH), adjusted-dose warfarin, fondaparinux or mechanical prophylaxis to be given within 24 hours prior to incision time or within 24 hours after surgery end time. |
| Preventive Care and Screening: Body Mass Index (BMI) Screening and Follow-Up Plan | Percentage of patients aged 18 years and older with a BMI documented during the current encounter or during the previous six months AND with a BMI outside of normal parameters, a follow-up plan is documented during the encounter or during the previous six months of the current encounter. Normal Parameters: Age 18 years and older BMI $\geq$ 18.5 and < 25 kg/m$^2$ |
| Preventive Care and Screening: Screening for High Blood Pressure and Follow-Up Documented | Percentage of patients aged 18 years and older seen during the reporting period who were screened for high blood pressure AND a recommended follow-up plan is documented based on the current blood pressure (BP) reading as indicated. |
| Preventive Care and Screening: Tobacco Use: Screening and Cessation Intervention | Percentage of patients aged 18 years and older who were screened for tobacco use one or more times within 24 months AND who received cessation counseling intervention if identified as a tobacco user. |
| Rheumatoid Arthritis (RA): Assessment and Classification of Disease Prognosis | Percentage of patients aged 18 years and older with a diagnosis of rheumatoid arthritis (RA) who have an assessment and classification of disease prognosis at least once within 12 months. |
| Rheumatoid Arthritis (RA): Functional Status Assessment | Percentage of patients aged 18 years and older with a diagnosis of rheumatoid arthritis (RA) for whom a functional status assessment was performed at least once within 12 months. |
| Rheumatoid Arthritis (RA): Glucocorticoid Management | Percentage of patients aged 18 years and older with a diagnosis of rheumatoid arthritis (RA) who have been assessed for glucocorticoid use and, for those on prolonged doses of prednisone $\geq$ 10 mg daily (or equivalent) with improvement or no change in disease activity, documentation of glucocorticoid management plan within 12 months. |
| Tobacco Use and Help with Quitting Among Adolescents | The percentage of adolescents aged 12-20 years with a primary care visit during the measurement year for whom tobacco use status was documented and received help with quitting if identified as a tobacco user. |
| Total Knee Replacement: Identification of Implanted Prosthesis in Operative Report | Percentage of patients regardless of age undergoing a total knee replacement whose operative report identifies the prosthetic implant specifications including the prosthetic implant manufacturer, the brand name of the prosthetic implant and the size of each prosthetic implant. |

*Continued on next page*

**TABLE 7-17.** MACRA's Quality Payment Program MIPS
Measures Relevant to Orthopedists (continued)

| MEASURE NAME | MEASURE DESCRIPTION |
| --- | --- |
| Total Knee Replacement: Preoperative Antibiotic Infusion with Proximal Tourniquet | Percentage of patients regardless of age undergoing a total knee replacement who had the prophylactic antibiotic completely infused prior to the inflation of the proximal tourniquet. |
| Total Knee Replacement: Shared Decision Making: Trial of Conservative (Non-surgical) Therapy | Percentage of patients regardless of age undergoing a total knee replacement with documented shared decision making with discussion of conservative (non-surgical) therapy (e.g., non-steroidal anti-inflammatory drug (NSAIDs), analgesics, weight loss, exercise, injections) prior to the procedure. |
| Total Knee Replacement: Venous Thromboembolic and Cardiovascular Risk Evaluation | Percentage of patients regardless of age undergoing a total knee replacement who are evaluated for the presence or absence of venous thromboembolic and cardiovascular risk factors within 30 days prior to the procedure (e.g. history of Deep Vein Thrombosis (DVT), Pulmonary Embolism (PE), Myocardial Infarction (MI), Arrhythmia and Stroke). |
| Use of Imaging Studies for Low Back Pain | Percentage of patients aged 18-50 years with a diagnosis of low back pain who did not have an imaging study (plain X-ray, MRI, CT scan) within 28 days of the diagnosis. |

# PEDIATRICIANS

I.  **Why and How You May Want to Utilize Pediatricians in Your CIN/ACO**

The development of APMs has been focused on adult care initiatives because they have been driven by the Medicare Shared Savings Program, which focuses on adults over 65. But the movement of state Medicaid programs to value-based payment for integrated population health thrusts pediatric care generally, and pediatric behavioral and mental health care specifically, from being an afterthought to the forefront of value-based care innovation and opportunity.

The opportunity arising from this movement regarding increased payer attention to care management for children is leveraged even more for child psychiatry as the integration of mental and physical health are also being recognized. Movement toward a family-centered pediatric ACO will benefit millions of children. Nationally, pediatricians provide a majority of all office visits for children enrolled in Medicaid. As of 2016, Medicaid provided health insurance to over 30 million children.[211]

A.  **Optimization of Pediatricians in Care for Children Depends on Recognition of the Distinctly Different Attributes Needed for High-Value Contributions** (Tables 6-18, 6-19)

**TABLE 7-18.** Relevant Clinical Distinctions Between Adult and Pediatric Patients

|  | ADULT | CHILDREN |
|---|---|---|
| Primary Care | Treatment and management of chronic diseases; "sickness care." | Focus on prevention including immunizations and checkups. |
| Admission Diagnoses | Heart disease, diabetes, pneumonia, stroke. | Newborn births, mood disorders, asthma, injury. |
| Physiology Variation | Adult; elderly adults generally most expensive. | Infants, children, adolescents, and some adults; 1st year of life especially critical. |

**TABLE 7-19.** Population Health Characteristics Compared

| TIER | ADULTS | CHILDREN |
|---|---|---|
| Highest-Cost Patients | Multiple chronic conditions such as heart disease and diabetes. With better management, patients can drop to the middle tier—often elderly. | Prematurity. Rare and complex congenital or genetic diseases. Good management can keep them out of the ED and hospital, but their conditions are generally lifelong. |
| Chronic Disease | Large population with varying degrees of disease control, big opportunity for cost savings. | Relatively small population with 1 or 2 chronic conditions such as asthma or ADHD. |
| Healthy Patients | Depending on whom you ask, 60%-75% of patients. | Most kids, with focus on prevention, growth and development. |

The HIMSS ACO Task Force noted the following unique attributes of care for children:

- "Kids' unique medical needs and social environment necessitate care from pediatric-trained physicians and child-specific community resources such as schools.
- It is essential to select performance metrics that are meaningful to pediatrics and that accurately measure the quality of pediatric care.
- Population characteristics and scarce subspecialists require a regional vs. local provider base.
- Technology needs to include functionality to support pediatric care.
- Children with medical complexity usually have many subspecialists and rely on community resources and will need special care throughout their lives.
- The family is generally responsible for a child's health care, rather than the patient him- or herself.
- Federal leadership provided by Medicare is lacking in Medicaid, but states have begun working with providers to form Medicaid ACOs.
- A largely healthy population means that a larger number of patients is needed to show significant cost savings."[212]

B. **Family-Centered "Pediatric Medical/Health Homes" Linked to Specialty Care for Complex Conditions**—The family-centered medical home is the foundation of a primary care-driven integrated delivery system that is anchoring the ACO. There must be a sufficient number of pediatric primary and specialty care pediatricians for the number of children managed by the ACO. In many parts of the country, medical homes or tightly integrated relationships between children's hospitals, pediatricians, and specialty care pediatricians may be the foundation for a network that can be strengthened further within the architecture of an ACO with strong pediatric capabilities.[213] The pediatric community's experience with care coordination, not only in the management of children with complex conditions but also in the daily encounters with children who may need short-term and intermediate care coordination, also supports the concept of a pediatric ACO value-adding contribution.[214]

Finally, social determinants such as integrating community, oral, and mental health into the ACO's delivery and payment structure is essential, because so much of a child's health and safety is affected by social determinants and because some of the most common major chronic care conditions children and adolescents experience are oral and mental health problems. For example, the pediatric ACO, University Hospitals Rainbow Care Connection, in Cleveland, Ohio, integrates behavioral health services with primary care using social workers and tele-behavioral health.

For more detail on integrating with behavioral health and community health resources, see TAC's *Accountable Care Manual for Psychiatrists* and

*Accountable Care Manual for Community Health Partners* at www.ncmedsoc. org/physician-resources/accountable-care/aco-toolkits.

According to research in New Orleans, families of children and youth with special healthcare needs in an underserved population experienced enhanced services from nurse care coordinator support.[215] In short, unmet needs for services decrease when primary care clinicians are sensitive to the culture and needs of children and youth with special healthcare needs and their families and incorporate levels of care coordination in care delivery.[216] Care coordination conducted as a standard of pediatric practice resulted in increased family satisfaction with the quality of care and also decreased barriers to care.[217]

A 2011 study in children and youth with special healthcare needs and their families who received care coordination and individualized care plans via a Medicaid managed-care plan study reported improved satisfaction with mental health services and specialized therapies and participants were observed to have a decline in unmet needs, improved satisfaction with specialty care, and improved ratings of child health and family functioning.[218]

C. **Specific Strategies for Premature Infants**—"In a population of pretty healthy people, children, we see the avoidable costs for premature deliveries as an area of savings opportunity."[219] Premature babies often become long-term chronic high-risk, high-cost patients. Fortunately, a number of straightforward proven initiatives can promote better health and reduce costs, particularly readmissions. Value-based payment for population management, such as in ACOs, has the potential to unleash these practices by making them financially feasible.

- Protocolize Neonatal Hospital Care—Neonatologist Docia Hickey, MD, noted that "set protocols in the hospital make a lot of difference." Especially beneficial is protocolized team care in the delivery room. Protocols can be instituted for feeding, monitoring oxygen levels, minimizing touching, keeping the infant calm, using the ventilator, central line care and removal, and minimizing interventricular hemorrhage (IVH), chronic lung disease, and central line infections. The children should be screened for IVH and retinopathy of prematurity (ROP), initially and during follow up.

- Home Care/Case Management—Significant benefits have been realized when a case manager is assigned to premature infants upon discharge. One Pediatric Accountable Care Workgroup member recounted particular success when former neonatology nurses were enlisted as case managers. The management specifically included home health. The babies were on monitors in all cases. This practice resulted in the ability to discharge infants at lower weights earlier, and significantly reduced readmission rates.

- Participate in National Database—Participation in a national database for premature infants allows you to benchmark yourself. The Workgroup recommended reviewing statistics, stratified according to gestational age, for mortality, IVH, ROP, central line infections, and rate of readmissions.

- Follow-Up Clinic—For an ACO with a large neonatal population, a follow-up clinic is suggested.

In summary, a specific neonatal strategy such as described above makes sense for ACOs with a patient population that includes children. However, these are strategies unique to this population. It can be said that just as children are not simply small adults, premature infants are not simply small children.

D. **Increased Focus on Asthma Care**—A randomized controlled study of a pediatric outreach program reported by Greineder DK demonstrated a 75% reduction in hospitalizations among children aged 1-15 years with asthma who participated in a comprehensive asthma outreach program.[220] The program was focused on ensuring that patients kept scheduled appointments, monitored their asthma, and took maintenance medications.[221] Reduced hospitalizations along with significant reductions in emergency department use and out-of-health-plan use including referrals, home care, and durable medical equipment contributed to an estimated direct savings of $7.69 to $11.67 for every dollar spent on the intervention.[222] Montefiore Medical Center, New York ACO, invests heavily in school-based healthcare centers, which reduces admissions for pediatric asthma tenfold and helps reduce teenage pregnancy by 47%.[223]

E. **Standardized Evidence-Based Best Practices and Data-Driven Research**—Health information technology can play a pivotal role in care coordination. Tracking and monitoring patients via the use of patient registries can support care-coordination activities and functions and improve patient safety. The Data Resource Center for Child and Adolescent Health (DRC) supports efforts to improve pediatric healthcare and quality by providing population-based child health from various national surveys that can be easily accessed through the DRC website.

Advantages of the DRC website include: (1) National standardization allows for consistent measurement and reporting across states and geographic areas within states; standardization of measurement is critical to allowing comparison across states and subgroups of children; (2) Comparison can be made across a wide array of demographic and health status subgroups of children and youth, including race/ethnicity, presence of a special healthcare need, household income, etc.; (3) Many topics relevant to national health goals for children are validly reported by parents and are not possible to access using other information systems, such as billing, administrative, clinical, or medical records; (4) An array of resources are available on how to use these data at the national, regional, state, and local level; (5) The role of evidence-based medicine in impacting patient care is noted among one of the expectations of the Patient Protection and Affordable Care Act.[224]

- **Pediatric Data is Different.** One Pediatrics Accountable Care Workgroup member commented, "One of the things we're finding in our experience is that we have to pull out pediatrics as a population; otherwise, the analytics are skewed." Adult data should focus on chronic disease management, sickness care, heart disease, diabetes, frail complex elderly care, with more widespread health concerns as a percent of the population. In contrast, data for population management for children should include well visits, immunizations, family communication, asthma, newborns, complex congenital or genetic diseases, and higher percentage of overall good health. Pediatric-appropriate data capture is tied to the need for unique performance metrics appropriate for pediatric care, for the purpose of data collection and measurement is to evaluate performance against clinically valid and appropriate structure, process, and outcome goals desired that are reflected in the set of metrics chosen. Both are essential and they are intertwined.

- **Evidence-Based Best Practices Work.** One Pediatrics Accountable Care Workgroup member noted, "Even in high-cost areas, we need to use what evidence we have. Don't just throw the kitchen sink at it." Another shared experience with the benefit of evidence-based approaches to premature infants, to reduce length of stay and improve others. "Many things can be protocolized. That translates into lower costs." Coordinated care for children is in its infancy. Consequently, evidence-based best practices are just now emerging, and principles-based guidelines are being initiated, starting the lifecycle toward becoming evidence-based. One example of evidence-based practices may be found in the suggestions of the American Academy of Pediatrics found in the Choosing Wisely® initiative[225]:

  1. **Antibiotics should not be used for apparent viral respiratory illnesses (sinusitis, pharyngitis, bronchitis).** Although overall antibiotic prescription rates for children have fallen, they still remain alarmingly high. Unnecessary medication use for viral respiratory illnesses can lead to antibiotic resistance and contributes to higher healthcare costs and the risks of adverse events.

  2. **Cough and cold medicines should not be prescribed or recommended for respiratory illnesses in children under four years of age.** Research has shown these products offer little benefit to young children and can have potentially serious side effects. Many cough and cold products for children have more than one ingredient, increasing the chance of accidental overdose if combined with another product.

  3. **Computed tomography (CT) scans are not necessary in the immediate evaluation of minor head injuries; clinical observation/Pediatric Emergency Care Applied Research Network (PECARN) criteria should be used to determine whether imaging is indicated.** Minor head

injuries occur commonly in children and adolescents. Approximately 50% of children who visit hospital emergency departments with a head injury are given a CT scan, many of which may be unnecessary. Unnecessary exposure to x-rays poses considerable danger to children, including increasing the lifetime risk of cancer because a child's brain tissue is more sensitive to ionizing radiation. Unnecessary CT scans impose undue costs to the healthcare system. Clinical observation prior to CT decision making for children with minor head injuries is an effective approach.

4. **Neuroimaging (CT, MRI) is not necessary in a child with simple febrile seizure.** CT scanning is associated with radiation exposure that may escalate future cancer risk. MRI also is associated with risks from required sedation and comes at a high cost. The literature does not support the use of skull films in the evaluation of a child with a febrile seizure. Clinicians evaluating infants or young children after a simple febrile seizure should direct their attention toward identifying the cause of the child's fever.

5. **CT scans are not necessary in the routine evaluation of abdominal pain.** Utilization of CT imaging in the emergency department evaluation of children with abdominal pain is increasing. The increased lifetime risk for cancer due to excess radiation exposure is of special concern given the acute sensitivity of children's organs. There also is the potential for radiation overdose with inappropriate CT protocols.

6. **Don't prescribe high-dose dexamethasone (0.5 mg/kg per day) for the prevention or treatment of bronchopulmonary dysplasia in pre-term infants.** High-dose dexamethasone (0.5 mg/kg per day) does not appear to confer additional therapeutic benefit over lower doses and is not recommended. High doses also have been associated with numerous short- and long-term adverse outcomes, including neurodevelopmental impairment.

7. **Don't perform screening panels for food allergies without previous consideration of medical history.** Ordering screening panels (IgE tests) that test for a variety of food allergens without previous consideration of the medical history is not recommended. Sensitization (a positive test) without clinical allergy is common. For example, about 8% of the population tests positive to peanuts, but only approximately 1% are truly allergic and exhibit symptoms upon ingestion. When symptoms suggest a food allergy, tests should be selected based on a careful medical history.

8. **Avoid using acid blockers and motility agents such as metoclopramide (generic) for physiologic gastroesophageal reflux (GER) that is effort-less, painless, and not affecting growth.** Do not use medication in the so-called "happy-spitter." There is scant evidence that gastroesophageal

reflux (GER) is a causative agent in many conditions though reflux may be a common association. There is accumulating evidence that acid-blocking and motility agents such as metoclopramide (generic) are not effective in physiologic GER. Long-term sequelae of infant GER is rare, and there is little evidence that acid blockade reduces these sequelae. The routine performance of upper gastrointestinal (GI) tract radiographic imaging to diagnose GER or gastroesophageal disease (BERD) is not justified. Parents should be counseled that GER is normal in infants and not associated with anything but stained clothes. GER that is associated with poor growth or significant respiratory symptoms should be further evaluated.

9. **Avoid the use of surveillance cultures for the screening and treatment of asymptomatic bacteriuria.** There is minimal evidence that surveillance urine cultures or treatment of asymptomatic bacteriuria is beneficial. Surveillance cultures are costly and produce both false positive and false negative results. Treatment of asymptomatic bacteriuria also increases exposure to antibiotics, which is a risk factor for subsequent infections with a resistant organism. This also results in the overall use of antibiotics in the community and may lead to unnecessary imaging.

10. **Infant home apnea monitors should not be routinely used to prevent sudden infant death syndrome (SIDS).** There is no evidence that the use of infant home apnea monitors decreases the incidence of SIDS. They might be of value for selected infants at risk for apnea or cardiovascular events after discharge but should not be used routinely. Editorial note by Pediatric Accountable Care Workgroup: Consider adding congestion and neonatal to the list of conditions for which home monitoring is of value.

F. **Incorporate Community-Based Resources**—Children are never cared for in isolation. The family, community, and educational system in which they live are natural extensions of accountable care principles that allow us to redefine the healthcare ecosystem. Schools, churches, healthy food choices, and daycares should be included in pediatric accountable care strategies.

II. **Metrics**

A. **Overview**—After determining the initiatives involving this specialty that are most appropriate for your CIN/ACO, to incentivize the desired behavior and outcomes, it is recommended that clinically valid metrics track adherence to the chosen activities and accomplishment of the desired results. Starting with the MACRA Quality Payment Program measures (Table 7-20), use the available array of measures from various sources as a "menu" from which to start, and then tailor, prioritize, and weight them to fit your incentivization goals.

**TABLE 7-20.** MACRA's Quality Payment Program MIPS Measures Relevant to Pediatrics

| MEASURE NAME | MEASURE DESCRIPTION |
|---|---|
| Acute Otitis Externa (AOE): Systemic Antimicrobial Therapy - Avoidance of Inappropriate Use | Percentage of patients aged 2 years and older with a diagnosis of AOE who were not prescribed systemic antimicrobial therapy |
| Acute Otitis Externa (AOE): Topical Therapy | Percentage of patients aged 2 years and older with a diagnosis of AOE who were prescribed topical preparations |
| ADHD: Follow-Up Care for Children Prescribed Attention-Deficit/Hyperactivity Disorder (ADHD) Medication | Percentage of children aged 6-12 years and newly dispensed a medication for attention-deficit/hyperactivity disorder (ADHD) who had appropriate follow-up care. Two rates are reported: 1. Percentage of children who had one follow-up visit with a practitioner with prescribing authority during the 30-Day Initiation Phase. 2. Percentage of children who remained on ADHD medication for at least 210 days and who, in addition to the visit in the Initiation Phase, had at least two additional follow-up visits with a practitioner within 270 days (9 months) after the Initiation Phase ended. |
| Appropriate Testing for Children with Pharyngitis | Percentage of children aged 3-18 years who were diagnosed with pharyngitis, ordered an antibiotic, and received a group A streptococcus (strep) test for the episode. |
| Appropriate Treatment for Children with Upper Respiratory Infection (URI) | Percentage of children aged 3 months-18 years who were diagnosed with upper respiratory infection (URI) and were not dispensed an antibiotic prescription on or three days after the episode. |
| Child and Adolescent Major Depressive Disorder (MDD): Suicide Risk Assessment | Percentage of patient visits for those patients aged 6-17 years with a diagnosis of major depressive disorder with an assessment for suicide risk. |
| Childhood Immunization Status | Percentage of children 2 years of age who had four diphtheria, tetanus, and acellular pertussis (DTaP); three polio (IPV), one measles, mumps and rubella (MMR); three H influenza type B (HiB); three hepatitis B (Hep B); one chicken pox (VZV); four pneumococcal conjugate (PCV); one hepatitis A (Hep A); two or three rotavirus (RV); and two influenza (flu) vaccines by their second birthday. |
| Chlamydia Screening for Women | Percentage of women aged 16-24 years who were identified as sexually active and who had at least one test for chlamydia during the measurement period |
| Follow-Up After Hospitalization for Mental Illness (FUH) | The percentage of discharges for patients 6 years of age and older who were hospitalized for treatment of selected mental illness diagnoses and who had an outpatient visit, an intensive outpatient encounter or partial hospitalization with a mental health practitioner. Two rates are reported: 1. The percentage of discharges for which the patient received follow-up within 30 days of discharge. 2. The percentage of discharges for which the patient received follow-up within 7 days of discharge. |
| HIV/AIDS: Pneumocystis Jiroveci Pneumonia (PCP) Prophylaxis | Percentage of patients aged 6 weeks and older with a diagnosis of HIV/AIDS who were prescribed *Pneumocystis jiroveci* pneumonia (PCP) prophylaxis. |

**TABLE 7-20.** MACRA's Quality Payment Program MIPS
Measures Relevant to Pediatrics (continued)

| MEASURE NAME | MEASURE DESCRIPTION |
| --- | --- |
| HIV/AIDS: Sexually Transmitted Disease Screening for Chlamydia, Gonorrhea, and Syphilis | Percentage of patients aged 13 years and older with a diagnosis of HIV/AIDS for whom chlamydia, gonorrhea, and syphilis screenings were performed at least once since the diagnosis of HIV infection. |
| Immunizations for Adolescents | The percentage of adolescents 13 years of age who had the recommended immunizations by their 13th birthday. |
| Medication Management for People with Asthma | The percentage of patients aged 5-64 years during the measurement year who were identified as having persistent asthma and were dispensed appropriate medications that they remained on for at least 75% of their treatment period. |
| Preventive Care and Screening: Influenza Immunization | Percentage of patients aged 6 months and older seen for a visit between October 1 and March 31 who received an influenza immunization OR who reported previous receipt of an influenza immunization. |
| Preventive Care and Screening: Screening for Clinical Depression and Follow-Up Plan | Percentage of patients aged 12 years and older screened for depression on the date of the encounter using an age-appropriate standardized depression screening tool AND if positive, a follow-up plan is documented on the date of the positive screen. |
| Primary Caries Prevention Intervention as Offered by Primary Care Providers, including Dentists | Percentage of children, age 0-20 years, who received a fluoride varnish application during the measurement period. |
| Tobacco Use and Help with Quitting Among Adolescents | The percentage of adolescents aged 12-20 years with a primary care visit during the measurement year for whom tobacco use status was documented and received help with quitting if identified as a tobacco user. |
| Weight Assessment and Counseling for Nutrition and Physical Activity for Children and Adolescents | Percentage of patients aged 3-17 years who had an outpatient visit with a primary care physician (PCP) or obstetrician/gynecologist (OB/GYN) and who had evidence of the following during the measurement period. Three rates are reported: 1. Percentage of patients with height, weight, and body mass index (BMI) percentile documentation. 2. Percentage of patients with counseling for nutrition. 3. Percentage of patients with counseling for physical activity. |

B. **Pediatric Measures List**—Community Care of North Carolina is a care-coordination organization administering the North Carolina Medicaid population, over half of whom are children. It developed measures specific to pediatric care that may be found at https://www.communitycarenc.org/quality-improvement/performance-measures/.

# PRIMARY CARE PHYSICIANS

I. **Why and How You May Want to Utilize Primary Care Physicians in Your CIN/ACO**

Any ACO strategy for any physician subspecialty begins with determining if there are high-impact, value-add contributions for patients they manage. Because primary care can impact all five of the high-impact target areas in population management—prevention, chronic care management, reduced hospitalizations, care transitions, and multispecialty coordination of complex patients—it is no wonder that internal medicine and the other primary care subspecialties are the only ones required by law to be included in all MSSP ACOs.

A. **Overview**

If primary care is in the "sweet spot," all the high-value areas for value-based care, what do you prioritize? An October 2014 study of high-performing ACOs found the following key attribute present: "All three organizations are building on past efforts to redesign and strengthen primary care."[226] Although there are unique attributes and strengths of each of the primary care sub-specialties, the commonalities predominate of opportunities for high-value contributions, and thus all primary strategies are collected in this chapter.

B. **The Primary Care Physician as PCMH Quarterback**

Primary care should head the Patient-Centered Medical Home to unleash its potential in the ACO setting. Unlike in fee-for-service, primary care's concerns now are *all* the patients attributed to you in your ACO's defined patient population(s), not just the ones presenting to your office. That population should be evaluated and stratified according to diagnosis and severity. As Figure 7-1 illustrates, separate ACO strategies unfold for each category of patient.

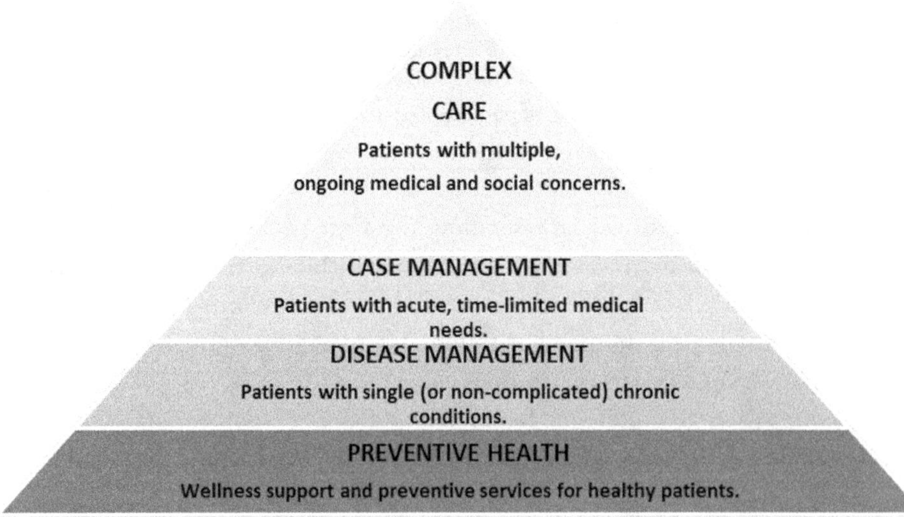

**COMPLEX CARE**
Patients with multiple, ongoing medical and social concerns.

**CASE MANAGEMENT**
Patients with acute, time-limited medical needs.

**DISEASE MANAGEMENT**
Patients with single (or non-complicated) chronic conditions.

**PREVENTIVE HEALTH**
Wellness support and preventive services for healthy patients.

**FIGURE 7-1.** Population Health Segmentation Strategies
*(California Quality Collaborative)*

Once the ACO provides the population stratification, the primary care physician and the PCMH team can create proactive care-management opportunities. Additional "face time" with patients during the initial visit pays dividends in compliance and rapport. Medication reconciliation and patient education and self-management tips can be introduced. One Workgroup member explained that this was a much more enjoyable way to practice. "Figure out what buttons to push for which patient and which resources to bring to them."

The high-risk complex patient receives special attention. Some others may be grouped for prevention/wellness/lifestyle management; some for management of their chronic diseases, and perhaps others for access to behavioral health, community health resources, transition management, or post-acute care management.

*Strategic Note:* Utilize "wellness visits" strategically. CMS reimburses for this smart value-building activity.[227] One Workgroup member in a large multispecialty, single tax identification number ACO commented that they have protocolized this population assessment methodology and found that it was also "a big source of revenue for us." Further, the CMS MSSP attribution calculations of assigning patients to the physician rendering the plurality of primary care services are notoriously fickle. The wellness visit is a good way to add a primary care "touch." Fee-for-service chronic care management and related codes also promote and compensate value-based care management by primary care. They are often a good on-ramp to promote behavior change and provide value-based care compensation to pay for ACO infrastructure costs.[228]

*Strategic Note:* Unleash the value of care coordinators. In the first several years of ACO operation, the high value of nurse care coordinators almost always catches the ACO by surprise. Once the patient population care-management plans have been determined, care coordinators usually play key roles. For example, one Workgroup member stated simply, "Figure out exactly what the patient's needs are and then pass that on to the care navigator. It could be as simple as helping the patient to stop eating Little Debbies at night."

Regardless of the care plan, the one-on-one staff reinforcement increases compliance and self-management substantially. Nurse navigators who follow up with a home visit or telephone call post-discharge have proven especially valuable in avoiding readmissions. Patients with chronic diseases are assigned care coordinators. The transition/coordination role for complex high-risk patient care is even higher.

One primary care ACO member estimated that the "ROI," or return on investment, for a nurse care coordinator is at least three-to-one. Another commented that the coordinators handled a lot of routine care, allowing the physician to practice at the top of his or her license and to actually increase fee-for-service compensation by being able to code for more severe and complex services. The Workgroup internists could not overemphasize the benefit of care coordinators.

- Disease Management. Many patients will be appropriate for disease management, such as for diabetes, congestive heart failure, asthma, and COPD.
- OK, but how do I know if our disease management protocol works? The more common protocols are publicly available. They should be collected and vetted by the Clinical Committee of the ACO, of which a primary care physician, preferably an internist, should be a member. For example, the nonprofit Community Care of North Carolina (CCNC) has honed disease management initiatives for a number of years and has posted them publicly, including:
  - Asthma Management
  - COPD
  - Diabetes Quality Initiative
  - Heart Failure Program
  - Pharmacy Initiative
  - Pregnancy Medical Home[229]
- Transition Management—Since the fee-for-service system is reactive, based on the patient self-selecting to see a physician or go to the emergency department, it is inevitable that effective transition management will be lacking when it comes to proactive coordination/transition/communication approach for patient transition among providers and facilities. The PCMH and the ACO's specialists can ameliorate this concern.

  One example is pre-operation evaluation and transition for a patient anticipating an inpatient procedure. Pre-anesthesia testing (PAT) coordination among primary care physicians, anesthesiologists, and surgeons has been shown to dramatically reduce the number of costly cancellations and the number of tests ordered.[230] It has been said that coordinating care across our fragmented system is the number one savings opportunity for ACOs. "The best bet for achieving returns from integration is to prioritize initiatives specifically targeting waste and inefficiency caused by fragmentation in today's delivery system, unnecessary spending allotted to substandard clinical coordination, aggravated by the complexity of navigating episodes of care, and unwanted variation in clinical outcomes driven by lack of adherence to best clinical practice."[231]

  *Strategic Note: Take advantage of transition support codes. As with wellness visits, CMS will* pay for certain care transition activities. CMS has figured out that the payback in improved care is well worth the investment. One ACO physician mentioned that coding for this ACO strategic value-add initiative resulted in over $250,000.00 per physician in increased Medicare payments in one year. One Workgroup member noted that her practice protocolized this process utilizing trained staffers. This greatly benefited their ACO population management, but also generated additional fee-for-service revenues. "We've used that money to expand our wellness and coordination programs," she said, "including hiring a nutritionist and more care navigators, and to expanding group education meetings."

The point is not the reimbursement, but that this is an intelligent incentivization to induce the right kind of population management behavior. Medicare has begun paying physicians and their staffs for 30 days of transition care management—the time spent following up with patients after their discharge from an inpatient hospital setting or nursing facility. It covers coordination as the patient transitions back into the home or assisted living environment. This service is covered by two new Current Procedure Terminology (CPT) Codes—99495 and 99496. They both require face-to-face visits after discharge, which do not have to be at the practice.

- Group Visits are Great—The Workgroup members strongly recommend group patient visits. One staffer can manage, and the benefits of patient engagement, self-management capability, medication reconciliations, and lifestyle improvement are "high impact," they report.

- Integrate with Behavioral Health—"Accountable care organizations (ACOs) may be well-positioned to increase the focus on managing behavioral health conditions . . . through integration of behavioral health treatment and primary care."[232] There is no clinical debate over the health delivery benefits of integrating mental and physical healthcare. As the National Alliance on Mental Illness puts it plainly in its family guide, *Integration of Mental Health and Primary Care*, "As individuals, we are not fragmented, we are whole people."[233] The separation has largely been driven by the checkered fee-for-service payment system and to a lesser degree, a lack of shared traditions. The ACO model finally removes the financial disincentives to work together.

> *"The ACO payment mechanism gives healthcare providers a new opportunity and incentives to rebuild the healthcare system in a way that reverses the separation between primary care and behavioral healthcare. . . . If ACOs can effectively integrate behavioral health services into their care and connect patients to these services, they can be better positioned to reach both cost and quality benchmarks."[234]*

The integration scheme will vary according to circumstances, but will develop along one of these general paths:

- Awareness—There is wide variance today in knowledge and awareness of potential synergies among the disciplines. Psychiatrists and internists can close the gap in an ACO by having joint planning and periodic "lunch-and-learn" sessions. Written protocols and guidelines can be developed.
- Four Models—ACOs incorporating primary care and behavioral health employed one of four models: (1) consulting; (2) co-location; (3) embedded; or (4) for Medicaid contracts with large disadvantaged populations, reverse integration (primary care physicians are integrated into existing behavioral health programs.[235] One psychiatrist practicing in an ACO environment commented that, "I participate in such a program and can attest to its effectiveness in three ways [medication management, earlier diagnosis, and identification and referral of severe mental disorders]. Almost all of my work is non-billable, but the ACO that employs me sees me as an important part of overall quality improvement and cost control."[236]

- Integrate with Community Resources—Dennis Weaver, MD, commented that, "At its most basic, population health means actively working to keep your community healthy. When you think about it that way, it makes you wonder, 'Who or what is influencing the health of individuals in my community the most?' To date, population healthcare strategy has focused mainly on the role healthcare providers themselves play as the main influencers of health outcomes. But the reality is that we are not the only ones influencing the health status of the people we serve . . . [Health] systems will need to engage with organizations that impact the health determinations in your community and influence individual's behavior when they're between provider visits."[237]

Many patients do not receive certain clinical preventive services, cannot access the medical system, and need help in self-management. Coordinating with external non-clinical organizations such as local health departments and community- and faith-based organizations can mitigate these problems. The MSSP requires ACOs to engage with community health resources. The benefits of such collaboration will be even more pronounced in inner-city and rural medically underserved areas. The Internal Medicine Accountable Care Workgroup recommends accessing the Agency on Aging for an inventory of available resources.

Remember, it is no longer just about the patient who shows up at your office, but your responsibility and opportunity now extend to your entire patient population. You can reach them so much better by integrating with community health resources. ACO president, Grace Terrell, MD, makes it clear: "Community partnerships MATTER MORE THAN

PRACTICALLY ANYTHING in the world of value-based care."[238] For more information, refer to the *Accountable Care Manual for Community Health Partners*, found at www.ncmedsoc.org/physician-resources/accountable-care/aco-toolkits.

- Utilize ED Avoidance Techniques—The gap analysis of a population's health as compared to the ideal invariably reveals overutilization of the emergency department (ED) for non-emergency services. Under pure fee-for-service, there are few adverse financial consequences for this, and it was a lot easier for providers to let this happen. Now, the ACO receives up to 50% of the savings through mitigation of inappropriate ED utilization. Simple measures have proven successful, such as extended hours, weekend hours, and walk-in urgent care clinics. A nurse triage "hotline" and embedded health professionals in the ED have also proven to be successful.

C. **Primary Care Physician as Complex Patient Care-Management Coach**
The level of coordination and transition management of complex high-risk patients is both one of the greatest failings of the fee-for-service system and one of the greatest opportunities under accountable care. These patients commonly comprise around 10% to 20% of the patient population yet consume 50% to 70% of the total costs (see Figure 7-2).

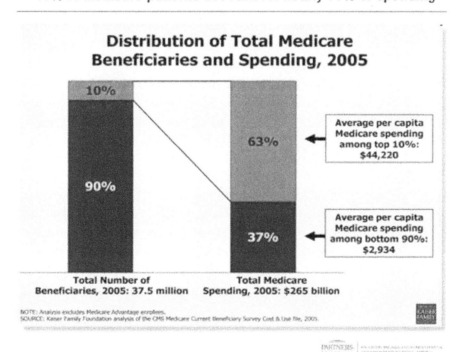

FIGURE 7-2. 10% of Medicare Patients Account for Nearly 70% of Spending

Because this management yields significant overall contributions to the Triple Aim, they are considered "low-hanging fruit" by ACOs. Primary care physicians are ideally suited to serve leadership roles in such efforts. They can be logical extensions of the PCMH concept with more intensity of multispecialty site-of-service coordination and care navigators/community outreach involvement.

The process begins with the aforementioned population stratification. Patients with certain diagnoses, severity of illnesses, and levels of resource utilization are assigned for structure intervention.

The October 2014 Commonwealth Fund study of common attributes of high-performing ACOs found the following:

> *"**Care management of patients with costly, complex needs.** All study sites have invested resources in deploying care managers, outreach workers, or virtual care teams to engage with and help improve outcomes for patients with complex needs or at risk of incurring high costs. All stress an individualized approach to identify and address unmet needs through in-person or telephone visits. For example, care teams that may include social workers as well as pharmacists and care coordinators have been deployed by urban safety-net clinics affiliated with Health Share and by Hill Physicians Medical Group to help address the psychosocial and clinical factors that play a role in improving patients' health and treatment adherence. Marshfield Clinic embedded nurse care coordinators in all its primary care clinics to help patients avoid unnecessary hospital use, with the expectation that shared savings would help fund this infrastructure. It subsequently discontinued the program because it was partially duplicating a service offered by its health plan and because the program's cost was not sustainable without support from other payers. The clinic retains a care-management program serving heart failure patients and is reconfiguring primary care teams to take over the care coordination responsibilities."[239]*

Other complex patient "best practices" of the high-performing ACOs revealed by the study included: (1) virtual care teams of pharmacists, social workers and case managers help primary care physicians manage the clinical and psychosocial needs of this population; (2) physicians are embedded in skilled nursing facilities to prevent avoidable hospital and emergency department admissions; (3) care-coordination nurses navigate care and provide individualized care management; and (4) nurses receive electronic alerts when patients visit an emergency department or are discharged.

One of our Accountable Care Workgroup members added that, "This is a much more enjoyable way to practice." Having navigators, nutritionists, mental health, and access to specialist input brings the right resources to the patient (and treating internist) at the right time and at the right place. Early and accurate intervention is enhanced, and offsite physical referral needs are diminished. Discharge planning and post-acute care coordination for these complex patients pay dividends. The skillsets of internists make them particularly suited to serve as team leaders. We are moving from fragmented care to team-oriented integrated care. Because of their concentration in adult medicine training, including particularly for elderly complex patients, primary care physicians are the most appropriate group to serve as a team leader who brings the disparate parts together.

*Strategic Note:* The better home health, rehab and skilled nursing providers can be identified, and made aware of the transition and coordination protocols. According to the Accountable Care Workgroup, they had no problem getting them onboard because, as one member noted, "They love the referrals." This is an example that the primary care physician, PCMH, and ACO can exercise value-based "narrow network" steering similar to those used by payers. Use your care coordinators to give you feedback on who are the best post-acute care providers.

*Strategic Note:* As noted, take advantage of chronic care-management codes. Eligible patients are those with multiple chronic conditions, often your identified high-risk patient. The assessment of medical, mental, and social needs care coordination and transition management should all be part of your ACO's high-risk patient management playbook.

### D. Reduced Unjustified Variability Against Best Practices

Primary care physicians in top practices are inevitably surprised with the variability in treatment approaches, outcomes, and costs for even common services, such as diabetes management. Population health shifts the culture from "I know I deliver high-quality care because I was well-trained," and the available scheduled time and memory of the physician; to standardized care following peer-vetted, clinically valid, evidence-based best practices.

An example of evidence-based best practices recommended by the American College of Physicians (ACP) may be found in the Choosing Wisely® Initiative:

- **Don't obtain screening exercise electrocardiogram testing in individuals who are asymptomatic and at low risk for coronary heart disease.** In asymptomatic individuals at low risk for coronary heart disease (10-year risk <10%) screening for coronary heart disease with exercise electrocardiography does not improve patient outcomes.

- **Don't obtain imaging studies in patients with nonspecific low back pain.** In patients with back pain that cannot be attributed to a specific disease or spinal abnormality following a history and physical examination (*e.g.*, nonspecific low back pain), imaging with plain radiography, computed tomography (CT) scan, or magnetic resonance imaging (MRI) does not improve patient outcomes.

- **In the evaluation of simple syncope and a normal neurological examination, don't obtain brain imaging studies (CT or MRI).** In patients with witnessed syncope but with no suggestion of seizure and no report of other neurologic symptoms or signs, the likelihood of a central nervous system (CNS) cause of the event is extremely low and patient outcomes are not improved with brain imaging studies.

- **In patients with low pretest probability of venous thromboembolism (VTE), obtain a high-sensitive D-dimer measurement as the initial diagnostic test; don't obtain imaging studies as the initial diagnostic test.** In patients with low pretest probability of VTE as defined by the Wells prediction rules, a negative high-sensitivity D-dimer measurement effectively excludes VTE and the need for further imaging studies.

- **Don't obtain preoperative chest radiography in the absence of a clinical suspicion for intrathoracic pathology imaging studies.**

- **Don't obtain preoperative chest radiography in the absence of a clinical suspicion for intrathoracic pathology.** In the absence of cardiopulmonary symptoms, preoperative chest radiography rarely provides any meaningful changes in management or improved patient outcomes.

Another example may be found in the following list published on the ACP website:

- **Non-surgical Management of Urinary Incontinence in Women.** Urinary incontinence contributes to high medical spending in the United States. Approximately $19.5 billion was spent on UI care in 2004, and UI accounts for 6% of nursing home admissions for elderly women, costing around $3 billion. Physicians should utilize non-drug treatments as much as possible for UI. Kegel exercises for stress UI, bladder training for urgency UI, and Kegel exercises with bladder training for mixed UI are effective, have few side effects, and are less expensive than medications. Although various drugs can improve UI and provide complete continence, adverse effects often lead many patients to stop taking their medication.

- **Diagnosis of Obstructive Sleep Apnea in Adults.** Prior to diagnosis, patients with obstructive sleep apnea (OSA) have higher rates of healthcare use, more frequent and longer hospital stays, and greater healthcare costs than after diagnosis. Assessing patients for OSA in the absence of daytime sleepiness or treating individuals with low apnea-hypopnea index (AHI) scores is low-value care because the evidence indicated that it does not improve clinical outcomes.

- **Screening Pelvic Examination in Adult Women.** Screening pelvic examination exposes adult, asymptomatic, average risk, non-pregnant women to unnecessary and avoidable harms, including anxiety, embarrassment, and discomfort, and may even prevent some women from getting needed medical care. False positive findings can lead to unnecessary tests or procedures, adding additional unnecessary costs to the healthcare system.

- **Treatment of Anemia in Patients with Heart Disease.** Current evidence does not support the benefit of liberal blood transfusions in patients with asymptomatic anemia and heart disease. Therefore, ACP does not support the liberal use of blood transfusions in the management of mild to moderate anemia in patients with cardiovascular disease. The probability that transfusion may be beneficial is higher in patients with lower hemoglobin levels (<7 g/dL) and lower in less anemic patients (hemoglobin >10 g/dL) (67). ACP does not support the use of ESAs for treating patients with mild to moderate anemia and heart disease because the harms outweigh the benefits for these patients.

- **Screening, Monitoring, and Treatment of Stage 1-3 Chronic Kidney Disease.** ACP found no evidence that screening for chronic kidney disease in patients without risk factors improves clinical outcomes. In the absence of any known benefits, ordering screening laboratory studies is not going to have any impact on the clinical outcomes of the patient and will add unnecessary costs to the healthcare system due to increased medical visits and unnecessary tests.

- **Obstructive Sleep Apnea.** Physicians should stress the importance of compliance with treatments, especially CPAP. Doctors should weigh patient preferences and the likelihood of therapy adherence against costs before initiating CPAP.

- **Inpatient Glycemic Control.** High blood glucose is associated with poor outcomes in hospitalized patients and use of intensive insulin therapy (IIT) to control hyperglycemia is a common practice in hospitals. But the recent evidence does not show a consistent benefit and even shows harms associated with the use of IIT.

- **Screening for Prostate Cancer.** Men between the ages of 50 and 69 should discuss the limited benefits and substantial harms of the prostate-specific antigen test with their doctor before undergoing screening for prostate cancer.

- **Diagnostic Imaging for Low Back Pain.** [See Choosing Wisely® list above.]

- **Oral Pharmacologic Treatment of Type 2 Diabetes Mellitus.** On the basis of the evidence reviewed in this paper, ACP has found strong evidence that in most patients with Type 2 diabetes in whom lifestyle modifications have failed to adequately improve hyperglycemia, oral pharmacologic therapy with metformin (unless contraindicated) is an effective management strategy. It is cheaper than most other pharmacologic agents, has better effectiveness, and is associated with fewer adverse effects; of note, it does not result in weight gain.

- **Screening for Colorectal Cancer.** Currently, no evidence shows that screening more frequently than recommended improves patient outcomes or reduces cancer-related deaths. On the other hand, screening more frequently than recommended can contribute substantially to avoidable healthcare costs.

- **Upper Endoscopy for Gastroesophageal Reflux Disease.** Upper endoscopy is commonly used in the diagnosis and management of gastroesophageal reflux disease (GERD). Evidence demonstrates that it is indicated only in certain situations and inappropriate use generates unnecessary costs and exposes patients to harm without improving outcomes.

E. **Other**—Please see *The Accountable Care Manual for Internal Medicine*, which may be downloaded at www.ncmedsoc.org/physician-resources/accountable-care/aco-toolkits.

F. **PCSP Standards**—The NCQA Patient-Centered Specialty Practice standards regarding care team and patient coordination are recommended generally for all specialists, including internists.

II. **Metrics**

A. **Overview**—After determining the initiatives involving this specialty that are most appropriate for your CIN/ACO, to incentivize the desired behavior and outcomes, it is recommended that clinically valid metrics track adherence to the chosen activities and accomplishment of the desired results. Starting with the MSSP and MACRA Quality Payment Program measures (Table 7-21), use the available array of measures from various sources as a "menu" from which to start, and then tailor, prioritize, and weight them to fit your incentivization goals.

**TABLE 7-21.** MACRA'S Quality Payment Program MIPS
Measures Relevant to Primary Care Medicine

| MEASURE NAME | MEASURE DESCRIPTION |
| --- | --- |
| Adult Sinusitis: Antibiotic Prescribed for Acute Sinusitis (Overuse) | Percentage of patients, aged 18 years and older, with a diagnosis of acute sinusitis who were prescribed an antibiotic within 10 days after onset of symptoms. |
| Adult Sinusitis: Appropriate Choice of Antibiotic: Amoxicillin with or Without Clavulanate Prescribed for Patients with Acute Bacterial Sinusitis (Appropriate Use) | Percentage of patients aged 18 years and older with a diagnosis of acute bacterial sinusitis that were prescribed amoxicillin, with or without clavulanate, as a first-line antibiotic at the time of diagnosis. |

**TABLE 7-21.** MACRA's Quality Payment Program MIPS Measures
Relevant to Primary Care Medicine (continued)

| MEASURE NAME | MEASURE DESCRIPTION |
|---|---|
| Adult Sinusitis: Computerized Tomography (CT) for Acute Sinusitis (Overuse) | Percentage of patients aged 18 years and older, with a diagnosis of acute sinusitis who had a computerized tomography (CT) scan of the paranasal sinuses ordered at the time of diagnosis or received within 28 days after date of diagnosis. |
| Adult Sinusitis: More than One Computerized Tomography (CT) Scan Within 90 Days for Chronic Sinusitis (Overuse) | Percentage of patients aged 18 years and older with a diagnosis of chronic sinusitis who had more than one CT scan of the paranasal sinuses ordered or received within 90 days after the date of diagnosis. |
| Annual Hepatitis C Virus (HCV) Screening for Patients who are Active Injection Drug Users | Percentage of patients, regardless of age, who are active injection drug users who received screening for HCV infection within the 12-month reporting period. |
| Anti-Depressant Medication Management | Percentage of patients aged 18 years and older who were treated with anti-depressant medication, had a diagnosis of major depression, and who remained on an anti-depressant medication treatment. Two rates are reported. a. Percentage of patients who remained on an anti-depressant medication for at least 84 days (12 weeks). b. Percentage of patients who remained on an anti-depressant medication for at least 180 days (6 months). |
| Atrial Fibrillation and Atrial Flutter: Chronic Anticoagulation Therapy | Percentage of patients aged 18 years and older with a diagnosis of nonvalvular atrial fibrillation (AF) or atrial flutter whose assessment of the specified thromboembolic risk factors indicate one or more high-risk factors or more than one moderate risk factor, as determined by CHADS2 risk stratification, who are prescribed warfarin OR another oral anticoagulant drug that is FDA approved for the prevention of thromboembolism. |
| Avoidance of Antibiotic Treatment in Adults with Acute Bronchitis | The percentage of adults aged 18-64 years with a diagnosis of acute bronchitis who were not dispensed an antibiotic prescription. |
| Breast Cancer Screening | Percentage of women aged 50-74 years who had a mammogram to screen for breast cancer. |
| Care Plan | Percentage of patients aged 65 years and older who have an advance care plan or surrogate decision maker documented in the medical record or documentation in the medical record that an advance care plan was discussed but the patient did not wish or was not able to name a surrogate decision maker or provide an advance care plan. |
| Colorectal Cancer Screening | Percentage of adults aged 50-75 years who had appropriate screening for colorectal cancer. |
| Controlling High Blood Pressure | Percentage of patients aged 18-85 years who had a diagnosis of hypertension and whose blood pressure was adequately controlled (<140/90mmHg) during the measurement period. |

*Continued on next page*

**TABLE 7-21.** MACRA'S Quality Payment Program MIPS Measures
Relevant to Primary Care Medicine (continued)

| MEASURE NAME | MEASURE DESCRIPTION |
|---|---|
| Diabetes: Eye Exam | Percentage of patients aged 18-75 years with diabetes who had a retinal or dilated eye exam by an eye care professional during the measurement period or a negative retinal exam (no evidence of retinopathy) in the 12 months prior to the measurement period. |
| Diabetes: Foot Exam | The percentage of patients aged 18-75 years with diabetes (type 1 and type 2) who received a foot exam (visual inspection and sensory exam with mono filament and a pulse exam) during the measurement year. |
| Diabetes: Hemoglobin A1c (HbA1c) Poor Control (>9%) | Percentage of patients aged 18-75 years with diabetes who had hemoglobin A1c > 9.0% during the measurement period. |
| Documentation of Current Medications in the Medical Record | Percentage of visits for patients aged 18 years and older for which the eligible professional attests to documenting a list of current medications using all immediate resources available on the date of the encounter. This list must include ALL known prescriptions, over-the-counters, herbals, and vitamin/mineral/dietary (nutritional) supplements AND must contain the medications' name, dosage, frequency and route of administration. |
| Documentation of Signed Opioid Treatment Agreement | All patients aged 18 and older prescribed opiates for longer than six weeks duration who signed an opioid treatment agreement at least once during Opioid Therapy documented in the medical record. |
| Elder Maltreatment Screen and Follow-Up Plan | Percentage of patients aged 65 years and older with a documented elder maltreatment screen using an Elder Maltreatment Screening tool on the date of encounter AND a documented follow-up plan on the date of the positive screen. |
| Evaluation or Interview for Risk of Opioid Misuse | All patients 18 and older prescribed opiates for longer than six weeks duration evaluated for risk of opioid misuse using a brief validated instrument (e.g. Opioid Risk Tool, SOAPP-R) or patient interview documented at least once during Opioid Therapy in the medical record. |
| Falls: Plan of Care | Percentage of patients aged 65 years and older with a history of falls that had a plan of care for falls documented within 12 months. |
| Falls: Risk Assessment | Percentage of patients aged 65 years and older with a history of falls that had a risk assessment for falls completed within 12 months. |
| Heart Failure (HF): Angiotensin-Converting Enzyme (ACE) Inhibitor or Angiotensin Receptor Blocker (ARB) Therapy for Left Ventricular Systolic Dysfunction (LVSD) | Percentage of patients aged 18 years and older with a diagnosis of heart failure (HF) with a current or prior left ventricular ejection fraction (LVEF) < 40% who were prescribed ACE inhibitor or ARB therapy either within a 12-month period when seen in the outpatient setting OR at each hospital discharge. |

**TABLE 7-21.** MACRA'S Quality Payment Program MIPS Measures
Relevant to Primary Care Medicine (continued)

| MEASURE NAME | MEASURE DESCRIPTION |
|---|---|
| Hepatitis C: Screening for Hepatocellular Carcinoma (HCC) in Patients with Cirrhosis | Percentage of patients aged 18 years and older with a diagnosis of chronic hepatitis C cirrhosis who underwent imaging with either ultrasound, contrast enhanced CT or MRI for hepatocellular carcinoma (HCC) at least once within the 12-month reporting period. |
| Ischemic Vascular Disease (IVD): Use of Aspirin or Another Antiplatelet | Percentage of patients aged 18 years and older who were diagnosed with acute myocardial infarction (AMI), coronary artery bypass graft (CABG) or percutaneous coronary interventions (PCI) in the 12 months prior to the measurement period, or who had an active diagnosis of ischemic vascular disease (IVD) during the measurement period, and who had documentation of use of aspirin or another antiplatelet during the measurement period. |
| One-Time Screening for Hepatitis C Virus (HCV) for Patients at Risk | Percentage of patients aged 18 years and older with one or more of the following: a history of injection drug use, receipt of a blood transfusion prior to 1992, receiving maintenance hemodialysis, OR birthdate in the years 1945-1965 who received one-time screening for hepatitis C virus (HCV) infection. |
| Opioid Therapy Follow-up Evaluation | All patients aged 18 and older prescribed opiates for longer than six weeks duration who had a follow-up evaluation conducted at least every three months during opioid therapy documented in the medical record. |
| Osteoarthritis (OA): Function and Pain Assessment | Percentage of patient visits for patients aged 21 years and older with a diagnosis of osteoarthritis (OA) with assessment for function and pain. |
| Osteoporosis Management in Women Who Had a Fracture | The percentage of women aged 50-85 years who suffered a fracture and who either had a bone mineral density test or received a prescription for a drug to treat osteoporosis in the six months after the fracture. |
| Preventive Care and Screening: Body Mass Index (BMI) Screening and Follow-Up Plan | Percentage of patients aged 18 years and older with a BMI documented during the current encounter or during the previous six months AND with a BMI outside of normal parameters, a follow-up plan is documented during the encounter or during the previous six months of the current encounter. Normal Parameters: Age 18 years and older BMI $\geq$ 18.5 and < 25 kg/m$^2$. |
| Preventive Care and Screening: Influenza Immunization | Percentage of patients aged 6 months and older seen for a visit between October 1 and March 31 who received an influenza immunization OR who reported previous receipt of an influenza immunization. |

*Continued on next page*

**TABLE 7-21.** MACRA'S Quality Payment Program MIPS Measures
Relevant to Primary Care Medicine (continued)

| MEASURE NAME | MEASURE DESCRIPTION |
|---|---|
| Preventive Care and Screening: Screening for Clinical Depression and Follow-Up Plan | Percentage of patients aged 12 years and older screened for depression on the date of the encounter using an age-appropriate standardized depression screening tool AND if positive, a follow-up plan is documented on the date of the positive screen. |
| Preventive Care and Screening: Screening for High Blood Pressure and Follow-Up Documented | Percentage of patients aged 18 years and older seen during the reporting period who were screened for high blood pressure AND a recommended follow-up plan is documented based on the current blood pressure (BP) reading as indicated. |
| Preventive Care and Screening: Tobacco Use: Screening and Cessation Intervention | Percentage of patients aged 18 years and older who were screened for tobacco use one or more times within 24 months AND who received cessation counseling intervention if identified as a tobacco user. |
| Preventive Care and Screening: Unhealthy Alcohol Use: Screening & Brief Counseling | Percentage of patients aged 18 years and older who were screened for unhealthy alcohol use using a systematic screening method at least once within the last 24 months AND who received brief counseling if identified as an unhealthy alcohol user. |
| Statin Therapy for the Prevention and Treatment of Cardiovascular Disease | Percentage of the following patients-all considered at high risk of cardiovascular events-who were prescribed or were on statin therapy during the measurement period: Adults aged ≥ 21 years who were previously diagnosed with or currently have an active diagnosis of clinical atherosclerotic cardiovascular disease (ASCVD); OR Adults aged ≥21 years who have ever had a fasting or direct low-density lipoprotein cholesterol (LDL-C) level ≥ 190 mg/dL or were previously diagnosed with or currently have an active diagnosis of familial or pure hypercholesterolemia; OR Adults aged 40-75 years with a diagnosis of diabetes with a fasting or direct LDL-C level of 70-189 mg/dL |
| Tobacco Use and Help with Quitting Among Adolescents | The percentage of adolescents aged 12- 20 years with a primary care visit during the measurement year for whom tobacco use status was documented and received help with quitting if identified as a tobacco user. |
| Urinary Incontinence: Plan of Care for Urinary Incontinence in Women Aged 65 Years and Older | Percentage of female patients aged 65 years and older with a diagnosis of urinary incontinence with a documented plan of care for urinary incontinence at least once within 12 months. |

# PSYCHIATRISTS

I.   **Why and How You May Want to Utilize Psychiatrists in Your CIN/ACO**
    A.  **Background: Psychiatry's Potential to Add Value**
        1.  **Psychiatric Illness as a Co-Morbidity**—The inclusion of the psychiatrist in the ACO team follows from the data about the prevalence of psychiatric disease and psychiatric co-morbidity with other illness, most commonly cardiorespiratory and metabolic disease. National Institute of Mental Health data states that one-quarter of adults suffer from a psychiatric illness in a given year and that some of these illnesses begin in childhood and adolescence. A Robert Wood Johnson synthesis of the data finds that co-morbidity "is the rule rather than the exception" in high-cost cases.[240]

            Studies have found that when asthma, cardiovascular disease, and diabetes have co-morbid psychiatric and substance abuse diagnoses, the cost of such care can double or triple, and the ability to deliver quality clinical outcomes is compromised. Data about post myocardial infarction (MI) deaths routinely show mortality is increased with co-morbid clinical depression.[241]

            In current primary care settings, the majority of care visits are due to psychosocial issues. Patients may present with "physical" complaints, but they are triggered by mental health or substance abuse conditions. The ACO approach accepts the premise that treatment for general physical care must be integrated with mental health and substance abuse treatment by a team that embraces the care of the whole person.[242]

            There are many studies that show the benefit of psychiatric involvement in specific populations in the primary care setting, most notably depression, and this is achieved through collaborative care. These results are found within several current collaborative care models such as the IMPACT Model, MacArthur Foundation approach, and the Respect Model. The work of the psychiatrist covers a range of activities from direct provider to supervisor to teacher. Additional information can be found at http://impact-uw.org.

        2.  **Select Most Appropriate Collaborative Care Model**—There are several examples of ways in which psychiatry can be involved in collaborative care.

            **Stepped Care (from IMPACT Model of Collaborative Care)**[243]— Psychiatrists can serve as part of a team that includes primary care physicians and care managers. Treatment can be adjusted based on clinical outcomes and according to an evidence-based algorithm.
            - Aim for a 50% reduction in symptoms within 10-12 weeks.
            - If patient is not significantly improved at 10-12 weeks after the start of a treatment plan, change the plan. The change can be an increase in medication dosage, a change to a different medication, addition of

psychotherapy, a combination of medication and psychotherapy, or other treatments suggested by the team psychiatrist.

**Systematic Screening for Psychiatric Illness in Primary Care—** Psychiatrist can help to develop a screening program in the primary care setting with use of evidence-based tools.

- Depression screening as part of routine primary care practice—Evidence basis for use of PHQ-9 as part of systematic focus on screening for depression with subsequent algorithm for intervention.
- Substance abuse screening as part of routine primary care practice.
- Screening for depression in high-risk groups—post-MI, post stroke, Diabetes Mellitus—Evidence that risk for depression is higher in these populations and outcomes can be improved with adequate intervention.

**Development of Treatment Guidelines Based on Primary Care Population Statistics,** including, but not limited to the following:

- Guidelines for treatment of common psychiatric disorders within primary care practices such as anxiety, depression, attention-deficit disorders.
- Guidelines for the process of referral to specialty psychiatric resources, including substance abuse facilities, when it is no longer appropriate to treat complex disorders in whole or in part within the primary care practice.
- Primary care practices with high utilization of atypical antipsychotics— make sure use is appropriate to diagnosis and alternatives are utilized when indicated.
- Guidelines for choosing the most cost-effective and clinically appropriate medication based on patient profile.

Choosing Wisely®, an initiative of the American Board of Internal Medicine (ABIM) Foundation, is a resource "to help physicians and patients engage in conversations to reduce overuse of tests and procedures, and support physician efforts to help patients make smart and effective care choices." (http://www.abimfoundation.org/Initiatives/Choosing-Wisely.aspx.)

The recommendations of the American Psychiatric Association to the Choosing Wisely® initiative can be accessed at: http://www.choosingwisely. org/doctor-patient-lists/american-psychiatric-association/. They include, among other suggestions, rethinking the use of atypical antipsychotics as a first-line intervention for insomnia in adults.

**Access to Psychiatric Care**

- Develop close relationships between psychiatry and primary care, including onsite collaboration, phone consultation and availability, and office-based consultation with referral back to primary care for ongoing management.

- Telepsychiatry is a medium to increase psychiatric access, especially in rural settings, but has applicability across settings.

**B. Other**—Please see *The Accountable Care Manual for Psychiatrists*, which may be downloaded at www.ncmedsoc.org/physician-resources/accountable-care/aco-toolkits.

**C. PCSP Standards**—The NCQA Patient-Centered Specialty Practice standards regarding care team and patient coordination are recommended generally for all specialists, including psychiatrists.

## II. Metrics

**A. Overview**—After determining the initiatives involving this specialty that are most appropriate for your CIN/ACO, to incentivize the desired behavior and outcomes, it is recommended that clinically valid metrics track adherence to the chosen activities and accomplishment of the desired results. Use the available array of measures from various sources as a "menu" from which to start, and then tailor, prioritize, and weight them to fit your incentivization goals (see Table 7-22).

**TABLE 7-22.** MACRA's Quality Payment Program MIPS Measures Relevant to Psychiatry

| MEASURE NAME | MEASURE DESCRIPTION |
|---|---|
| ADHD: Follow-Up Care for Children Prescribed Attention-Deficit/ Hyperactivity Disorder (ADHD) Medication | Percentage of children 6-12 years of age and newly dispensed a medication for attention-deficit/hyperactivity disorder (ADHD) who had appropriate follow-up care. Two rates are reported: 1. Percentage of children who had one follow-up visit with a practitioner with prescribing authority during the 30-Day Initiation Phase. 2. Percentage of children who remained on ADHD medication for at least 210 days and who, in addition to the visit in the Initiation Phase, had at least two additional follow-up visits with a practitioner within 270 days (9 months) after the Initiation Phase ended. |
| Adherence to Antipsychotic Medications for Individuals with Schizophrenia | Percentage of individuals at least 18 years of age as of the beginning of the measurement period with schizophrenia or schizoaffective disorder who had at least two prescriptions filled for any antipsychotic medication and who had a Proportion of Days Covered (PDC) of at least 0.8 for antipsychotic medications during the measurement period (12 consecutive months). |
| Adult Major Depressive Disorder (MDD): Coordination of Care of Patients with Specific Co-morbid Conditions | Percentage of medical records of patients aged 18 years and older with a diagnosis of major depressive disorder (MDD) and a specific diagnosed co-morbid condition (diabetes, coronary artery disease, ischemic stroke, intracranial hemorrhage, chronic kidney disease [stages 4 or 5], End-Stage Renal Disease [ESRD] or congestive heart failure) being treated by another clinician with communication to the clinician treating the co-morbid condition. |
| Care Plan | Percentage of patients aged 65 years and older who have an advance care plan or surrogate decision maker documented in the medical record or documentation in the medical record that an advance care plan was discussed but the patient did not wish or was not able to name a surrogate decision maker or provide an advance care plan. |

*Continued on next page*

**TABLE 7-22.** MACRA's Quality Payment Program MIPS
Measures Relevant to Psychiatry (continued)

| MEASURE NAME | MEASURE DESCRIPTION |
|---|---|
| Depression Remission at Six Months | Adult patients age 18 years and older with major depression or dysthymia and an initial PHQ-9 score > 9 who demonstrate remission at six months defined as a PHQ-9 score less than 5. This measure applies to both patients with newly diagnosed and existing depression who's current PHQ-9 score indicates a need for treatment. This measure additionally promotes ongoing contact between the patient and provider as patients who do not have a follow-up PHQ-9 score at six months (+/− 30 days) are also included in the denominator. |
| Depression Remission at Twelve Months | Patients age 18 and older with major depression or dysthymia and an initial Patient Health Questionnaire (PHQ-9) score greater than nine who demonstrate remission at twelve months (+/− 30 days after an index visit) defined as a PHQ-9 score less than five. This measure applies to both patients with newly diagnosed and existing depression who's current PHQ-9 score indicates a need for treatment. |
| Depression Utilization of the PHQ-9 Tool | Patients age 18 and older with the diagnosis of major depression or dysthymia who have a Patient Health Questionnaire (PHQ-9) tool administered at least once during a 4-month period in which there was a qualifying visit |
| Documentation of Current Medications in the Medical Record | Percentage of visits for patients aged 18 years and older for which the eligible professional attests to documenting a list of current medications using all immediate resources available on the date of the encounter. This list must include ALL known prescriptions, over-the-counters, herbals, and vitamin/mineral/dietary (nutritional) supplements AND must contain the medications' name, dosage, frequency and route of administration. |
| Follow-Up After Hospitalization for Mental Illness (FUH) | The percentage of discharges for patients 6 years of age and older who were hospitalized for treatment of selected mental illness diagnoses and who had an outpatient visit, an intensive outpatient encounter or partial hospitalization with a mental health practitioner. Two rates are reported: The percentage of discharges for which the patient received follow-up within 30 days of discharge. The percentage of discharges for which the patient received follow-up within 7 days of discharge. |
| Preventive Care and Screening: Screening for Clinical Depression and Follow-Up Plan | Percentage of patients aged 12 years and older screened for depression on the date of the encounter using an age-appropriate standardized depression screening tool AND if positive, a follow-up plan is documented on the date of the positive screen. |

# PULMONOLOGISTS

I.  **Why and How You May Want to Utilize Pulmonologists in Your CIN/ACO**

- With pulmonologist's (1) diagnostic skills, (2) experience balancing multiple medical concerns and competing co-morbid conditions, and (3) experience leading interdisciplinary teams, they bring helpful skillsets to successful ACO population management.

- With pulmonary diseases imposing significant and growing economic burden on the U.S. healthcare system, a pulmonologist's specialized expertise is critical to improving under-diagnosis and for developing options that reduce deleterious and costly exacerbations.

- The ability to access an ACO's electronic data registry places pulmonologists in position to be an ACO's early warning system and care coordinator, especially for patients with chronic obstructive pulmonary disease (COPD).

- Pulmonologists can use their experience in chronic care management to drive significant outcome improvements and reduce population costs in accountable care.

A.  **Accurate Diagnosis of Chronic Obstructive Pulmonary Disease**—For pulmonologists, the "low-hanging fruit" and the area where the practice can make the greatest impact is in how it addresses management of COPD of a population. COPD is a progressive disease impacting over 11 million Americans.[244] The disease is frequently untreated until later stages of progression, and was classified (along with the larger grouping of chronic lower respiratory diseases) as the third-leading cause of death in the United States in 2013.[245] As an irreversible, progressive disease, frequently found with multiple co-morbidities (common culprits including heart disease, diabetes, and depression), effective treatment of COPD is predicated on an accurate diagnosis followed by appropriate disease management.

Despite its widespread prevalence, COPD is under-diagnosed. Results from a 2000 Centers for Disease Control and Prevention (CDC) report indicate that roughly 24 million people appeared to have COPD, but the disease was only diagnosed in about half of them.[246] However, over-diagnosis is a concern as well; there can be multiple reasons for shortness of breath. Input from pulmonologists will enable the ACO to appropriately identify patients within the early stages of COPD to optimize outcomes.

For example, family physicians often rely on symptoms and chest x-rays to make a COPD diagnosis whereas studies have demonstrated that spirometry services can be incorporated into family medicine practice with acceptable levels of technical adequacy and accurate interpretation that the results influence management of patients previously diagnosed with COPD.[247]

As expressed by the Workgroup, spirometry is essential for both diagnosis and for determining the severity of disease. As the gold standard for diagnosing COPD, the use of spirometers are not as common as they should be in primary care physician offices.[248] The prevalence of COPD and its role in driving avoidable healthcare costs means that practicing physicians have much to gain by adopting strategies for properly diagnosing and developing effective interventions for this chronic disease.[249]

B. **Coordination and Collaboration with the Primary Care Team**—Larger market forces and regulatory policy actions are encouraging team approaches to primary care, which can be helpful in addressing chronic health conditions. Effective treatment of pulmonary diseases is predicated on management. There are opportunities for pulmonologists to contribute to better primary care for patients managing certain diseases which may manifest in certain lung-related issues or problems.

With a pulmonologist working in a systemized care approach with the primary care provider as part of an ACO, early and accurate intervention is enhanced, and offsite physical referral needs are diminished. Discharge planning and post-acute care coordination for these complex patients pay dividends. As pointed out by a member of the TAC Consortium Physician Advisory Committee, care coordination in transitions of care from the hospital to the home setting is a crucial component of decreasing the risk of readmission. As this is already the way pulmonologists practice themselves, the ACO provides the opportunity to remove some of the frustrations many pulmonologists expressed in terms of the "too many handoffs" of a patient, leading to duplicative processes and missed opportunities.

C. **Use of Best Practices**—Core best practices are articulated within guidelines, classification, and statements provided by the Global Initiative for Chronic Obstructive Lung Disease (GOLD), the American Thoracic Society (ATS), the European Respiratory Society (ERS), and the American College of Chest Physicians (CHEST). An example of a useful source of core best practices provided below may be found in the recommendations of the American College of Chest Physicians and American Thoracic Society to the Choosing Wisely® program sponsored by the ABIM Foundation:

1. "Don't perform computed tomography (CT) surveillance for evaluation of indeterminate pulmonary nodules at more frequent intervals or for a longer period of time than recommended by established guidelines.

2. Don't routinely order imaging tests for patients without symptoms or signs of significant lung disease. Don't routinely offer pharmacologic treatment with advanced vasoactive agents approved only for the management of pulmonary arterial hypertension to patients with pulmonary hypertension resulting from left heart disease or hypoxemic lung diseases (Groups II or III pulmonary hypertension).

3. For patients recently discharged on supplemental home oxygen following hospitalization for an acute illness, don't renew the prescription without assessing the patient for ongoing hypoxemia.

4. Don't perform chest computed tomography (CT angiography) to evaluate for possible pulmonary embolism in patients with a low clinical probability and negative results of a highly sensitive D-dimer assay.

5. Don't perform CT screening for lung cancer among patients at low risk for lung cancer."

Additionally, in a U.S. Preventive Services Task Force special communication, the Task Force concluded with moderate certainty that screening for COPD in asymptomatic persons has no net benefit and therefore recommended against such screening in such patients. The recommendation was based on the evidence of both the benefits and harms of the service and an assessment of balance without considering the costs of providing the service. The special communication included a recognition that clinical decisions involve more consideration than evidence alone and therefore prompts clinicians to understand the evidence but to individualize decisions to the specific patient or situation.[250]

**D. Patient and Family Education and Communication**—The quality and integrity of long-term care for chronic illnesses such as COPD depends on a patient's informed participation and the ability to articulate priorities and decisions in advance of crisis events. Allowing patients to be part of the care plan development helps ensure their ongoing engagement and investment in their healthcare needs. In addition, patient adherence to a care plan and self-management help drive down healthcare costs.

Patient-centered care also emphasizes patient and family education as a means of achieving patient-centered goals of care and preventing unnecessary or unwanted care. The ACO model provides opportunities for pulmonologists to receive greater institutional support and recognition for their contribution in helping patients articulate their health goals and priorities. Providers can initiate and/or facilitate these sometimes-challenging, time-consuming, and yet vital discussions around goals of care.

A continuum of self-management for COPD patients provided by a trained health professional can significantly reduce the utilization of healthcare services and improve health status.[251] This approach to care can be implemented within normal practice.

In COPD, as in any chronic disease, day-to-day care responsibilities fall most heavily on patients and their families. Interventions to improve outcomes of chronic disease and/or reduce hospital readmissions have been developed on the basis of self-management principles.[252] One study showed that patients with COPD who received an education intervention with supervision and support based on disease-specific self-management principles had a better outcome than the usual care group with respect to hospital admissions, emergency department and unscheduled family physician visits, and health-related quality of life. These differences, especially those on healthcare utilization, are important and worth considering. These benefits to the health system could potentially add to the patients' quality of life by avoiding institutionalization.[253]

E. **Drug Management**—Use of best practices and effectiveness evidence in determining the best drug for treatment may lead to cost reductions. Medication adherence by patients and effective internal protocols within a provider system to ensure safety and optimization of pharmaceuticals. An ACO's use of pulmonologists will likely have an impact on prescribing trends as payers and providers alike see chronic lung disorders as a treatment arena ripe for improvements in both cost savings and health outcomes. Your ACO can create an environment where the pulmonologists are more conscious of long-term consequences of each prescribing decision by linking their reimbursement to the achievement of goals such as reducing hospital admissions as well as saving on prescription drug costs. Appropriate management requires a recognition that the prescription and use of more medications earlier in the course of treatment may lead to fewer hospitalizations.

F. **Optimize Site-of-Service**—Providers are encouraged to move procedures to lower-cost facilities or outpatient sites when consistent with best practices. Particular opportunity exists for providing alternatives to the emergency department, which has a pronounced patient engagement aspect. For example, the cost for treatment or maintenance of pulmonary disease with an emergency department as the first option is expensive to the system and often provides less optimal results than if the patient is seen in the pulmonologists' office. One way this can be accomplished is by offering after-hours access for patients to avoid potentially unnecessary emergency department use. Additionally, pulmonologists should focus on avoiding expensive in-hospital procedures when the same procedure can be done in a less-expensive setting with the same or better-quality outcomes, such as a physician's office or ambulatory surgical center.

G. **Use of Telehealth**—With the multitude of telehealth technology options entering the market, pulmonologists may find the use of telehealth technology to increase access to care and improve the patient experience. Telemedicine possibilities for patients with COPD include medical consultations, in-home patient monitoring, and remote rehabilitation. Teleconsultations have been used successfully, saving time and travel costs for patients, with only a few subsequently requiring face-to-face visits. Despite many reports, the impact of telemonitoring on the detection of exacerbations, reductions in healthcare utilization, and cost savings is equivocal. As emerging evidence from preliminary trials of tele-rehabilitation for the pulmonary patient is encouraging, it may represent a useful tool for increasing access and building capacity, especially in remote areas.[254]

Broad functions of telehealth interventions for COPD include the ability to:

- Monitor vital signs or biological health data (*e.g.*, oxygen saturation).
- Monitor symptoms, medication, or other non-biologic endpoints (*e.g.*, exercise adherence).
- Provide information (education) and/or other support services (such as reminders to exercise or positive reinforcement).
- Establish a communication link between patient and provider.[255]

Additionally, as previously discussed, spirometry is an important tool for diagnosis and management of respiratory diseases. A web-based application was tested for development of high-quality spirometry skills in community/ primary care settings. Researchers examined the efficacy, acceptability, and usability of a web-based application covering three main functions: 1) accessibility to educational material for continuous professional development; 2) remote support for quality assurance of tests performed by non-experts; and 3) remote assistance for lung function interpretation. This research indicated sustained benefit of online intervention by increasing high-quality spirometry tests, and professionals acknowledged the usefulness of a web-based tool for remote assistance with interpretation of the results as well as to increase non-expert professionals' skills for performing high-quality forced spirometry in primary care.[256]

**H. Prevention and Tobacco Cessation**—Pulmonologists can be a critical part of the care team working on patient education and prevention by urging patients to quit smoking and to follow up with their primary care provider where necessary. As a specialty, pulmonologist have decades of experience in promoting adaptive behavior in patients across populations. In roughly 85% of those whom COPD has been diagnosed, cigarette smoking is a primary cause, according to the American Lung Association.

According to Jeffrey Cain, MD, president of the American Academy of Family Physicians, doctors also need to adjust their own views of tobacco use and look at it as a chronic rather than acute problem. "Tobacco use is much more like a rheumatoid arthritis that tends to flux and flare," he says. "We have to think of this as an ongoing management issue. So even though the patient in front of you may not have changed at this visit, if you're using the stages-of-change model, giving them effective counseling even in early stages helps move people forward."[257] Pulmonologists have been at the forefront of the movement to address public health epidemics. As the vanguard in this area, they are highly valuable to ACOs for this soft skill in communicating to patients individually and across populations.

    **I.** **Other**—Please see *The Accountable Care Manual for Pulmonologists*, which may be downloaded at www.ncmedsoc.org/physician-resources/accountable-care/aco-toolkits.

    **J.** **PCSP Standards**—The NCQA Patient-Centered Specialty Practice standards regarding care team and patient coordination are recommended generally for all specialists, including pulmonologists.

**II.** **Metrics**

    **A.** **Match Metrics to Plans**—After determining the initiatives involving this specialty that are most appropriate for your CIN/ACO, to incentivize the desired behavior and outcomes, it is recommended that clinically valid metrics track adherence to the chosen activities and accomplishment of the desired results. Use available measures from various sources as a "menu" from which to start, and then tailor, prioritize, and weight them to fit your incentivization goals (see Table 7-23).

**TABLE 7-23.** MACRA'S Quality Payment Program MIPS Measures Relevant to Pulmonology

| MEASURE NAME | MEASURE DESCRIPTION |
|---|---|
| Appropriate Testing for Children with Pharyngitis | Percentage of children 3-18 years of age who were diagnosed with pharyngitis, ordered an antibiotic and received a group A streptococcus (strep) test for the episode. |
| Appropriate Treatment for Children with Upper Respiratory Infection (URI) | Percentage of children 3 months-18 years of age who were diagnosed with upper respiratory infection (URI) and were not dispensed an antibiotic prescription on or three days after the episode. |
| Avoidance of Antibiotic Treatment in Adults with Acute Bronchitis | The percentage of adults 18-64 years of age with a diagnosis of acute bronchitis who were not dispensed an antibiotic prescription. |
| Care Plan | Percentage of patients aged 65 years and older who have an advance care plan or surrogate decision maker documented in the medical record or documentation in the medical record that an advance care plan was discussed but the patient did not wish or was not able to name a surrogate decision maker or provide an advance care plan. |
| Controlling High Blood Pressure | Percentage of patients 18-85 years of age who had a diagnosis of hypertension and whose blood pressure was adequately controlled (<140/90mmHg) during the measurement period. |
| Documentation of Current Medications in the Medical Record | Percentage of visits for patients aged 18 years and older for which the eligible professional attests to documenting a list of current medications using all immediate resources available on the date of the encounter. This list must include ALL known prescriptions, over-the-counters, herbals, and vitamin/mineral/dietary (nutritional) supplements AND must contain the medications' name, dosage, frequency and route of administration. |

**TABLE 7-23.** MACRA'S Quality Payment Program MIPS
Measures Relevant to Pulmonology (continued)

| MEASURE NAME | MEASURE DESCRIPTION |
|---|---|
| Elder Maltreatment Screen and Follow-Up Plan | Percentage of patients aged 65 years and older with a documented elder maltreatment screen using an Elder Maltreatment Screening tool on the date of encounter AND a documented follow-up plan on the date of the positive screen. |
| Falls: Plan of Care | Percentage of patients aged 65 years and older with a history of falls that had a plan of care for falls documented within 12 months. |
| Falls: Risk Assessment | Percentage of patients aged 65 years and older with a history of falls that had a risk assessment for falls completed within 12 months. |
| Medication Reconciliation Post-Discharge | The percentage of discharges from any inpatient facility (e.g. hospital, skilled nursing facility, or rehabilitation facility) for patients 18 years and older of age seen within 30 days following discharge in the office by the physician, prescribing practitioner, registered nurse, or clinical pharmacist providing ongoing care for whom the discharge medication list was reconciled with the current medication list in the outpatient medical record. This measure is reported as three rates stratified by age group: Reporting Criteria 1: 18-64 years of age Reporting Criteria 2: 65 years and older Total Rate: All patients 18 years of age and older |
| Optimal Asthma Control | Composite measure of the percentage of pediatric and adult patients whose asthma is well-controlled as demonstrated by one of three age-appropriate patient-reported outcome tools and not at risk for exacerbation. |
| Pain Assessment and Follow-Up | Percentage of visits for patients aged 18 years and older with documentation of a pain assessment using a standardized tool(s) on each visit AND documentation of a follow-up plan when pain is present. |
| Pain Brought Under Control Within 48 Hours | Patients aged 18 and older who report being uncomfortable because of pain at the initial assessment (after admission to palliative care services) that report pain was brought to a comfortable level within 48 hours. |
| Use of High-Risk Medications in the Elderly | Percentage of patients 66 years of age and older who were ordered high-risk medications. Two rates are reported. a. Percentage of patients who were ordered at least one high-risk medication. b. Percentage of patients who were ordered at least two different high-risk medications. |

# RADIOLOGISTS

I.  **Why and How You May Want to Utilize Radiologists in Your CIN/ACO**

A.  **Diagnostic Direction**—Radiologists regularly support your CIN/ACO, primary care, and other referring physicians across a wide spectrum of disease states. As part of this systematic diagnostic support, many radiology practices have useful technologies, such as data-mining capabilities with voice recognition. In a CIN/ACO context, radiologists can be an important part of the consultation to manage a variety of medical conditions, particularly the most appropriate use of imaging studies to limit unnecessary referrals and procedures.[258] The benefit of such guidance will increase as value-based care models will elevate the role of allied providers.

Relatedly, their experience with widespread decision support makes radiologists good candidates to participate in the design and implementation of the CIN/ACO information and decision-support infrastructure.

B.  **Standardization of Image Management Best Practices**—The fee-for-service system has fostered over-referral of high-cost and low-value imaging services, even when there are multiple high-value imaging services available. Radiologists are in the best position to manage an ACO's imaging within a tight band of evidence-based best practices. The increased quality and savings stand to be significant if this initiative is deployed.

ACOs usually start with radiologist education, then nonbinding review, then binding authorization, once efficiency is shown. In a show of leadership, the American College of Radiology (ACR) has developed "The ACR Appropriateness Criteria,"[259] which are evidence-based guidelines to assist referring physicians and others in making the most appropriate and effective imaging or treatment decision for a given clinical showing. There are 186 topics and over 900 variants in the February 2013 version, which are posted on the National Guidelines Clearinghouse (NGC) website: http://www.guideline.gov/; search "ACR Appropriateness Criteria." The NGC is an initiative of the Agency for Healthcare Research and Quality (AHRQ).

Choosing Wisely®, an initiative of the American Board of Internal Medicine (ABIM) Foundation (http://www.abimfoundation.org/Initiatives/Choosing-Wisely.aspx) that focuses on encouraging physicians and patients to think about tests and procedures that may be unnecessary, places a strong emphasis on imaging. The ACR's recommendations on the Choosing Wisely® initiative can be accessed at: http://www.choosingwisely.org/doctor-patient-lists/american-college-of-radiology/. The Choosing Wisely® campaign now receives input from 24 medical societies, each of which puts out a list that highlight low-value, overused tests. Nearly every society included at least one imaging study on their list. Examples include imaging for lower back pain,

MRI for syncope, and unnecessary prostate cancer imaging for older men. On the other hand, existing evidence suggests high cost-effectiveness for the following: CCTA for mild-moderate chest pain patients, preoperative MRI, spectroscopy for prostate cancer patients undergoing prostatectomy, and CT colonoscopy for men over 60 who refuse traditional colonoscopy.

1. **Radiologist Imaging Management—Case Study**—The following example illustrates radiologists' value-added leadership in establishing a best practice and educating ordering physicians. It also shows the benefit of transparently showing outliers and documenting benefits. Vanderbilt University Medical Center engaged its radiologists to review literature regarding use of CT for head trauma patients in the emergency department. They found that such scans do not affect treatment decisions. A mandatory radiologist nonbinding consult was instituted with all referring physicians who have ordered such imaging. CT head trauma orders declined by more than 50%. This success helped the department later get to the point that radiologist recommendations be binding.[260]

   *Take-Away*—The radiologist's value in this non-interpretive context is clear. This type of best practice consult, monitor, and measure progression can be repeated for many imaging scenarios and contrasts sharply with the siloed economic pressure under the fee-for-service system in which interpretation of images predominates.

2. **Utilization Management Assisted by Decision Support**—Radiologists can guide appropriate utilization in an ACO using tools such as computerized order entry (OE) and through implementation of decision support (DS) protocols in close collaboration and consultation with referring physicians. State-of-the-art DS systems incorporate evidence-based guidelines, such as the ACR's appropriateness criteria, to assist referring physicians and other providers to select the most appropriate imaging studies for given clinical conditions. The use of such systems can reduce costs and radiation exposure through the elimination of unnecessary imaging studies as well as untoward complications resulting from unnecessary interventions based on inappropriate imaging.

   The most effective systems provide real-time clinical guidance by basing the decision algorithm on patient complaints, actual clinical data, or diagnosis input by physicians. The system recommends potentially useful imaging studies, rates their appropriateness, and indicates the resulting level of radiation exposure. These systems can track imaging of multiple physicians, providing valuable feedback to reduce unwarranted variation in care. The consulting firm, The Advisory Board, suggests that, "Imaging expertise on efficiency and productivity should be shared with other [hospital] departments to improve radiology's image as a valuable collaborator."[261] The ACR goes further and states that, "A radiologist-managed OE/DS system should be central to the decision-support 'hub' of an ACO,"[262] predicting financial rewards to radiologists when this happens. Many believe that this will drive the quality and efficiency that preauthorization has not done successfully.

3. **Expert Consultation**—Radiologists not only can introduce and educate referring physicians on the best practice guidelines, they also can provide ongoing consultation for cases that are unusual or for which the DS system does not offer clear guidance. By providing effective imaging advice, radiologists increase quality, decrease costs, and save time—a referring physician's most precious resource. One ACO found significant efficiencies through the simple practice of monthly multispecialty service-line meetings to discuss unusual cases and best practices, including referral management.

4. **Guideline Management**—Job one still is radiologist-led intra-ACO adherence to a tight band of best practices, with as many reduced to written guidelines as possible; however, clinically valid guidelines will generate the additional benefit of reducing the urge to order unnecessary images due to fear of malpractice liability. Also, if self-referral for imaging is allowed within the ACO, adherence to guidelines must be closely monitored. Working with referring physicians, radiologists can set up imaging algorithms for common clinical problems, including The ACR Appropriateness Criteria. This can be plugged into the DS system.

C. **Other**—Please see *The Accountable Care Manual for Radiologists*, which may be downloaded at www.ncmedsoc.org/physician-resources/accountable-care/aco-toolkits.

D. **PCSP Standards**—The NCQA Patient-Centered Specialty Practice standards regarding care team and patient coordination are recommended generally for all specialists, including radiologists.

II. **Metrics**

A. **Overview**—After determining the initiatives involving this specialty that are most appropriate for your CIN/ACO, to incentivize the desired behavior and outcomes, it is recommended that clinically valid metrics track adherence to the chosen activities and accomplishment of the desired results. Starting with the MACRA measures in Table 7-24, use the available array of measures from various sources as a "menu" from which to start, and then tailor, prioritize, and weight them to fit your incentivization goals.

TABLE 7-24. MACRA's Quality Payment Program MIPS Measures Relevant to Radiology

| MEASURE NAME | MEASURE DESCRIPTION |
|---|---|
| Appropriate Assessment of Retrievable Inferior Vena Cava (IVC) Filters for Removal | Percentage of patients in whom a retrievable IVC filter is placed who, within 3 months post-placement, have a documented assessment for the appropriateness of continued filtration, device removal or the inability to contact the patient with at least two attempts |
| Appropriate Follow-up Imaging for Incidental Abdominal Lesions | Percentage of final reports for abdominal imaging studies for asymptomatic patients aged 18 years and older with one or more of the following noted incidentally with follow-up imaging recommended: Liver lesion ≤ 0.5 cm Cystic kidney lesion < 1.0 cm Adrenal lesion ≤ 1.0 cm |
| Nuclear Medicine: Correlation with Existing Imaging Studies for All Patients Undergoing Bone Scintigraphy | Percentage of final reports for all patients, regardless of age, undergoing bone scintigraphy that include physician documentation of correlation with existing relevant imaging studies (e.g., x-ray, MRI, CT, etc.) that were performed |
| Optimizing Patient Exposure to Ionizing Radiation: Appropriateness: Follow-up CT Imaging for Incidentally Detected Pulmonary Nodules According to Recommended Guidelines | Percentage of final reports for computed tomography (CT) imaging studies of the thorax for patients aged 18 years and older with documented follow-up recommendations for incidentally detected pulmonary nodules (e.g., follow-up CT imaging studies needed or that no follow-up is needed) based at a minimum on nodule size AND patient risk factors |
| Optimizing Patient Exposure to Ionizing Radiation: Computed Tomography (CT) Images Available for Patient Follow-up and Comparison Purposes | Percentage of final reports for computed tomography (CT) studies performed for all patients, regardless of age, which document that Digital Imaging and Communications in Medicine (DICOM) format image data are available to non-affiliated external healthcare facilities or entities on a secure, media-free, reciprocally searchable basis with patient authorization for at least a 12-month period after the study |
| Optimizing Patient Exposure to Ionizing Radiation: Count of Potential High-Dose Radiation Imaging Studies: Computed Tomography (CT) and Cardiac Nuclear Medicine Studies | Percentage of computed tomography (CT) and cardiac nuclear medicine (myocardial perfusion studies) imaging reports for all patients, regardless of age, that document a count of known previous CT (any type of CT) and cardiac nuclear medicine (myocardial perfusion) studies that the patient has received in the 12-month period prior to the current study |
| Optimizing Patient Exposure to Ionizing Radiation: Reporting to a Radiation Dose Index Registry | Percentage of total computed tomography (CT) studies performed for all patients, regardless of age, that are reported to a radiation dose index registry that is capable of collecting at a minimum selected data element |
| Optimizing Patient Exposure to Ionizing Radiation: Search for Prior Computed Tomography (CT) Studies Through a Secure, Authorized, Media-Free, Shared Archive | Percentage of final reports of computed tomography (CT) studies performed for all patients, regardless of age, which document that a search for Digital Imaging and Communications in Medicine (DICOM) format images was conducted for prior patient CT imaging studies completed at non-affiliated external healthcare facilities or entities within the past 12-months and are available through a secure, authorized, media-free, shared archive prior to an imaging study being performed |

*Continued on next page*

**TABLE 7-24.** MACRA's Quality Payment Program MIPS
Measures Relevant to Radiology (continued)

| MEASURE NAME | MEASURE DESCRIPTION |
|---|---|
| Optimizing Patient Exposure to Ionizing Radiation: Utilization of a Standardized Nomenclature for Computed Tomography (CT) Imaging Description | Percentage of computed tomography (CT) imaging reports for all patients, regardless of age, with the imaging study named according to a standardized nomenclature and the standardized nomenclature is used in institution's computer systems |
| Radiation Consideration for Adult CT: Utilization of Dose Lowering Techniques | Percentage of final reports for patients aged 18 years and older undergoing CT with documentation that one or more of the following dose reduction techniques were used: Automated exposure control Adjustment of the mA and/or kV according to patient size Use of iterative reconstruction technique |
| Radiology: Exposure Dose or Time Reported for Procedures Using Fluoroscopy | Final reports for procedures using fluoroscopy that document radiation exposure indices, or exposure time and number of fluorographic images (if radiation exposure indices are not available) |
| Radiology: Inappropriate Use of "Probably Benign" Assessment Category in Screening Mammograms | Percentage of final reports for screening mammograms that are classified as "probably benign" |
| Radiology: Reminder System for Screening Mammograms | Percentage of patients undergoing a screening mammogram whose information is entered into a reminder system with a target due date for the next mammogram |
| Radiology: Stenosis Measurement in Carotid Imaging Reports | Percentage of final reports for carotid imaging studies (neck magnetic resonance angiography [MRA], neck computed tomography angiography [CTA], neck duplex ultrasound, carotid angiogram) performed that include direct or indirect reference to measurements of distal internal carotid diameter as the denominator for stenosis measurement |

# RHEUMATOLOGISTS

I.  **Why and How You May Want to Utilize Rheumatologists in Your CIN/ACO**

A.  **Co-Management of RA**—Rheumatoid arthritis (RA) and its frequent co-morbidities are often chronic, complex, and expensive conditions. The new collaborative nature of integrated population health, contrasted with the fragmented fee-for-service delivery paradigm, presents high-value opportunities for better diagnosis, treatment, and monitoring of those patients with RA.

   •  **Rheumatologists' Empowerment of Primary Care for Early Diagnosis and Treatment**—Early diagnosis and treatment avoids disabilities that compromise their ability to perform activities related to daily living. Appropriate and timely application of disease-modifying therapy can reduce that potential and slow the progression of joint damage.[263] Yet, in our traditional siloed system, primary care physicians are often unaware of incipient RA symptoms, do not have access to a rheumatologist, and do not know when to refer or co-manage the patient. They are often uncomfortable managing RA with disease-modifying anti-rheumatic drugs.[264]

   In the CIN/ACO setting, the systemic barriers are removed and rheumatologists can provide diagnostic information through written materials or "lunch-and-learn" sessions. They can establish ready access via telephone, email, or telemedicine. General indicators of when to refer and when to co-manage can be established. The rheumatologist should agree to coordinate with the primary care medical home and the rest of the care team.

   In the treatment of RA, it is important to monitor disease progression, adverse events, and changes in the patient's general health. This is another element of care appropriate for co-management, with the primary care team including this awareness in its regular laboratory testing, infection monitoring, and routine screening. The patient's care plan and engagement strategy should include integrated behavioral health strategies, an understanding of community resources available, such as transportation, and a drug management reconciliation, compliance, efficiency to cost, and number of expensive medications.

B.  **Best Practices**—While there are multiple resources that provide clinically developed and proven best practice guidelines, one example of a useful source of core best practices may be found in the recommendations of the American College of Rheumatology to the Choosing Wisely® program sponsored by the ABIM Foundation and is included below:

   1.  **"Don't test ANA sub-serologies without a positive ANA and clinical suspicion of immune-mediated disease.** Tests for anti-nuclear antibody (ANA) sub-serologies (including antibodies to double-stranded DNA, Smith, RNP, SSA, SSB, Scl-70, centromere) are usually negative if the

ANA is negative. Exceptions include anti-Jo1, which can be positive in some forms of myositis, or occasionally, anti-SSA, in the setting of lupus or Sjögren's syndrome. Broad testing of autoantibodies should be avoided; instead the choice of autoantibodies should be guided by the specific disease under consideration.

2. **Don't test for Lyme disease as a cause of musculoskeletal symptoms without an exposure history and appropriate exam findings.** The musculoskeletal manifestations of Lyme disease include brief attacks of arthralgia or intermittent or persistent episodes of arthritis in one or a few large joints at a time, especially the knee. Lyme testing in the absence of these features increases the likelihood of false positive results and may lead to unnecessary follow-up and therapy. Diffuse arthralgias, myalgias or fibromyalgia alone are not criteria for musculoskeletal Lyme disease.

3. **Don't perform MRI of the peripheral joints to routinely monitor inflammatory arthritis.** Data evaluating MRI for the diagnosis and prognosis of rheumatoid arthritis are currently inadequate to justify widespread use of this technology for these purposes in clinical practice. Although bone edema assessed by MRI on a single occasion may be predictive of progression in certain RA populations, using MRI routinely is not cost-effective compared with the current standard of care, which includes clinical disease activity assessments and plain film radiography.

4. **Don't prescribe biologics for rheumatoid arthritis before a trial of methotrexate (or other conventional non-biologic DMARDs).** High-quality evidence suggests that methotrexate and other conventional non-biologic disease-modifying anti-rheumatic drugs (DMARD) are effective in many patients with rheumatoid arthritis (RA). Initial therapy for RA should be a conventional non-biologic DMARDs unless these are contraindicated. If a patient has had an inadequate response to methotrexate with or without other non-biologic DMARDs during an initial 3-month trial, then biologic therapy can be considered. Exceptions include patients with high disease activity and poor prognostic features (functional limitations, disease outside the joints, seropositivity or bony damage), where biologic therapy may be appropriate first-line treatment.

5. **Don't routinely repeat DXA scans more often than once every two years.** Initial screening for osteoporosis should be performed according to National Osteoporosis Foundation recommendations. The optimal interval for repeating Dual-energy X-ray Absorptiometry (DXA) scans is uncertain, but because changes in bone density over short intervals are often smaller than the measurement error of most DXA scanners, frequent testing (e.g., <2 years) is unnecessary in most patients. Even in high-risk patients receiving drug therapy for osteoporosis, DXA changes do not always correlate with

probability of fracture. Therefore, DXAs should only be repeated if the result will influence clinical management or if rapid changes in bone density are expected. Recent evidence also suggests that healthy women age 67 and older with normal bone mass may not need additional DXA testing for up to ten years provided osteoporosis risk factors do not significantly change."[265]

C. **Optimize Site-of-Service**—Providers are encouraged to seek to move procedures to lower-cost facilities or outpatient sites when consistent with best practices. Particular opportunity exists for providing alternatives to the emergency department, which has a pronounced patient engagement aspect, discussed below. For example, when a patient presents at an emergency department with pain associated with rheumatoid arthritis, the patient will likely need to undergo a series of expensive tests to rule out a variety of causes. However, if seen in the Rheumatologists' office, the specialized expertise of the clinician can rule out certain conditions and thereby reduce the number of tests that may need to be completed. One way this can be accomplished is by offering after-hours access for patients to avoid potentially unnecessary emergency department use. Additionally, rheumatologists should focus on avoidance of expensive in-hospital procedures when the same procedure can be done in a less-expensive setting with the same or better-quality outcomes, such as a physician's office or ambulatory surgical center. Practice based infusion therapy is typically less expensive than when performed in a hospital outpatient facility.

D. **Other**—For more detail on the above-prioritized initiatives and information on others, please refer to the *Accountable Care Manual for Rheumatologists* at www.ncmedsoc.org/physician-resources/accountable-care/aco-toolkits.

E. **PCSP Standards**—The NCQA Patient-Centered Specialty Practice standards regarding care team and patient coordination are recommended generally for all specialists, including rheumatologists.

II. **Metrics**

A. **Overview**—After determining the initiatives involving this specialty that are most appropriate for your CIN/ACO, to incentivize the desired behavior and outcomes, it is recommended that clinically valid metrics track adherence to the chosen activities and accomplishment of the desired results. With the MACRA measures in Table 7-25 as a start, use the available array of measures from various sources as a "menu" from which to start, and then tailor, prioritize, and weight them to fit your incentivization goals.

**TABLE 7-25.** MACRA's Quality Payment Program MIPS Measures Relevant to Rheumatology

| MEASURE NAME | MEASURE DESCRIPTION |
|---|---|
| Care Plan | Percentage of patients aged 65 years and older who have an advance care plan or surrogate decision maker documented in the medical record or documentation in the medical record that an advance care plan was discussed but the patient did not wish or was not able to name a surrogate decision maker or provide an advance care plan |
| Closing the Referral Loop: Receipt of Specialist Report | Percentage of patients with referrals, regardless of age, for which the referring provider receives a report from the provider to whom the patient was referred |
| Documentation of Current Medications in the Medical Record | Percentage of visits for patients aged 18 years and older for which the eligible professional attests to documenting a list of current medications using all immediate resources available on the date of the encounter. This list must include ALL known prescriptions, over-the-counters, herbals, and vitamin/mineral/dietary (nutritional) supplements AND must contain the medications' name, dosage, frequency and route of administration. |
| Preventive Care and Screening: Body Mass Index (BMI) Screening and Follow-Up Plan | Percentage of patients aged 18 years and older with a BMI documented during the current encounter or during the previous six months AND with a BMI outside of normal parameters, a follow-up plan is documented during the encounter or during the previous six months of the current encounter Normal Parameters: Age 18 years and older BMI ≥ 18.5 and < 25 kg/m$^2$ |
| Preventive Care and Screening: Screening for High Blood Pressure and Follow-Up Documented | Percentage of patients aged 18 years and older seen during the reporting period who were screened for high blood pressure AND a recommended follow-up plan is documented based on the current blood pressure (BP) reading as indicated |
| Preventive Care and Screening: Tobacco Use: Screening and Cessation Intervention | Percentage of patients aged 18 years and older who were screened for tobacco use one or more times within 24 months AND who received cessation counseling intervention if identified as a tobacco user |
| Rheumatoid Arthritis (RA): Assessment and Classification of Disease Prognosis | Percentage of patients aged 18 years and older with a diagnosis of rheumatoid arthritis (RA) who have an assessment and classification of disease prognosis at least once within 12 months |
| Rheumatoid Arthritis (RA): Functional Status Assessment | Percentage of patients aged 18 years and older with a diagnosis of rheumatoid arthritis (RA) for whom a functional status assessment was performed at least once within 12 months |
| Rheumatoid Arthritis (RA): Glucocorticoid Management | Percentage of patients aged 18 years and older with a diagnosis of rheumatoid arthritis (RA) who have been assessed for glucocorticoid use and, for those on prolonged doses of prednisone ≥ 10 mg daily (or equivalent) with improvement or no change in disease activity, documentation of glucocorticoid management plan within 12 months |
| Rheumatoid Arthritis (RA): Periodic Assessment of Disease Activity | Percentage of patients aged 18 years and older with a diagnosis of rheumatoid arthritis (RA) who have an assessment and classification of disease activity within 12 months |

**TABLE 7-25.** MACRA's Quality Payment Program MIPS
Measures Relevant to Rheumatology (continued)

| MEASURE NAME | MEASURE DESCRIPTION |
|---|---|
| Rheumatoid Arthritis (RA): Tuberculosis Screening | Percentage of patients aged 18 years and older with a diagnosis of rheumatoid arthritis (RA) who have documentation of a tuberculosis (TB) screening performed and results interpreted within 6 months prior to receiving a first course of therapy using a biologic disease-modifying anti-rheumatic drug (DMARD) |
| Tobacco Use and Help with Quitting Among Adolescents | The percentage of adolescents 12 to 20 years of age with a primary care visit during the measurement year for whom tobacco use status was documented and received help with quitting if identified as a tobacco user |
| Tuberculosis (TB) Prevention for Psoriasis, Psoriatic Arthritis and Rheumatoid Arthritis Patients on a Biological Immune Response Modifier | Percentage of patients whose providers are ensuring active tuberculosis prevention either through yearly negative standard tuberculosis screening tests or are reviewing the patient's history to determine if they have had appropriate management for a recent or prior positive test |

# UROLOGISTS

I.   **Why and How You May Want to Utilize Urologists in Your CIN/ACO**

A.  **Site-of-Service**—As the following excerpt shows, an unexpected finding by the Urology Accountable Care Workgroup of practicing urologists in the development of *The Accountable Care Manual for Urologists* was the prioritization of mindful site-of-service selection for urologists:

What is the least expensive site of treatment consistent with best practices? This applies for both acute and subacute. Many benefits in value-based care are hard to measure—like the infection that did not happen. But an equally effective treatment in a lower-cost setting is readily measurable. The Urology Accountable Care Workgroup recommends such things as: (1) outpatient access to the ACO's same-day clinic in lieu of referral to the emergency department, (2) select procedures in an office-based setting in lieu of an ambulatory surgery center, and (3) utilize ambulatory surgery centers in lieu of hospitalization, all as clinically appropriate.

One Urology Accountable Care Workgroup member noted that, "This is the number one-way subspecialists can help ACOs bend the cost curve, without question." For years, when a patient came in who was not scheduled, the mantra was 'send him to the ER.'" One ACO instituted a same-day clinic and found a direct correlation between the opening of the same-day clinic and reduced ER usage.

Site-of-service guidelines must be built upon urologist-vetted and approved evidence-based best practices. Implementing site-of-service guidelines might be more difficult, however, in states with certificate of need (CON) laws.

B.  **Standardization Around Best Practices**—To find the biggest "bang for the buck," look for the diagnoses with the highest avoidable costs for patients seen by urologists. This is not the same as the ones with the highest urology fees involved, as the greatest savings urologists drive will likely be in things like avoided hospitalization, infections, readmissions, inappropriate referrals, or misdiagnoses.

Practice variation is another factor to consider. As one urologist put it, "This is a shift from what we've seen before—six partners treating six different ways. The name of the game is avoiding variability." Urologists determine the best way particular diagnoses should be addressed across the continuum and the urologist's optimum role in that treatment.

The Urology Accountable Care Workgroup suggests that in practice, the relative adherence to the practice guidelines be closely monitored and be transparent. Ideally, associated costs and savings also will be tracked. One Workgroup member stated, "If you're an outlier, you're in trouble. That's when we'll see behavior change." Next, urologists should look for those high-cost events that can most effectively have the quickest and easiest impact. Lastly, be biased toward the ones with existing nationally recognized metrics, as they can be implemented most rapidly.

Applying these screens, the Urology Accountable Care Workgroup suggests that urologists consider whether any of the American Urological Association's (AUA) Clinical Practice Guidelines meet those criteria for their local situations. The AUA Guidelines provide evidence-based guidance with an explicit clinical scope and purpose (http://www.auanet.org/education/aua-guidelines.cfm).

Examples from the extensive offering include:
- Bladder cancer
- Interstitial cystitis/bladder pain syndrome
- Incontinence
- Prostate cancer
- Renal cancer

Urology Accountable Care Workgroup members also noted that opportunities exist to decrease use of ancillary services such as imaging, laboratory services, and pathology. While many decisions are based on individual patient needs, broad considerations include use of CT scans vs. plain films, indications for biopsy and number of biopsies, PSA screening into advanced age, and repeated testosterone testing.

C. **Coordination Across Specialties**—Remember, the highest impact may be in influencing the patient and primary care physician through "upstream" education and navigation and the coordinated care of high-cost, chronically ill patients with co-morbidities. Urologists have found the AUA Guidelines useful here as well. Examples are asymptomatic micro-hematuria, erectile dysfunction, initial management of benign prostatic hypertrophy, and PSA screenings for advanced-age men.

Practically speaking, urologists in ACOs have found monthly care continuum meetings to be valuable for coordinating implementation of clinical protocols across specialties and settings. These meetings provide a means for urologists to: (1) push knowledge "upstream"; (2) advise when and where primary care should refer; and (3) communicate information needed at the time of referral.

For example, using the AUA Guidelines as reference, discussion of asymptomatic hematuria treatment identified a knowledge gap in care, which led to education of the primary care physicians regarding initial evaluation and appropriate imaging. Research suggests that communication with primary care physicians can result in high-value outcomes, better diagnosis, and treatment design. To increase adherence, the Geisinger Clinic's ACO embeds as much of the agreed-upon clinical protocol support as possible into their electronic health record (EHR) system so that it is available at the point of care across the continuum.

This coordination can be aided through access via telephone, email, video conferencing, and telemedicine consults.

D. **Other**—For more detail on the above-prioritized initiatives and information on others, please refer to the *Accountable Care Manual for Urologists* at www.ncmedsoc.org/physician-resources/accountable-care/aco-toolkits.

E. **PCSP Standards**—The NCQA Patient-Centered Specialty Practice standards regarding care team and patient coordination are recommended generally for all specialists, including urologists.

II. **Metrics**

A. **Overview**—After determining the initiatives involving this specialty that are most appropriate for your CIN/ACO, to incentivize the desired behavior and outcomes, it is recommended that clinically valid metrics track adherence to the chosen activities and accomplishment of the desired results. Starting with the MACRA measures in Table 7-25, use the available array of measures from various sources as a "menu" from which to start, and then tailor, prioritize, and weight them to fit your incentivization goals.

**TABLE 7-26.** MACRA's Quality Payment Program MIPS Measures Relevant to Urology

| MEASURE NAME | MEASURE DESCRIPTION |
|---|---|
| Biopsy Follow-Up | Percentage of new patients whose biopsy results have been reviewed and communicated to the primary care/referring physician and patient by the performing physician |
| Care Plan | Percentage of patients aged 65 years and older who have an advance care plan or surrogate decision maker documented in the medical record or documentation in the medical record that an advance care plan was discussed but the patient did not wish or was not able to name a surrogate decision maker or provide an advance care plan |
| Closing the Referral Loop: Receipt of Specialist Report | Percentage of patients with referrals, regardless of age, for which the referring provider receives a report from the provider to whom the patient was referred |
| Documentation of Current Medications in the Medical Record | Percentage of visits for patients aged 18 years and older for which the eligible professional attests to documenting a list of current medications using all immediate resources available on the date of the encounter. This list must include ALL known prescriptions, over-the-counters, herbals, and vitamin/mineral/dietary (nutritional) supplements AND must contain the medications' name, dosage, frequency and route of administration. |

**TABLE 7-26.** MACRA's Quality Payment Program MIPS
Measures Relevant to Urology (continued)

| MEASURE NAME | MEASURE DESCRIPTION |
|---|---|
| Patient-Centered Surgical Risk Assessment and Communication | Percentage of patients who underwent a non-emergency surgery who had their personalized risks of post-operative complications assessed by their surgical team prior to surgery using a clinical data-based, patient-specific risk calculator and who received personal discussion of those risks with the surgeon |
| Preventive Care and Screening: Screening for High Blood Pressure and Follow-Up Documented | Percentage of patients aged 18 years and older seen during the reporting period who were screened for high blood pressure AND a recommended follow-up plan is documented based on the current blood pressure (BP) reading as indicated |
| Preventive Care and Screening: Tobacco Use: Screening and Cessation Intervention | Percentage of patients aged 18 years and older who were screened for tobacco use one or more times within 24 months AND who received cessation counseling intervention if identified as a tobacco user |
| Prostate Cancer: Adjuvant Hormonal Therapy for High Risk or Very High-Risk Prostate Cancer | Percentage of patients, regardless of age, with a diagnosis of prostate cancer at high or very high risk of recurrence receiving external beam radiotherapy to the prostate who were prescribed adjuvant hormonal therapy (GnRH [gonadotropin-releasing hormone] agonist or antagonist) |
| Prostate Cancer: Avoidance of Overuse of Bone Scan for Staging Low-Risk Prostate Cancer Patients | Percentage of patients, regardless of age, with a diagnosis of prostate cancer at low (or very low) risk of recurrence receiving interstitial prostate brachytherapy, OR external beam radiotherapy to the prostate, OR radical prostatectomy, OR cryotherapy who did not have a bone scan performed at any time since diagnosis of prostate cancer |
| Tobacco Use and Help with Quitting Among Adolescents | The percentage of adolescents 12 to 20 years of age with a primary care visit during the measurement year for whom tobacco use status was documented and received help with quitting if identified as a tobacco user |
| Urinary Incontinence: Assessment of Presence or Absence of Urinary Incontinence in Women Aged 65 Years and Older | Percentage of female patients aged 65 years and older who were assessed for the presence or absence of urinary incontinence within 12 months |
| Urinary Incontinence: Plan of Care for Urinary Incontinence in Women Aged 65 Years and Older | Percentage of female patients aged 65 years and older with a diagnosis of urinary incontinence with a documented plan of care for urinary incontinence at least once within 12 months |

# CHAPTER EIGHT

# Conclusion

"We always overestimate the change that will occur in the next two years and under-estimate the change that will occur in the text ten. Don't let yourself be lulled into inaction."[266]

When Bill Gates made that now famous quote in 1996, there were only 100,000 websites worldwide. The Macarena had just become a worldwide hit. Major league soccer had made its debut in the U.S. eBay had just started its online auction. And the Hoover Institution released an optimistic report that global warming would probably reduce mortality in the United States and provide Americans with valuable benefits. Steve Jobs' company NeXT was bought by Apple. The human genome project was seven years away from completion. Healthcare costs per capita were around $4,000, and electronic health records were used in fewer than 5% of health systems nationwide. The U.S. was experiencing a stock market surge due to the growth of dot.com businesses.[267]

In 2006, Apple introduced the iPhone, whose operating system was built on the so-called "failed" NeXT technology. Facebook opened to the public, Google bought YouTube for $1.65 billion, and the very first Tweet was sent. The country had recovered from the dot.com bust but was in the middle of a stock market surge due to exponential growth in the housing market. Total national healthcare costs per capita were greater than $7,000.[268] About 10% of health systems were using integrated electronic medical record systems.

When we look back on these major cultural and technological changes, we can see the massive changes that occurred over that 10-year period, but during it all, it was hard to perceive the extent of these changes, even as the pace of change accelerated. Now, more than 10 years later, healthcare costs likely have reached the tipping point of economic sustainability for the country as the $10,000 per capita cost of healthcare reached 19% of the gross domestic product.

We believe the pressures these financial forces will exert on our healthcare system will lead to massive changes in the healthcare delivery system that will be amplified by new technologies such as artificial intelligence, block chain technology, and genomic, proteomic, and metabolomic technologies encompassing personalized medicine. Ten years from now this changed world may have a very different healthcare delivery system. Irrespective of the details of how it is designed, we believe the basic tenants of value-based payment systems in integrated models of care will be essential components.

Our objective in writing this book has been to compile the collective experience, knowledge, and wisdom of the many people who have been working on the cutting edge of health system delivery change, including countless physician specialists, payment system reformers, care model designers, and change management and leadership experts with whom we have had the privilege to work or who have influenced our thinking through their written work and policy contributions. We hope the format will be a useful tool for those who are passionate about improving the healthcare delivery system in our country and are committed to the journey to do so.

This metaphor of the move to value as a journey is applied to health system delivery reform perhaps more than any other, to the point it has almost become a cliché. Nonetheless, we still believe the metaphor is fitting because we must all travel from the fee-for-service, siloed healthcare delivery system of the past 75 years to a new one that is more efficient, more effective, and more equitable. This journey is an opportunity to improve the care of the patients we serve, with new models of care, new payment models, new technology, new successes, and new challenges.

We hope the material we have provided here, based on the experiences of value-based care pioneers, will help your journey as you gain your own expertise in the opportunity of a lifetime to improve our healthcare system.

# REFERENCES

1. Muhlestein D, Saunders RS, Richards R, McClellan MB. Recent Progress in the Value Journey: Growth of ACOs and Value-based Payment Models in 2018. *Health Affairs Blog*, August 14, 2018. www.healthaffairs.org/do/10.1377/hblog20180810.481968/full.

2. Leavitt Partners. https://leavittpartners.com.

3. The Commonwealth Fund. US Health System Ranks Last Among Eleven Countries on Measures of Access, Equity, Quality, Efficiency, and Healthy Lives. The Commonwealth Fund, June 16, 2014. www.commonwealthfund.org/publications/press-releases/2014/jun/us-health-system-ranks-last

4. Congress of the United States, Congressional Budget Office. *Budget Options, Vol 1.: Healthcare.* December 2008:72

5. Muhlestein D, Garner P, Caughley W, de Lisle K. Projected Growth of Accountable Care Organizations. White Paper. Leavitt Partners; Dec 2015. www.leavittpartners.com.

6. Goodman JC, Wedekind LJ. How the Trump Administration Is Reforming Medicare. *Health Affairs Blog*, May 3, 2019. www.healthaffairs.org/do/10.1377/hblog20190501.529581.

7. HITC Staff. Survey: Less Than 1 in 4 Physicians Are Well Prepared to Meet MACRA Requirements. *HIT Consultant.* June 29, 2017. www.hitconsultant.net/2017/06/29/ama-kpmg-macra-qpp/.

8. Mostashari F, Sanghavi D, McClellan M. Health Reform and Physician-Led Accountable Care: The Paradox of Primary Care Physician Leadership. *JAMA.* 2014;311(18):1855-56.

9. The Medicare Access and CHIP Reauthorization Act of 2015 (MACRA) was passed in April 2015 with a 92-8 Senate vote and 392-3 House of Representatives vote.

10. During the Obama Administration, the Final Rule implemented by the law was published on October 14, 2106. During the Trump Administration, a Proposed Rule to ease administrative burdens was published on June 30, 2017.

11. The Commonwealth Fund. *US Health System Ranks Last Among Eleven Countries on Measures of Access, Equity, Quality, Efficiency, and Healthy Lives.* The Commonwealth Fund, June 16, 2014. www.commonwealthfund.org/publications/press-releases/2014/jun/us-health-system-ranks-last

12. NEJM. *Unlocking the Opportunities for Health Care Delivery Transformation.* NEJM; May 2019. http://join.catalyst.nejm.org/download/understanding-barriers-unlocking-opportunity-ebook2019/register

13. Roning P. *Becoming Accountable, HFMA Compendium—Contemplating the ACO Opportunity,* Appendix; November 2010:40.

14. Lazerow R. Toward Accountable Payment. The Advisory Board Company blog; 2010

15. Roning P. *Becoming Accountable, HFMA Compendium—Contemplating the ACO Opportunity,* Appendix; November 2010: 40.

16. NEJM. *Unlocking the Opportunities for Health Care Delivery Transformation.* NEJM; May 2019:11. http://join.catalyst.nejm.org/download/understanding-barriers-unlocking-opportunity-ebook2019/register

17. Compton-Phillips A, *et al.* Care Redesign Survey: How Design Thinking Can Transform Healthcare. *NEJM Catalyst,* June 7, 2018.

18. Shortell SM, Schmittdiel J, Wang MC, Li R, *et al.* An Empirical Assessment of High-Performing Medical Groups: Results from a National Study. *Med Care Res Rev.* 2005 Aug;62(4):407-434.

19. Dunn L. 6 Characteristics of High-Performing Healthcare Organizations. *Becker's Hospital Review.* August 1, 2012. www.beckershospitalreview.com/hospital-management-administration/6-characteritcs-of-high-performing-healthcare-organizations.

20. White KR, Griffith JR. *The Well-Managed Healthcare Organization.* Chicago: Health Administration Press, 2019:1-38.

21. GE Healthcare Partners. 10 Emerging Characteristics of High-Performing Hospitals. GE Healthcare Partners. June 05, 2015. https://uscan.gehealthcarepartners.com/insight-detail/10-emerging-characteristics-of-high-performing-hos

22. Mongan J. Framework for a High-Performance Health System for the United States. The Commonwealth Fund. August 1, 2006. www.commonwealthfund.org/publications/fund-reports/2006/aug/framework-high-performance-health-system-united-states

23. American Medical Group Association. High-Performing Health Systems. https://www.amga.org/wcm/ADV/wcm/Advocacy/HPHS/index_HPHS.aspx

24. American Medical Group Association. AMGA Analytics/Benchmarking website. www.amga.org/wcm/PI/ATC/wcm/PI/analytics_pi.aspx?hkey=e85d7417-8446-4b18-9c4e-3a9d4f911675

25. Abbott A. *The System of Professions: An Essay on the Division of Expert Labor.* Chicago: University of Chicago Press, 1988:188.

26. Ackoff R. The Future of Operational Research Is Past. *Journal of the Operational Research Society.* 1979 Feb;30(2):93-104.

27. James P, Magee L, Scerri A, Steger MB. *Urban Sustainability in Theory and Practice: Circles of Sustainability.* London: Routledge, 2015:53.

28. Leicht KT, Fennell ML. *Professional Work: A Sociological Approach.* Malden, MA: Blackwell Publishers, 2001:87.

29. Mitchell M. *Complexity: A Guided Tour.* Oxford: Oxford University Press, 2009:13.

30. Complex Adaptive Systems. Wikipedia accessed July 22, 2016.

31. Mitchell M. *Complexity: A Guided Tour.* Oxford: Oxford University Press, 2009:297.

32. Meadows DH. *Thinking in Systems: A Primer.* White River Junction, VT: Chelsea Green Publishing, 2008.

33. Rosen E. *The Culture of Collaboration: Maximizing Time, Talent, and Tools to Create Value in the Global Economy.* San Francisco: Red Ape Publishing; 2007:57.

34. Hansen MT. *Collaboration: How Leaders Avoid the Traps, Create Unity, and Reap Big Results.* Boston: Harvard Business Review Press, 2009.

35. Johansen B. *Leaders Make the Future.* San Francisco: Berrett-Koehler Publishers, Inc., 2012.

36. Johansen B. *Leaders Make the Future.* San Francisco: Berrett-Koehler Publishers, Inc., 2012:183.

37. Kotter JP. What Leaders Really Do. *Harvard Business Review.* 2001 Dec.; 68:103-11.

38. Lopez B. *Crow and Weasel,* NY: Farrar, Straus, and Giroux, 1998.

39. Abbott A. *The System of Professions: An Essay on the Division of Expert Labor.* Chicago: University of Chicago Press, 1988:323.

40. Freidson E. *Professionalism: The Third Log.* Chicago: University of Chicago Press, 2001: 122.

41. *Webster's Third International Dictionary.* 1967;2:1811.

42. Freidson E. *Professional Powers: A Study of the Institutionalization of Formal Knowledge.* Chicago: University of Chicago Press, 1986: 46.

43. Delong TJ, Gabarro JJ, Lees RJ. *When Professionals Have to Lead: A New Model for High Performance.* Boston: Harvard Business School Press, 2007:14-42.

44. Doukas DL. Professionalism: Curriculum Goals and Meeting their Challenges. In Wear D, Aultman JM, eds. *Professionalism in Medicine: Critical Perspectives.* New York: Springer Science+Business, LLC, 2007:44.

45. Zaffron S, Logan D. *The Three Laws of Performance: Rewriting the Future of Your Organization and Your Life.* San Francisco: Josey Bass 2009:70.

46. Horwath R. *Sculpting Air: The Executive's Guide to Shaping Strategy.* Barrington Hills, Ill: Sculptura Consulting, Inc., 2006.

47. Leinwand P, Mainardi C. *The Essential Advantage: How to Win with a Capabilities-Driven Strategy.* Boston: Harvard Business Review Press, 2011.

48. Olson M, van Bever D, Verry S. When Growth Stalls. *Harvard Business Review*, 2008 March;86(3):51-61.

49. Horwath R. *Elevate: The Three Disciplines of Advanced Strategic Thinking.* Hoboken, NJ. John Wiley and Sons, 2014.

50. Horwath R. *Elevate: The Three Disciplines of Advanced Strategic Thinking.* Hoboken, NJ: John Wiley and Sons, 2014.

51. Magretta J. *Understanding Michael Porter: The Essential Guide to Competition and Strategy.* Boston: Harvard Business Review Press, 2011:32.

52. Govindarajan V, Trimble C. *Beyond the Idea: How to Execute Innovation in Any Organization.* New York: St. Martin's Press, 2012.

53. Govindarajan V, Trimble C. *The Other Side of Innovation: Solving the Execution Challenge.* Boston: Harvard Business Review Press, 2010.

54. Anthony SD. *The Little Black Book of Innovation: How It Works, How to Do It,* Boston: Harvard Business Review Press, 2012.

55. Markman AB, Wood KL. *Tools for Innovations: The Science Behind the Practical Methods that Drive New Ideas.* Oxford: Oxford University Press, 2009.

56. Merrifield R. *Re-think: A Business Manifesto for Cutting Costs and Boosting Innovation.* Upper Saddle River, NJ: Pearson FT Press, 2009.

57. Lockwood T. *Design Thinking: Integrating Innovation, Customer Experience, and Brand Value.* New York: Allworth Press: 81-95.

58. Porter M. "What is Strategy?" *Harvard Business Review.* 1996 Nov.-Dec. 1996;74(6):61-78.

59. McCarthy C, Eastman D, Garets DE. *Effective Strategies for Change.* New York: HIMSS, 2014: 4.

60. Kotter JP. *Leading Change.* Boston: Harvard Business School Press, 1996.

61. Kotter JP. *Leading Change.* Boston: Harvard Business School Press, 1996: 40.

62. Kotter JP, Cohen, DS. *The Heart of Change.* Boston: Harvard Business Review Press, 2002.

63. Kotter JP, Cohen, DS. *The Heart of Change.* Boston: Harvard Business Review Press, 2002: X.

64. Bridges W. *Managing Transition,* 3rd ed. Philadelphia: DeCapo Press Books, 2009.

65. Langley, GJ, Moen, RD, Nolan, KM Nolan, TW, Norman, CL, Provost, LP. *The Improvement Guide: A Practical Approach to Enhancing Organizational Performance.* San Francisco: Jossey Bass, 2009.

66. Kotter JP. *Leading Change.* Boston: Harvard Business School Press, 1996: 72.

67. McCarthy C, Eastman D, Garets DE. *Effective Strategies for Change.* New York: HIMSS, 2014: 4.

68. Langley, GJ, Moen, RD, Nolan, KM Nolan, TW, Norman, CL, Provost, LP. *The Improvement Guide: A Practical Approach to Enhancing Organizational Performance.* San Francisco: Jossey Bass, 2009.

69. Luecke R. *Managing Change and Transition.* Boston, MA: Harvard Business School Press, 2003.

70. Kotter JP. *Leading Change.* Boston: Harvard Business School Press, 1996: 21.

71. Bridges W. *Managing Transition,* 3rd ed. Philadelphia: DeCapo Press Books, 2009.

72. Kübler-Ross E. *On Death and Dying.* New York: Simon and Schuster, 1969.

73. Machiavelli N. *The Prince.* Indianapolis, IN: Hackett Pub. Co., 1995.

74. Bridges W. *Managing Transition,* 3rd ed. Philadelphia: DeCapo Press Books, 2009.

75. Gardner H. *Changing Minds: The Art and Science of Changing Our Own and Other People's Minds.* Boston: Harvard Business School Publishing, 2006.

76. Bossidy L, Charan R. *Execution: The Discipline of Getting Things Done.* New York: Random House, 2009.

77. Horwath R. *Deep Dive: The Proven Method for Building Strategy, Focusing Your Resources, and Taking Smart Action.* Austin, TX: Greenleaf Book Club Press, 2009: 134.

78. Ridgley SK. *Strategic Thinking Skills.* Chantilly, VA: Great Courses Teaching Company, 2012: 85.

79. Belsky S. *Making Ideas Happen.* New York: Penguin Group, 2010.

80. Kindig D, Stoddart G. What Is Population Health? *Am J Public Health.* 2003;93(3):380-383.

81. Kindig D, Asada Y, Booske B. A Population Health Framework for Setting National and State Health Goals. *JAMA.* 2008;299(17):2081-2083.

82. Nash D, Reifsnyder J, Fabius R, Pracilio V. *Population Health: Creating a Culture of Wellness.* Sudbury, MA: Jones & Bartlett Learning, LLC, 2011: xxxvi.

83. The Advisory Board Company. How to Prioritize Population Health Interventions. *Executive Research Briefing.* The Advisory Board Company, 2013.

84. Raab J, Kenis P. Heading Toward a Society of Networks Empirical Developments and Theoretical Challenges. *J of Manage Inquiry.* 2009 Sep;18(3):198-210.

85. Spooner B, Reese B, Konschak C. *Accountable Care: Bridging the Health Information Technology Divide.* Virginia Beach, VA: Convergent Publishing, 2012.

86. Healthcare Information and Management Systems Society. www.himss.org.

87. OHSU Clinical Informatics Wiki. EMR Adoption Model. http://clinfowiki.org/wiki/index.php/EMR_Adoption_Model

88. American Medical Group Association. www.amga.org.

89. Certification Commission for Health Information Technology. A Health IT Framework for Accountable Care. CCHIT, 2013. www.healthit.gov/FACAS/sites/faca/files/a_health_it_framework_for_accountable_care_0.pdf

90. Weill P, Ross JW. *IT Governance: How Top Performers Manage IT Decision Rights for Superior Results*. Boston: Harvard Business School Press, 2004.

91. Davenport TH, Harris JG, Morison R. *Analytics at Work: Smart Decisions, Better Results*. Boston: Harvard Business Press, 2010.

92. Boland P. *The Capitation Sourcebook: A Practical Guide to Managing At-Risk Arrangements*. Berkeley, CA: Boland Health Care, 1996.

93. Kaiser Family Foundation. Distribution of Health Care Expenditures by Service by State of Residence (in millions). 2014. www.kff.org.

94. Kahneman D, Tversky A. Prospect Theory: An Analysis of Decisions Under Risk. *Econometrica* (2): 263-91.

95. Slywotzky AJ. *Value Migration: How to Think Several Moves Ahead of the Competition*. Boston, MA: Harvard Business School Press, 1996.

96. Porter ME. *Redefining Health Care: Creating Value-Based Competition on Results*. Boston: Harvard Business School Press, 2006.

97. Kohn LT, Corrigan JM, Donaldson MS, eds. *To Err is Human: Building a Better Health System*. Washington, DC: Institute of Medicine, 1999.

98. U.S. Department of Health and Human Services, Office of Inspector General. *Adverse Events in Hospitals: National Incidence Among Medicare Beneficiaries*. Washington, DC: U.S. Department of Health and Human Services, Nov. 2010. (27% of patients suffered adverse events or temporary harm; 44% of those were clearly or likely preventable; $4.4 billion in added costs per annum.)

99. "Two-thirds of adults and nearly one in three children are overweight or obese. . . . The sobering impact of these numbers is reflected in the nation's concurrent epidemics of diabetes, heart disease, and other chronic diseases. . . . This future is unacceptable." (Message from the Surgeon General, *The Surgeon General's Vision for a Healthy and Fit Nation*, 2010, U.S. Dept. of Health and Human Services.) See, The Hot Spotters—Can We Lower Medical Costs by Giving the Neediest Patients Better Care? (Atul Gawande, *The New Yorker*, January 24, 2011.) "Spending per capita for obese adults exceeded spending for adults of normal weight by about 8% in 1987, and by about 38% in 2007." (The Congressional Budget Office, *How Does Obesity in Adults Affect Spending on Health Care?* September 8, 2010.)

100. "There is little or no coordination between primary care physicians and specialists, or between multiple specialists seeing the same patient . . . rather than having the specialist separately manage a portion of the care." Harold Miller, *How to Create Accountable Care Organizations*, Center for Healthcare Quality and Payment Reform.

101. Centers for Disease Control and Prevention. Heart Disease Facts. www.cdc.gov/heart-disease/facts.htm.

102. The Advisory Board Company Cardiovascular Roundtable. *Power Up Your CV Care Management Strategy*. Infographic. Jan. 2, 2014. www.advisory.com/research/cardiovascular-roundtable/resources/2013/posters/power-up-your-cardiovascular-care-management-strategy.

103. BlueCross BlueShield of North Carolina. Tiered Network Product, 2014. www.bcbsnc.com/content/providers/quality-based-networks/tiered-network.htm.

104. American Health Association. The American Heart Association Metrics for Ideal Health.

105. The Advisory Board Company. *The Population Health Manager's Playbook for Avoidable Costs*, 2012: 32.

106. Rokos I. Creating "Turbo" Accountable Care Organizations for Time Critical Diagnoses. *Circ Cardiovasc Qual Outcomes.* 2011 Nov 1;4(6):647-9.

107. Molden M, Brown CL, Griffith BE. At the Heart of Integration: Aligning Physicians and Administrators to Create New Value. *Front Health Serv Manage. 2013* Summer; 29(4):3-16.

108. The Advisory Board Company Cardiovascular Roundtable. *Securing Physician Alignment.* Slide 109, 2011.

109. The Advisory Board Company Cardiovascular Roundtable. *Securing Physician Alignment.* Slide 116.

110. The Advisory Board Company Cardiovascular Roundtable. *Securing Physician Alignment.* Slide 118.

111. The Advisory Board Company Cardiovascular Roundtable. *Securing Physician Alignment.* Slides 120-122.

112. Goodman P. Roles for Specialty Societies and Vascular Surgeons in Accountable Care Organizations. *J Vas Surg.* 2012 Mar;55(3):875-82.

113. Molden M, Brown CL, Griffith BE. At the Heart of Integration: Aligning Physicians and Administrators to Create New Value. *Front Health Serv Manage. 2013* Summer;29(4):7-9.

114. National Cardiovascular Data Registry. Metrics and Measures. www.ncdr.com/WebNCDR/home/metrics-and-measures.

115. BlueCross BlueShield of North Carolina. Tiered Network Product, 2014. www.bcbsnc.com/content/providers/quality-based-networks/tiered-network.htm.

116. CMS Quality Payment Program. Quality Measures Requirements. https://qpp.cms.gov/mips/quality-measures.

117. Lewis V, Colla CH, Tierney, *et al.* Few ACOs Pursue Innovative Models That Integrate Care for Mental Illness and Substance Abuse with Primary Care. *Health Aff* (Millwood). 2014 Oct;33(10):1808-16.

118. Lewis V, Colla CH, Tierney, *et al.* Few ACOs Pursue Innovative Models That Integrate Care for Mental Illness and Substance Abuse with Primary Care. *Health Aff* (Millwood). 2014 Oct;33(10):1808-16.

119. Richardson L, McCauley E, Katon W. Collaborative Care for Adolescent Depression: A Pilot Study. *Gen Hosp Psych.* 2009 Jan-Feb;31(1):36-45.

120. Richardson L, McCauley E, Katon W. Collaborative Care for Adolescent Depression: A Pilot Study. *Gen Hosp Psych.* 2009 Jan-Feb;31(1):36-45.

121. Brown N, Green JC, Desai MM, *et al.* Need and Unmet Need for Care Coordination Among Children with Mental Health Conditions. *Pediatrics.* 2014 Mar;133(3):e530-7.

122. Scott D, Happell B. The High Prevalence of Poor Physical Health and Unhealthy Lifestyle Behaviors in Individuals with Severe Mental Illness. *Issues Ment Health Nurs.* 2011;32(9):589-97.

123. Gruttadaro D, Markey D. *Integrating Mental Health and Pediatric Primary Care.* National Alliance on Mental Illness, 2011.

124. Gabel S. The Integration of Mental Health into Pediatric Practice: Pediatricians and Child and Adolescent Psychiatrists Working Together in New Models of Care. *J Pediatr.* 2010 Nov;157(5):848-51.

125. Reeves GM, Riddle MA. A Practical and Effective Primary Care Intervention for Treating Adolescent Depression. *JAMA*. 2014 Aug 27;312(8):797-8.

126. The AIMS Center, University of Washington. IMPACT: Improving Mood—Promoting Access to Collaborative Treatment. Website. http://aims.uw.edu/impact-improving-mood-promoting-access-collaborative-treatment.

127. Gruttadaro D, Markey D. *Integrating Mental Health and Pediatric Primary Care*. National Alliance on Mental Illness, 2011.

128. *Sample Basic Criteria*: *Is the differential diagnosis list long? *Does the diagnosis involve morbidity or mortality? *Has the patient failed initial therapy? *Does the treatment have a significant risk of adverse effects?

129. The American Telemedicine Association. *Practice Guidelines for Teledermatology*. www.americantelemed.org/?s=Guidelines+for++Teledermatology

130. American Board of Internal Medicine Foundation, Choosing Wisely. Ten Things Physicians and Patients Should Question. www.choosingwisely.org/societies/american-academy-of-dermatology.

131. The Advisory Board Company. Is Your ED Consumed with Non-Emergent Visits? June 22, 2012. www.advisory.com/research/physician-executive-council/expert-insights/2012/is-your-ED-consumed-with-non-emergent-visits.

132. American College of Emergency Physicians. Accountable Care Organizations: What Do They Mean for Emergency Medicine? 2012 Sep: 4.

133. American College of Emergency Physicians. Accountable Care Organizations: What Do They Mean for Emergency Medicine? 2012 Sep: 5.

134. Morganti KG, Bauhoff S, Blanchard C, *et al. The Evolving Role of Emergency Departments in the United State*. RAND Corporation, 2013.

135. American College of Emergency Physicians. Accountable Care Organizations: What Do They Mean for Emergency Medicine? 2012 Sep: 5.

136. The Advisory Board Company. Is Your ED Consumed with Non-Emergent Visits? June 22, 2012. www.advisory.com/research/physician-executive-council/expert-insights/2012/is-your-ED-consumed-with-non-emergent-visits.

137. American College of Emergency Physicians. Accountable Care Organizations: What Do They Mean for Emergency Medicine? 2012 Sep: 4.

138. MJH Life Sciences. Young Minority Women Bypass Primary Care for OB/GYN. *Medical Economics*, March 2013. www.medicaleconomics.com/obstetrics-gynecology-womens-health/young-minority-women-bypass-primary-care-obgyn

139. Askren H. Health Question for Women: Two Doctors or One? *Womens News*, November 21, 2012. https://womensenews.org/2012/11/health-question-women-two-doctors-or-one/.

140. Askren H. Health Question for Women: Two Doctors or One? *Womens News*, November 21, 2012. https://womensenews.org/2012/11/health-question-women-two-doctors-or-one/.

141. American College of Obstetricians and Gynecologists. OB/GYNs Urged to Help Reduce Health Disparities for Rural Women. ACOG News Release, February 2009.

142. American College of Obstetricians and Gynecologists. OB/GYNs Urged to Help Reduce Health Disparities for Rural Women. ACOG News Release, February 2009.

143. BlueCross BlueShield of North Carolina. Tiered Network Product, 2014. www.bcbsnc.com/content/providers/quality-based-networks/tiered-network.htm.

144. Knowledge@Wharton. Are 'Hospitalists' a Key to Saving Health Care? *The Fiscal Times*. February 26, 2014. www.thefiscaltimes.com/Articles/2014/02/26/Are-Hospitalists-Key-Saving-Health-Care.

145. Gamble M. Hospitalists and ACOs: The Perfect Fit? *Becker's Hospital Review*, March 21, 2011. www.beckershospitalreview.com/hospital-physician-relationships/hospitalists-and-acos-the-perfect-fit.html.

146. Beresford L. ONLINE EXCLUSIVE: Co-management Business Models. *The Hospitalist*. 2011(4).

147. Friedman SM, Mendelson DA, Bingham KW, Kates SL. Impact of Co-Managed Geriatric Fracture Center on Short-Term Hip Fracture Outcomes. *Arch Intern Med*. 2009;169(18):1712-17.

148. Beresford L. The Co-management Conundrum. *The Hospitalist*. 2011(4).

149. Beresford L. The Co-management Conundrum. *The Hospitalist*. 2011(4).

150. Shu, CC, Hsu NC, Lin YF, Wang Jy, *et al*. Integrated Postdischarge Transitional Care in a Hospitalist System to Improve Discharge Outcome: An Experimental Study. *BMC Med*. 2011 Aug 17;9:96.

151. Goldman L, Pantilat SZ, Whitcomb WF. Passing the Clinical Baton: 6 Principles to Guide the Hospitalist. *Am J Med*. 2001 Dec 21;111(9B):36S-39S.

152. Darves B. Hospitalists on the Move. NEJM CareerCenter. New England Journal of Medicine website, December 12, 2012. www.nejmcareercenter.org/article/hospitalists-on-the-move.

153. Quinn R. High-Value Care Program Puts Hospital on Path to Savings. *The Hospitalist*. 2014(7).

154. Darves B. Hospitalists on the Move. NEJM CareerCenter. The New England Journal of Medicine website, December 12, 2012. www.nejmcareercenter.org/article/hospitalists-on-the-move.

155. ABIM Foundation. "About." *Choosing Wisely* website.

156. Bendix J. Making Sense of the New Transitional Care Codes. How to Maximize Revenue Related to the Federal Government's Drive to Reduce Rehospitalizations. *Med Econ*. 2013 Mar 10;90(5):40,42-4.

157. Howell EE, Bessman ES, Rubin HR. Hospitalists and an Innovative Emergency Department Admission Process. *J Gen Intern Med*. 2004 Mar;19(3):266-8.

158. Maa J, Carter JT, Gosnell JE, Wachter R, Harris HW. The Surgical Hospitalist: A New Model for Emergency Surgical Care. *J Am Coll Surg*. 2007 Nov;205(5):704-11.

159. Pham HH, Devers KJ, Kuo S, Berenson R. Health Care Market Trends and the Evolution of Hospitalist Use and Roles. *J Gen Intern Med*. 2005 Feb;20(2):101-7.

160. Pittman D. SNFs: New Turf for Hospitalists? *MedPage Today*, 24 May 2013. www.medpagetoday.com/hospitalbasedmedicine/hospitalists/39401.

161. Kisuule F, Minter-Jordan M, Zenilman J, Wright SM. Expanding the Roles of Hospitalist Physicians to Include Public Health. *J Hosp Med*. 2007 Mar;2(2):93-101.

162. Kisuule F, Minter-Jordan M, Zenilman J, Wright SM. Expanding the Roles of Hospitalist Physicians to Include Public Health. *J Hosp Med*. 2007 Mar;2(2):93-101.

163. Muir JC, Arnold RM. Palliative Care and the Hospitalist: An Opportunity for Cross-fertilization. *Dis Mon*. 2002 Apr:48(4):207-16.

164. Muir JC, Arnold RM. Palliative Care and the Hospitalist: An Opportunity for Cross-fertilization. *Dis Mon.* 2002 Apr:48(4):207-16.

165. Beresford L. Hospitalist/Palliative-Care Collaboration Aims to Reduce Readmissions. *The Hospitalist.* 31 Jan. 2012.

166. Wyatt Matas. *The Hospitalist Group Model for Value-Based Care.*

167. See for example: Kinchen KS, Sadler J, Fink N. *et al.,* The Timing of a Specialist Evaluation in Chronic Kidney Disease and Mortality. *Ann Intern Med.* 2002;137:479-486; Junger P, Massy ZA, Nguyen-Khoa T. *et al.* Longer Duration of Predialysis Nephrological Care Is Associated with Improved Long-term Survival of Dialysis Patients. *Nephrol Dial Transplant.* 2001;16:2357-64; Stack AG. Impact of Timing of Nephrology Referral and Pre-ESRD Care on Mortality Risk Among New ESRD Patients in the United States. *Am. J. Kidney Dis.* 2003;41:310-18.

168. Grace Terrell, MD. email to Melanie Phelps, *et al.,* Feb. 23, 2015.

169. Rettig RA, Norris K, Nissenson AR. Chronic Kidney Disease in the United State: A Public Policy Imperative. *Clin J Am Soc Nephrol.* 2008 Nov;3(6):1902-10.

170. Rettig RA, Norris K, Nissenson AR. Chronic Kidney Disease in the United State: A Public Policy Imperative. *Clin J Am Soc Nephrol.* 2008 Nov;3(6):1902-10.

171. Epstein M. Non-steroidal Anti-inflammatory Drugs and the Continuum of Renal Dysfunction. *J Hypertens.* 2002;20[Suppl 6].

172. Rettig RA, Norris K, Nissenson AR. Chronic Kidney Disease in the United State: A Public Policy Imperative. *Clin J Am Soc Nephrol.* 2008 Nov;3(6):1902-10.

173. As one example, a member of the Workgroup identified the impact reliable transportation can have on improving care and reducing hospitalizations. This correlation between (1) access to a dialysis center through such reliable transportation and (2) reduction of hospitalizations was demonstrated forcefully by the anecdotal observation of an annual increase in admissions around the Christmas holidays of around 10%, reportedly attributable to the change in scheduling and the interruption in a patient's support network of family and friends.

174. Nissenson AR, Maddux FW, Velez RL, Mayne TJ, Parks J. Accountable Care Organizations and ESRD: The Time Has Come. *Am J Kidney Dis.* 2012 May;59(5):724-33.

175. Parker MG, Ibrahim T, Shaffer R, Rosner MH, Molitoris BA. The Future Nephrology Workforce: Will There Be One? *Clin J Am Soc Nephrol.* 2011 Jun;6(6):1501-6.

176. Cohen LM, Moss AH, Weisbord SD, Germain MJ. Renal Palliative Care. *J Palliat Med.* 2006 Aug;9(4):977-92.

177. Yard DH. Nephrologists Expand the Use of Palliative Care in ESRD. *Renal & Urology News,* April 1, 2010. www.renalandurologynews.com/home/news/nephrology/hemodialysis/nephrologists-expand-the-use-of-palliative-care-in-esrd.

178. The Renal Palliative Care Institute (RPCI) based out of the Baystate Medical Center in Massachusetts is one example of such an initiative. Founded in part through a 2003 grant from the Robert Wood Johnston Foundation, and recipient of the 2003 Circle of Life Award honoring innovations in palliative and end-of-life care, RPCI fosters collaboration between families, physicians, nurses, and social workers in developing and implementing protocols in end-of-life care. *See* www.promotingexcellence.org/baystate.

179. Yard DH. Nephrologists Expand the Use of Palliative Care in ESRD. *Renal & Urology News*, April 1, 2010. Quoting Dr. Moss, Professor of Medicine and Director of the Center for Health Ethics & Law at West Virginia University: "One major catalyst in the decision to rework the dialysis-withholding/withdrawal guideline is the fact that more than half a dozen studies demonstrate that select patients may live just as long with medical management alone as with dialysis." *See also* Germain M. *Supportive Care for the Renal Patient.* Oxford: Oxford University Press, 2010.

180. See for example, Krishnan *M. What's Wrong with the 5-star Rating System for the Renal Community. Nephrology News & Issues,* July 16, 2014. *See also* www.promotingexcellence. org/baystate.

181. The risk factors for stroke are well-known, and include high blood pressure, high cholesterol, diabetes, atrial fibrillation, carotid artery disease, and diet/smoking/alcohol consumption. High blood pressure is the single most important modifiable risk factor for stroke. It is estimated that high blood pressure affects 65 million Americans, and that number appears to be growing. Despite the efficacy of antihypertensive therapy and the ease of diagnosis and monitoring, a large proportion of the population still has undiagnosed or inadequately treated hypertension. Blood pressure must be regularly monitored, and high blood pressure must be aggressively treated, especially for those patients with additional stroke risk factors. For patients with diabetes, tight control of high blood pressure and high cholesterol are the most effective ways of preventing stroke. Atrial fibrillation is another significant risk factor. Patients over 65 years of age should be screened for atrial fibrillation. Patients with atrial fibrillation should be risk-stratified using predictive indices for stroke risk. Treatment is targeted to a given risk profile if a given atrial fibrillation patient, and ranges from aspirin for low risk patient to warfarin to high risk patients who can receive it safely. [Sources: Guidelines for the Primary Prevention of Stroke; Secondary Stroke Prevention; A Review of the Use of Telemedicine Within Stroke Systems of Care; Prevention of Stroke: Canadian Best Practices.]

182. The Mayo Clinic. Guidelines for the Primary Prevention of Stroke; Secondary Stroke Prevention.

183. England MJ, Liverman CT, Schultz AM, Strawbridge LM eds. *Epilepsy Across the Spectrum: Promoting Health and Understanding.* Institute of Medicine Committee on the Public Health Dimensions of the Epilepsies. Washington DC: National Academies Press, 2012. www.ncbi.nlm.nih.gov/pubmed/22993876

184. England MJ, Liverman CT, Schultz AM, Strawbridge LM eds. *Epilepsy Across the Spectrum: Promoting Health and Understanding.* Institute of Medicine Committee on the Public Health Dimensions of the Epilepsies. Washington DC: National Academies Press, 2012.

185. von Bruenigen VE, Deveny TC. Health Care Reform: Will Quality Remodeling Affect Obstetrician-Gynecologists in Addition to Patients? *Obstet Gynecol.* 2001 May:117(5):1167-9. "It is anticipated that patient requests to be induced because of fatigue or obstetricians scheduling inductions for patient convenience will be prohibited by value-based purchasing and accountable care organizations."

186. Janakiraman V, Ecker J. Quality in Obstetric Care: Measuring What Matters. *Obstet Gynecol.* 2010 Sep;116(3):728-32.

187. Janakiraman V, Ecker J. Quality in Obstetric Care: Measuring What Matters. *Obstet Gynecol.* 2010 Sep;116(3): 732.

188. Deline M. The Advisory Board Company Oncology Roundtable. *The New Rules of Oncology Service Line Growth*, Slide 10, (2012).

189. Blair K. 2013 Cancer Center Business Summit, Innovative Cancer Care Initiative # 2: The Oncology ACO. November 2013.

190. Barkley R, Cancer Center Business Summit, Oncologist-Hospital Alignment for Accountable Cancer Care: Hospital/Health System, Community Oncology and ACOs. November 2013.

191. The Advisory Board Company Oncology Roundtable, *Redesigning Cancer Care Delivery for the Era of Accountability.* 2012:76.

192. The Advisory Board Company Oncology Roundtable. *Redesigning Cancer Care Delivery for the Era of Accountability.* 2012:76.

193. Mayo Clinic Orientation DVD Components:
    Welcome to cancer center
    Introduction to philosophy of care
    Orientation to physical layout
    Encourages patient participation
    Patient testimonials
    Sources for obtaining education and support information

194. The Advisory Board Company Oncology Roundtable. *Redesigning Cancer Care Delivery for the Era of Accountability.* 2012:78.

195. The Advisory Board Company Oncology Roundtable. *Redesigning Cancer Care Delivery for the Era of Accountability.* 2012:17.

196. American Society of Clinical Oncology. *Shaping the Future of Oncology: Envisioning Cancer Care in 2030.* Alexandria, VA: ASCO, 2012. p. 13.

197. Samuels M. 2013 Cancer Center Business Summit: Transforming Oncology Through Innovation. Innovative Cancer Care Initiative # 2: The Oncology ACO. November 2013. www.cancerbusinesssummit.com/program.htm.

198. Blair, Kelly, 2013 Cancer Center Business Summit, Innovative Cancer Care Initiative # 2: The Oncology ACO. November 2013. www.cancerbusinesssummit.com/program.htm.

199. Grace Terrell, MD, President, Cornerstone Health Care.

200. American Board of Internal Medicine Foundation, Choosing Wisely. Five Things Physicians and Patients Should Question. American Academy of Ophthalmology. www.choosingwisely.org/societies/american-academy-of-ophthalmology.

201. American Academy of Ophthalmology Guidelines. www.aao.org/guidelines-browse?filter=preferredpracticepatterns.

202. National Institutes of Health. Comparison of AMD Treatments Trials (CATT): Lucentis—Avasti Trial. News Release. February 22, 2008. www.nih.gov/news-events/news-releases/comparison-amd-treatments-trials-catt-lucentis-avastin-trial

203. Whited JD. Accuracy and Reliability of Teleophthalmology for Diagnosing Diabetic Retinopathy and Macular Edema: A Review of the Literature. *Diabetes Technol Ther.* 2006 Feb;8(1):102-11.

204. Wakefield BJ, Holman JE, Ray A. *et al.* Effectiveness of Home Telehealth in Comorbid Diabetes and Hypertension: A Randomized, Controlled Trial. *Telemed J E Health.* 2011 May;17(4):254-61.

205. American Academy of Ophthalmology IRIS Registry. www.aao.org/iris-registry.

206. Butts DK, Cameron DJ, Hohenstein K, Banjer R. *et al. The Future of Accountable Care Organizations.* Navigant Issue Brief. 2016. www.navigant.com/-/media/www/site/insights/healthcare/2016/ppc_issuebriefaco2_nsl_0516.pdf

207. Dyrda L. Where Orthopedic Surgeons Fit in ACOs: Experts Weigh-in. *Becker's Spine Review.* October 2012. www.beckersspine.com/orthopedic-spine-practices-improving-profits/item/13549-where-orthopedic-surgeons-fit-in-acos-3-experts-weigh-in.html?tmpl=component&print=1.

208. Dyrda L. Where Orthopedic Surgeons Fit in ACOs: Experts Weigh-in. *Becker's Spine Review.* October 2012. www.beckersspine.com/orthopedic-spine-practices-improving-profits/item/13549-where-orthopedic-surgeons-fit-in-acos-3-experts-weigh-in.html?tmpl=component&print=1

209. Dyrda L. Where Orthopedic Surgeons Fit in ACOs: Experts Weigh-in. *Becker's Spine Review.* October 2012. www.beckersspine.com/orthopedic-spine-practices-improving-profits/item/13549-where-orthopedic-surgeons-fit-in-acos-3-experts-weigh-in.html?tmpl=component&print=1

210. Dyrda L. Where Orthopedic Surgeons Fit in ACOs: Experts Weigh-in. *Becker's Spine Review.* October 2012. www.beckersspine.com/orthopedic-spine-practices-improving-profits/item/13549-where-orthopedic-surgeons-fit-in-acos-3-experts-weigh-in.html?tmpl=component&print=1.

211. Congressional Budget Office. *Detail of Spending and Enrollment for Medicaid for CBO's March 2016 Baseline.* Congressional Budget Office, March 2016.

212. HIMSS ACO Task Force. Pediatric ACOs. April 2014.

213. American Academy of Pediatrics. Accountable Care Organizations (ACOs) and Pediatricians: Evaluation and Engagement. *APP News.* December 27, 2010. www.aap-publications.org/content/32/1/1.6.

214. American Academy of Pediatrics. Accountable Care Organizations (ACOs) and Pediatricians: Evaluation and Engagement. *APP News.* December 27, 2010. www.aap-publications.org/content/32/1/1.6.

215. American Academy of Pediatrics Counsel on Children with Disabilities and Medical Home Implementation Project Advisory Committee. Patient- and Family-Centered Care Coordination: A Framework for Integrating Care for Children and Youth Across Multiple Systems. *Pediatrics.* 2014 May;133(5):e1451-60.

216. American Academy of Pediatrics Counsel on Children with Disabilities and Medical Home Implementation Project Advisory Committee. Patient- and Family-Centered Care Coordination: A Framework for Integrating Care for Children and Youth Across Multiple Systems. *Pediatrics.* 2014 May;133(5):e1451-60.

217. American Academy of Pediatrics Counsel on Children with Disabilities and Medical Home Implementation Project Advisory Committee. Patient- and Family-Centered Care Coordination: A Framework for Integrating Care for Children and Youth Across Multiple Systems. *Pediatrics.* 2014 May;133(5):e1451-60.

218. American Academy of Pediatrics Counsel on Children with Disabilities and Medical Home Implementation Project Advisory Committee. Patient- and Family-Centered Care Coordination: A Framework for Integrating Care for Children and Youth Across Multiple Systems. *Pediatrics*. 2014 May;133(5):e1451-60.

219. Telephone interview with Pediatrics Accountable Care Workgroup member, neonatologist Docia Hickey, MD, September 10, 2014.

220. Mellon, M, Parasuraman B. Pediatric Asthma: Improving Management to Reduce Cost of Care. *J Manag Care Pharm*. 2004 Mar-Apr;10(2):130-41.

221. Mellon, M, Parasuraman B. Pediatric Asthma: Improving Management to Reduce Cost of Care. *J Manag Care Pharm*. 2004 Mar-Apr;10(2):130-41.

222. Mellon, M, Parasuraman B. Pediatric Asthma: Improving Management to Reduce Cost of Care. *J Manag Care Pharm*. 2004 Mar-Apr;10(2):130-41.

223. Robert Wood Johnson Foundation. Faces of Public Health: NY State Health Commissioner Nirav Shah. Robert Wood Johnson Foundation, April 2013.

224. Data Resource Center for Child & Adolescent Health, Child and Adolescent Health Measurement Initiative. *Pediatric Health Care Quality Measurement and Improvement*. www.childhealthdata.org.

225. American Board of Internal Medicine Foundation, Choosing Wisely. Ten Things Physicians and Patients Should Question. www.choosingwisely.org/societies/american-academy-of-pediatrics.

226. American Board of Internal Medicine Foundation, Choosing Wisely. Ten Things Physicians and Patients Should Question. www.choosingwisely.org/societies/american-academy-of-pediatrics.

227. The Wellness CPT codes are: G0402 IPPE Initial Preventative Physical Exam, G0438 Initial Annual Wellness, and G0439 Subsequent Annual Wellness.

228. Bobbitt J. How to Harness Value-Based Care Codes. *Family Practice News*, May 15, 2018.

229. Community Care of North Carolina. What We Do. www.communitycarenc.org/what-we-do.

230. Perrin Jones, MD email to Melanie Phelps, *et al.*, March 4, 2015.

231. The Advisory Board Company, *Toward Accountable Care*, 2010.

232. Lewis V, *et al.* Few ACOs Pursue Innovative Models That Integrate Care for Mental Illness and Substance Abuse with Primary Care. *Hlth Aff (Millwood)*. 2014 Oct;10:1808.

233. Grattadago D, *et al.* Integrating Mental Health into Primary Care. NAMI, November 2011.

234. Lewis V, Colla CH, Tierney K, *et al.* Few ACOs Pursue Innovative Models That Integrate Care for Mental Illness and Substance Abuse with Primary Care. *Hlth Aff (Millwood)*. 2014 Oct;33(10): 1814.

235. Lewis V, Colla CH, Tierney K, *et al.* Few ACOs Pursue Innovative Models That Integrate Care for Mental Illness and Substance Abuse with Primary Care. *Hlth Aff (Millwood)*. 2014 Oct;33(10): 1814.

236. Interview with Arthur Kelley, MD.

237. Weaver D. The Advisory Board Company. Who Really Influences a Population's Health? (Hint: It's Not Just Providers). The Care Transformation Center Blog, July 30,

2014. www.advisory.com/research/care-transformation-center/care-transformation-center-blog/2014/07/sw-what-really-influences-population-health.

238. Email from Grace Terrell, MD, to the TAC Physician Advisory Committee.

239. Lewis VA, CH, Tierney R, *et al.* Few ACOs Pursue Innovative Models That Integrate Care for Mental Illness and Substance Abuse with Primary Care. *Health Aff (Millwood).* 2014 Oct; 33(10):1808-16.

240. Goodell S, Druss BG, Walker ER. Mental Disorders and Medical Comorbidity. The Synthesis Project, Robert Wood Johnson Foundation. February 1, 2011. www.rwjf.org/en/library/research/2011/02/mental-disorders-and-medical-comorbidity.html.

241. Irvine J, Basinski A, Baker B, *et al.* Depression and Risk of Sudden Cardiac Death After Acute Myocardial Infarction: Test for the Confounding Effect of Fatigue. *Psychosom Med. 1999* Nov-Dec; 61:729-37.

242. Collins C, Hewson DL, Munger R, Wade T. *Evolving Models of Behavioral Health Integration in Primary Care.* New York: Milbank Memorial Fund, 2010. www.milbank.org/publications/evolving-models-of-behavioral-health-integration-in-primary-care.

243. Boyd C, Leff B, Weiss C, *et al. Full Report: Clarifying Multimorbidity to Improve Targeting and Delivery of Clinical Services for Medicaid Populations.* Center for Health Care Strategies, Inc., December 2010. For the full analysis and corresponding materials, visit www.chcs.org.

244. American Lung Association. Learn about COPD. Webpage. www.lung.org/lung-health-and-diseases/lung-disease-lookup/copd/learn-about-copd

245. Nichols H. What Are the Leading Causes of Death in the US. *Medical News Today,* July 4, 2019. www.medicalnewstoday.com/articles/282929.php.

246. Zamosky L. COPD: Exploring the Value of Care. *Modern Medicine Network.* 2013 Apr 10. http://medicaleconomics.modernmedicine.com/medical-economics/RC/tags/business-health/copd-exploring-value-care.

247. Yawn, BP, Enright PL, Lemanske RF, *et. al.* Spirometry Can Be Done in Family Physicians' Offices and Alters Clinical Decisions in Management of Asthma and COPD. *Chest.* 2007;132:1162-68.

248. Zamosky L. COPD: Exploring the Value of Care. *Modern Medicine Network.* 2013 Apr 10. http://medicaleconomics.modernmedicine.com/medical-economics/RC/tags/business-health/copd-exploring-value-care.

249. Zamosky L. COPD: Exploring the Value of Care. *Modern Medicine Network.* 2013 Apr 10. http://medicaleconomics.modernmedicine.com/medical-economics/RC/tags/business-health/copd-exploring-value-care.

250. Martinez FJ, O'Connor GT. Screening, Case-Finding, and Outcomes for Adults with Unrecognized COPD. *JAMA.* 2016:315(13): 1343-44.

251. Bourbeau J, Julien M, Maltais F, *et al.* Reduction of Hospital Utilization in Patients with Chronic Obstructive Pulmonary Disease A Disease-Specific Self-management Intervention. *Arch Intern Med.* 2003 Mar 10;163(5):585-91.

252. Bourbeau J, Julien M, Maltais F, *et al.* Reduction of Hospital Utilization in Patients with Chronic Obstructive Pulmonary Disease A Disease-Specific Self-management Intervention. *Arch Intern Med.* 2003 Mar 10;163(5):585-91.

253. Bourbeau J, Julien M, Maltais F, *et al*. Reduction of Hospital Utilization in Patients with Chronic Obstructive Pulmonary Disease A Disease-Specific Self-management Intervention. *Arch Intern Med*. 2003 Mar 10;163(5):585-91.

254. Goldstein RS, H'Oski S. Telemedicine in COPD: Time to Pause. *Chest*. 2014 May;145(5):945-9.

255. Franek J. Home Telehealth for Patients with Obstructive Pulmonary Disease (COPD*). Ont Health Technol Assess Ser*. 2012;12(11):1-58. www.ncbi.nlm.nih.gov/pmc/articles/ PMC3384362.

256. Hernandez C, Mallow J, Narsavage GL. Delivering Telemedicine Interventions in Chronic Respiratory Disease. Breathe. 2014;10:198-212. http://breathe.ersjournals.com/ content/10/3/198.

257. Zamosky L. COPD: Exploring the Value of Care. *Modern Medicine Network* 2013 Apr 10. http://medicaleconomics.modernmedicine.com/medical-economics/RC/tags/ business-health/copd-exploring-value-care.

258. Allen B Jr, Levin DC, Brant-Zawadski M, Lexa FJ, *et al*. ACR White Paper: Strategies for Radiologists in the Era of Health Care Reform and Accountable Care Organizations: A Report from the ACR Future Trends Committee. *J Am Coll Radiol*. 2011 May;8(5):311.

259. The Advisory Board Company. *A Growing Mandate—The Role of Radiology in the Care Continuum*. Slide 62; Nov. 2012.

260. The Advisory Board Company. *A Growing Mandate—The Role of Radiology in the Care Continuum*. Slide 62; Nov. 2012.

261. The Advisory Board Company. *A Growing Mandate—The Role of Radiology in the Care Continuum*. Slide 30; Nov 2012.

262. Allen B Jr, Levin DC, Brant-Zawadski M, Lexa FJ, *et al*. ACR White Paper: Strategies for Radiologists in the Era of Health Care Reform and Accountable Care Organizations: A Report from the ACR Future Trends Committee. *J Am Coll Radiol*. 2011 May;8(5):311.

263. Kosinski M, Kujawski SC, Martin R, *et al*. Health-Related Quality of Life in Early Rheumatoid Arthritis: Impact of Disease and Treatment Response. *Am J Manag Care*. 2002 Mar; 8(3):231-40.

264. Garneau KL, Iversen MD, Tsau H, Solomon DH. Primary Care Physicians' Perspectives Towards Managing Rheumatoid Arthritis: Room for Improvement. *Arthritis Res Ther*. 2011;13(6):R189. www.ncbi.nlm.nih.gov/pmc/articles/PMC3334638.

265. American Board of Internal Medicine Foundation, Choosing Wisely. Five Things Physicians and Patients Should Question. February 1, 2013. www.choosingwisely.org/ societies/american-college-of-rheumatology.

266. Gates B. The Road Ahead, 2nd ed. Seattle, WA: Viking Press, 1995.

267. Watts C. 20 Things That Happened in 1996. DDC. https://ddcpublicaffairs. com/20-things-in-1996.

268. Peterson-Kaiser. Health System Tracker. www.healthsystemtracker.org.

# INDEX

CPSIA information can be obtained
at www.ICGtesting.com
Printed in the USA
BVHW051332110820
586024BV00003B/8

9 780984 831012